BRITISH ENGLISH

GW00630805

ENGLISH
AZERBAIJANI

THEME-BASED
DICTIONARY

Contains over 9000 commonly
used words

T&P BOOKS PUBLISHING

Theme-based dictionary British English-Azerbaijani - 9000 words
British English collection

By Andrey Taranov

T&P Books vocabularies are intended for helping you learn, memorize and review foreign words. The dictionary is divided into themes, covering all major spheres of everyday activities, business, science, culture, etc.

The process of learning words using T&P Books' theme-based dictionaries gives you the following advantages:

- Correctly grouped source information predetermines success at subsequent stages of word memorization
- Availability of words derived from the same root allowing memorization of word units (rather than separate words)
- Small units of words facilitate the process of establishing associative links needed for consolidation of vocabulary
- Level of language knowledge can be estimated by the number of learned words

Copyright © 2013 T&P Books Publishing

All rights reserved No part of this book may be reproduced or utilized in any form or by any means, electronic or mechanical, including photocopying, recording or by information storage and retrieval system, without permission in writing from the publishers.

T&P Books Publishing
www.tpbooks.com

ISBN: 978-1-78314-672-7

This book is also available in E-book formats.
Please visit www.tpbooks.com or the major online bookstores.

AZERBAIJANI THEME-BASED DICTIONARY
British English collection

T&P Books vocabularies are intended to help you learn, memorize, and review foreign words. The vocabulary contains over 9000 commonly used words arranged thematically.

- Vocabulary contains the most commonly used words
- Recommended as an addition to any language course
- Meets the needs of beginners and advanced learners of foreign languages
- Convenient for daily use, revision sessions, and self-testing activities
- Allows you to assess your vocabulary

Special features of the vocabulary

- Words are organized according to their meaning, not alphabetically
- Words are presented in three columns to facilitate the reviewing and self-testing processes
- Words in groups are divided into small blocks to facilitate the learning process
- The vocabulary offers a convenient and simple transcription of each foreign word

The vocabulary has 256 topics including:

Basic Concepts, Numbers, Colors, Months, Seasons, Units of Measurement, Clothing & Accessories, Food & Nutrition, Restaurant, Family Members, Relatives, Character, Feelings, Emotions, Diseases, City, Town, Sightseeing, Shopping, Money, House, Home, Office, Working in the Office, Import & Export, Marketing, Job Search, Sports, Education, Computer, Internet, Tools, Nature, Countries, Nationalities and more ...

TABLE OF CONTENTS

Job. Business. Part 2 105

Professions and occupations 110

Sports 117

Education 125

PRONUNCIATION GUIDE

Letter	Azerbaijani example	T&P phonetics alphabet	English example
A a	stabil	[a]	shorter than in ask
B b	boksçu	[b]	baby, book
C c	Ceyran	[dʒ]	joke, general
Ç ç	Çay	[tʃ]	church, French
D d	daraq	[d]	day, doctor
E e	fevral	[e]	elm, medal
Ə ə	Əncir	[æ]	chess, man
F f	fokus	[f]	face, food
G g	giriş	[g]	game, gold
Ğ ğ	Çağırmaq	[ɣ]	between [g] and [h]
H h	həkim	[h]	home, have
X x	Xanım	[h]	huge, hat
I ı	Qarı	[ı]	big, America
İ i	dimdik	[i]	shorter than in feet
J j	Janr	[ʒ]	forge, pleasure
K k	kaktus	[k]	karate, keep
Q q	Qravüra	[g]	game, gold
L l	liman	[l]	lace, people
M m	mavi	[m]	magic, milk
N n	nömrə	[n]	name, normal
O o	okean	[o]	pod, John
Ö ö	Göbələk	[ø]	eternal, church
P p	parça	[p]	pencil, private
R r	rəng	[r]	rice, radio
S s	sap	[s], [θ]	think, sue
Ş ş	Şair	[ʃ]	machine, shark
T t	tarix	[t]	tourist, trip
U u	susmaq	[u]	book
Ü ü	Ümid	[y]	fuel, tuna
V v	varlı	[v]	very, river
Y y	Yaponiya	[j]	yes, New York
Z z	zarafat	[z], [ð]	then, zone

ABBREVIATIONS
used in the dictionary

ab.	-	about
adj	-	adjective
adv	-	adverb
anim.	-	animate
as adj	-	attributive noun used as adjective
e.g.	-	for example
etc.	-	et cetera
fam.	-	familiar
fem.	-	feminine
form.	-	formal
inanim.	-	inanimate
masc.	-	masculine
math	-	mathematics
mil.	-	military
n	-	noun
pl	-	plural
pron.	-	pronoun
sb	-	somebody
sing.	-	singular
sth	-	something
v aux	-	auxiliary verb
vi	-	intransitive verb
vi, vt	-	intransitive, transitive verb
vt	-	transitive verb

BASIC CONCEPTS

Basic concepts. Part 1

1. Pronouns

I, me	mən	[mæn]
you	sən	[sæn]
he, she, it	o	[o]
we	biz	[biz]
you (to a group)	siz	[siz]
they	onlar	[on'lar]

2. Greetings. Salutations. Farewells

Hello! (fam.)	Salam!	[sa'lam]
Hello! (form.)	Salam!	[sa'lam]
Good morning!	Sabahın xeyir!	[saba'hın he'jır]
Good afternoon!	Günortan xeyir!	[gynor'tan he'jır]
Good evening!	Axşamın xeyir!	[ahʃa'mın he'jır]
to say hello	salamlaşmaq	[salamlaʃ'mag]
Hi! (hello)	Salam!	[sa'lam]
greeting (n)	salam	[sa'lam]
to greet (vt)	salamlamaq	[salamla'mag]
How are you?	Necəsən?	[ne'dʒæsæn]
What's new?	Nə yenilik var?	['næ eni'lik 'var]
Bye-Bye! Goodbye!	Xudahafiz!	[hudaha'fiz]
See you soon!	Tezliklə görüşənədək!	[tez'liklæ gøryʃæ'nædæk]
Farewell! (to a friend)	Sağlıqla qal!	[saɣ'lıgla 'gal]
Farewell (form.)	Sağlıqla qalın!	[saɣ'lıgla 'galın]
to say goodbye	vidalaşmaq	[vidalaʃ'mag]
Cheers!	Hələlik!	[hælæ'lik]
Thank you! Cheers!	Sağ ol!	['saɣ 'ol]
Thank you very much!	Çox sağ ol!	['tʃoh 'saɣ 'ol]
My pleasure!	Buyurun	['buyrun]
Don't mention it!	Dəyməz	[dæj'mæz]
It was nothing	Bir şey deyil	['bir 'ʃəj 'dejıl]
Excuse me! (fam.)	Bağışla!	[baɣıʃ'la]
Excuse me! (form.)	Bağışlayın!	[baɣıʃ'lajın]
to excuse (forgive)	Bağışlamaq	[baɣıʃla'mag]
to apologize (vi)	üzr istəmək	['yzr istæ'mæk]
My apologies	Üzrümü qəbul et	[yzry'my gæ'bul 'æt]

13

I'm sorry!	Bağışlayın!	[baɣɯʃ'lajɯn]
to forgive (vt)	bağışlamaq	[baɣɯʃla'mag]
please (adv)	rica edirəm	[ri'dʒa æ'diræm]

Don't forget!	Unutmayın!	[u'nutmajɯn]
Certainly!	Əlbəttə!	[æl'battæ]
Of course not!	Əlbəttə yox!	[æl'battæ 'joh]
Okay! (I agree)	Razıyam!	[ra'zɯjam]
That's enough!	Bəsti!	['bæsti]

3. How to address

mister, sir	Cənab	[dʒæ'nab]
madam	Xanım	[ha'nɯm]
miss	Ay qız	['aj 'gɯz]
young man	Cavan oğlan	[dʒa'van oɣ'lan]
young man (little boy)	Ay oğlan	['aj oɣ'lan]
miss (little girl)	Ay qız	['aj 'gɯz]

4. Cardinal numbers. Part 1

0 zero	sıfır	['sɯfɯr]
1 one	bir	[bir]
2 two	iki	[i'ki]
3 three	üç	[ytʃ]
4 four	dörd	['dørd]

5 five	beş	[beʃ]
6 six	altı	[al'tɯ]
7 seven	yeddi	[ed'di]
8 eight	səkkiz	[sæk'kiz]
9 nine	doqquz	[dog'guz]

10 ten	on	[on]
11 eleven	on bir	['on 'bir]
12 twelve	on iki	['on i'ki]
13 thirteen	on üç	['on 'ytʃ]
14 fourteen	on dörd	['on 'dørd]

15 fifteen	on beş	['on 'beʃ]
16 sixteen	on altı	['on al'tɯ]
17 seventeen	on yeddi	['on ed'di]
18 eighteen	on səkkiz	['on sæk'kiz]
19 nineteen	on doqquz	['on dog'guz]

20 twenty	iyirmi	[ijɯr'mi]
21 twenty-one	iyirmi bir	[ijɯr'mi 'bir]
22 twenty-two	iyirmi iki	[ijɯr'mi i'ki]
23 twenty-three	iyirmi üç	[ijɯr'mi 'ytʃ]

| 30 thirty | otuz | [o'tuz] |
| 31 thirty-one | otuz bir | [o'tuz 'bir] |

| 32 thirty-two | otuz iki | [o'tuz i'ki] |
| 33 thirty-three | otuz üç | [o'tuz 'ytʃ] |

40 forty	qırx	[gırh]
41 forty-one	qırx bir	['gırh 'bir]
42 forty-two	qırx iki	['gırh i'ki]
43 forty-three	qırx üç	['gırh 'ytʃ]

50 fifty	əlli	[æl'li]
51 fifty-one	əlli bir	[æl'li 'bir]
52 fifty-two	əlli iki	[æl'li i'ki]
53 fifty-three	əlli üç	[æl'li 'ytʃ]

60 sixty	altmış	[alt'mıʃ]
61 sixty-one	altmış bir	[alt'mıʃ 'bir]
62 sixty-two	altmış iki	[alt'mıʃ i'ki]
63 sixty-three	altmış üç	[alt'mıʃ 'ytʃ]

70 seventy	yetmiş	[et'miʃ]
71 seventy-one	yetmiş bir	[et'miʃ 'bir]
72 seventy-two	yetmiş iki	[et'miʃ i'ki]
73 seventy-three	yetmiş üç	[et'miʃ 'ytʃ]

80 eighty	səksən	[sæk'sæn]
81 eighty-one	səksən bir	[sæk'sæn 'bir]
82 eighty-two	səksən iki	[sæk'sæn i'ki]
83 eighty-three	səksən üç	[sæk'sæn 'ytʃ]

90 ninety	doxsan	[doh'san]
91 ninety-one	doxsan bir	[doh'san 'bir]
92 ninety-two	doxsan iki	[doh'san i'ki]
93 ninety-three	doxsan üç	[doh'san 'ytʃ]

5. Cardinal numbers. Part 2

100 one hundred	yüz	[yz]
200 two hundred	iki yüz	[i'ki 'yz]
300 three hundred	üç yüz	['ytʃ 'yz]
400 four hundred	dörd yüz	['dørd 'yz]
500 five hundred	beş yüz	['beʃ 'yz]

600 six hundred	altı yüz	[al'tı 'yz]
700 seven hundred	yeddi yüz	[ed'di 'yz]
800 eight hundred	səkkiz yüz	[sæk'kiz 'yz]
900 nine hundred	doqquz yüz	[dog'guz 'yz]

1000 one thousand	min	[min]
2000 two thousand	iki min	[i'ki 'min]
3000 three thousand	üç min	['ytʃ 'min]
10000 ten thousand	on min	['on 'min]
one hundred thousand	yüz min	['yz 'min]

| million | milyon | [miʎ'jon] |
| billion | milyard | [miʎ'jard] |

15

6. Ordinal numbers

first (adj)	birinci	[birin'dʒi]
second (adj)	ikinci	[ikin'dʒi]
third (adj)	üçüncü	[ytʃun'dʒy]
fourth (adj)	dördüncü	[dørdyn'dʒy]
fifth (adj)	beşinci	[beʃin'dʒi]
sixth (adj)	altıncı	[altın'dʒı]
seventh (adj)	yeddinci	[eddin'dʒi]
eighth (adj)	səkkizinci	[sækkizin'dʒi]
ninth (adj)	doqquzuncu	[dogguzun'dʒu]
tenth (adj)	onuncu	[onun'dʒu]

7. Numbers. Fractions

fraction	kəsr	[kæsr]
one half	ikidə bir	[iki'dæ 'bir]
one third	üçdə bir	[ytʃ'da 'bir]
one quarter	dörddə bir	[dørd'da 'bir]
one eighth	səkkizdə bir	[sækkiz'dæ 'bir]
one tenth	onda bir	[on'da 'bir]
two thirds	üçdə iki	[ytʃ'dæ i'ki]
three quarters	dörddə üç	[dørd'dæ 'ytʃ]

8. Numbers. Basic operations

subtraction	çıxma	[tʃıh'ma]
to subtract (vi, vt)	çıxmaq	[tʃıh'mag]
division	bölmə	[bøl'mæ]
to divide (vt)	bölmək	[bøl'mæk]
addition	toplama	[topla'ma]
to add up (vt)	toplamaq	[topla'mag]
to add (vi)	artırmaq	[artır'mag]
multiplication	vurma	[vur'ma]
to multiply (vt)	vurmaq	[vur'mag]

9. Numbers. Miscellaneous

digit, figure	rəqəm	[ræ'gæm]
number	say	[saj]
numeral	say	[saj]
minus	minus	['minus]
plus	plyus	['plys]
formula	düstur	[dys'tur]
calculation	hesab	[he'sab]
to count (vt)	saymaq	[saj'mag]

| to count up | hesablamaq | [hesabla'mag] |
| to compare (vt) | müqayise etmek | [mygajı'sæ æt'mæk] |

How much?	Ne qeder?	['næ gæ'dær]
How many?	Neçe?	[ne'ʧə]
sum, total	mebleğ	[mæb'læɣ]
result	netice	[næti'dʒæ]
remainder	qalıq	[ga'lıg]

a few ...	bir neçe	[bir ne'ʧə]
few, little (adv)	bir az ...	['bir 'az]
the rest	qalanı	[gala'nı]
one and a half	bir yarım	['bir ja'rım]
dozen	on iki	['on i'ki]

in half (adv)	ten yarı	['tæn ja'rı]
equally (evenly)	tenberaber	[tænbæra'bær]
half	yarım	[ja'rım]
time (three ~s)	defe	[dæ'fæ]

10. The most important verbs. Part 1

to advise (vt)	meslehet vermek	[mæslæ'hæt ver'mæk]
to agree (say yes)	razı olmaq	[ra'zı ol'mag]
to answer (vi, vt)	cavab vermek	[dʒa'vab ver'mæk]

to apologize (vi)	üzr istemek	['yzr istæ'mæk]
to arrive (vi)	gelmek	[gæl'mæk]
to ask (~ oneself)	soruşmaq	[soruʃ'mag]
to ask (~ sb to do sth)	xahiş etmek	[ha'iʃ æt'mæk]

to be (vi)	olmaq	[ol'mag]
to be afraid	qorxmaq	[gorh'mag]
to be hungry	yemek istemek	[e'mæk iste'mæk]
to be interested in ...	maraqlanmaq	[maraglan'mag]
to be needed	teleb olunmaq	[tæ'læb olun'mag]
to be surprised	teeccüblenmek	[tæ:dʒyblæn'mæk]
to be thirsty	içmek istemek	[iʧ'mæk istæ'mæk]

to begin (vt)	başlamaq	[baʃla'mag]
to belong to ...	mensub olmaq	[mæn'sub ol'mag]
to boast (vi)	lovğalanmaq	[lovɣalan'mag]
to break (split into pieces)	qırmaq	[gır'mag]

to call (for help)	çağırmaq	[ʧaɣır'mag]
can (v aux)	bacarmaq	[badʒar'mag]
to catch (vt)	tutmaq	[tut'mag]
to change (vt)	deyişmek	[dæiʃ'mæk]
to choose (select)	seçmek	[seʧ'mæk]

to come down	aşağı düşmek	[aʃaɣ'ı dyʃ'mæk]
to come in (enter)	daxil olmaq	[da'hil ol'mag]
to compare (vt)	müqayise etmek	[mygajı'sæ æt'mæk]
to complain (vi, vt)	şikayet etmek	[ʃika'jət æt'mæk]

to confuse (mix up)	dolaşıq salmaq	[dola'ʃɪg sal'mag]
to continue (vt)	davam etdirmək	[da'vam ætdir'mæk]
to control (vt)	nəzarət etmək	[næza'ræt æt'mæk]
to cook (dinner)	hazırlamaq	[hazırla'mag]
to cost (vt)	qiyməti olmaq	[gijmæ'ti ol'mag]

to count (add up)	saymaq	[saj'mag]
to count on ...	bel bağlamaq	['bel bayla'mag]
to create (vt)	yaratmaq	[jarat'mag]
to cry (weep)	ağlamaq	[ayla'mag]

11. The most important verbs. Part 2

to deceive (vi, vt)	aldatmaq	[aldat'mag]
to decorate (tree, street)	bəzəmək	[bæzæ'mæk]
to defend (a country, etc.)	müdafiyə etmək	[mydafi'jə æt'mæk]
to demand (request firmly)	tələb etmək	[tæ'læb æt'mæk]

to dig (vt)	qazmaq	[gaz'mag]
to discuss (vt)	müzakirə etmək	[myzaki'ræ æt'mæk]
to do (vt)	etmək	[æt'mæk]
to doubt (have doubts)	şübhələnmək	[ʃybhælæn'mæk]
to drop (let fall)	yerə salmaq	[e'ræ sal'mag]

to exist (vi)	mövcud olmaq	[møv'dʒud ol'mag]
to expect (foresee)	qabaqcadan görmək	[ga'bagdʒadan gør'mæk]
to explain (vt)	izah etmək	[i'zah æt'mæk]

to fall (vi)	yıxılmaq	[jıhıl'mag]
to fancy (vt)	xoşuna gəlmək	[hoʃu'na gæl'mæk]
to find (vt)	tapmaq	[tap'mag]
to finish (vt)	qurtarmaq	[gurtar'mag]
to fly (vi)	uçmaq	[utʃ'mag]

to follow ... (come after)	ardınca getmək	[ar'dındʒa get'mæk]
to forget (vi, vt)	unutmaq	[unut'mag]
to forgive (vt)	bağışlamaq	[bayıʃla'mag]

to give (vt)	vermək	[ver'mæk]
to give a hint	eyham vurmaq	[æj'ham vur'mag]
to go (on foot)	getmək	[get'mæk]
to go for a swim	çimmək	[tʃim'mæk]
to go out (from ...)	çıxmaq	[tʃıh'mag]
to guess right	tapmaq	[tap'mag]

to have (vt)	malik olmaq	['malik ol'mag]
to have breakfast	səhər yeməyi yemək	[sæ'hær emæ'jı e'mæk]
to have dinner	axşam yeməyi yemək	[ah'ʃam emæ'jı e'mæk]
to have lunch	nahar etmək	[na'har æt'mæk]

to hear (vt)	eşitmək	[æʃit'mæk]
to help (vt)	kömək etmək	[kø'mæk æt'mæk]
to hide (vt)	gizlətmək	[gizlæt'mæk]
to hope (vi, vt)	ümid etmək	[y'mid æt'mæk]

to hunt (vi, vt)	ova çıxmaq	[o'va tʃıh'mag]
to hurry (vi)	tələsmək	[tælæs'mæk]

12. The most important verbs. Part 3

to inform (vt)	məlumat vermək	[mælu'mat ver'mæk]
to insist (vi, vt)	təkid etmək	[tæ'kid æt'mæk]
to insult (vt)	təhkir etmək	[tæh'kir æt'mæk]
to invite (vt)	dəvət etmək	[dæ'væt æt'mæk]
to joke (vi)	zarafat etmək	[zara'fat æt'mæk]

to keep (vt)	saxlamaq	[sahla'mag]
to keep silent	susmaq	[sus'mag]
to kill (vt)	öldürmək	[øldyr'mæk]
to know (sb)	tanımaq	[tanı'mag]
to know (sth)	bilmək	[bil'mæk]

to laugh (vi)	gülmək	[gyʎ'mæk]
to liberate (city, etc.)	azad etmək	[a'zad æt'mæk]
to look for ... (search)	axtarmaq	[ahtar'mag]
to love (sb)	sevmək	[sev'mæk]

to make a mistake	səhv etmək	['sæhv æt'mæk]
to manage, to run	idarə etmək	[ida'ræ æt'mæk]
to mean (signify)	ifadə etmək	[ifa'dæ æt'mæk]
to mention (talk about)	adını çəkmək	[adı'nı tʃək'mæk]
to miss (school, etc.)	buraxmaq	[burah'mag]
to notice (see)	görmək	[gør'mæk]

to object (vi, vt)	etiraz etmək	[æti'raz æt'mæk]
to observe (see)	müşaidə etmək	[myʃai'dæ æt'mæk]
to open (vt)	açmaq	[atʃ'mag]
to order (meal, etc.)	sifariş etmək	[sifa'riʃ æt'mæk]
to order (mil.)	əmr etmək	['æmr æt'mæk]
to own (possess)	sahib olmaq	[sa'hib ol'mag]

to participate (vi)	iştirak etmək	[iʃti'rak æt'mæk]
to pay (vi, vt)	pulunu ödəmək	[pulu'nu ødæ'mæk]
to permit (vt)	icazə vermək	[idʒa'zæ ver'mæk]
to plan (vt)	planlaşdırmaq	[planlaʃdır'mag]
to play (children)	oynamaq	[ojna'mag]
to pray (vi, vt)	dua etmək	[du'a æt'mæk]
to prefer (vt)	üstünlük vermək	[ystyn'lyk ver'mæk]

to promise (vt)	vəd etmək	['væd æt'mæk]
to pronounce (vt)	tələffüz etmək	[tælæf'fyz æt'mæk]
to propose (vt)	təklif etmək	[tæk'lif æt'mæk]
to punish (vt)	cəzalandırmaq	[dʒæzalandır'mag]
to read (vi, vt)	oxumaq	[ohu'mag]
to recommend (vt)	məsləhət görmək	[mæslæ'hæt gør'mæk]

to refuse (vi, vt)	imtina etmək	[imti'na æt'mæk]
to regret (be sorry)	heyfsilənmək	[hejfsilæn'mæk]
to rent (sth from sb)	kirayə etmək	[kira'jə æt'mæk]

to repeat (say again)	təkrar etmək	[tæk'rar æt'mæk]
to reserve, to book	sifariş etmək	[sifa'riʃ æt'mæk]
to run (vi)	qaçmaq	[gatʃ'mag]

13. The most important verbs. Part 4

to save (rescue)	xilas etmək	[hi'las æt'mæk]
to say (~ thank you)	demək	[de'mæk]
to scold (vt)	danlamaq	[danla'mag]
to see (vt)	görmək	[gør'mæk]

to sell (vt)	satmaq	[sat'mag]
to send (vt)	göndərmək	[gøndær'mæk]
to shoot (vi)	atəş açmaq	[a'tæʃ atʃ'mag]
to shout (vi)	çığırmaq	[tʃɪɣɪr'mag]
to show (vt)	göstərmək	[gøstær'mæk]

to sign (document)	imzalamaq	[imzala'mag]
to sit down (vi)	oturmaq	[otur'mag]
to smile (vi)	gülümsəmək	[gylymsæ'mæk]
to speak (vi, vt)	danışmaq	[danɪʃ'mag]

to steal (money, etc.)	oğurlamaq	[oɣurla'mag]
to stop (cease)	kəsmək	[kæs'mæk]
to stop (for pause, etc.)	dayanmaq	[dajan'mag]
to study (vt)	öyrənmək	[øjræn'mæk]
to swim (vi)	üzmək	[yz'mæk]

to take (vt)	almaq	[al'mag]
to think (vi, vt)	düşünmək	[dyʃyn'mæk]
to threaten (vt)	hədələmək	[hædælæ'mæk]
to touch (by hands)	əl vurmaq	['æl vur'mag]
to translate (vt)	tərcümə etmək	[tærdʒy'mæ æt'mæk]
to trust (vt)	etibar etmək	[æti'bar æt'mæk]
to try (attempt)	sınamaq	[sɪna'mag]
to turn (~ to the left)	döndərmək	[døndær'mæk]

to underestimate (vt)	lazımi qədər qiymətləndirməmək	[lazɪ'mi gæ'dær gijmætlæn'dirmæmæk]
to understand (vt)	başa düşmək	[ba'ʃa dyʃ'mæk]
to unite (vt)	birləşdirmək	[birlæʃdir'mæk]
to wait (vt)	gözləmək	[gøzlæ'mæk]
to want (wish, desire)	istəmək	[istæ'mæk]
to warn (vt)	xəbərdarlıq etmək	[hæbærdar'lɪg æt'mæk]
to work (vi)	işləmək	[iʃlæ'mæk]
to write (vt)	yazmaq	[jaz'mag]
to write down	yazmaq	[jaz'mag]

14. Colours

| colour | rəng | [ræŋ] |
| shade (tint) | çalar | [tʃa'lar] |

hue	ton	[ton]
rainbow	qövsi-quzeh	['gøvsi gy'zeh]

white (adj)	ağ	[aɣ]
black (adj)	qara	[ga'ra]
grey (adj)	boz	[boz]

green (adj)	yaşıl	[ja'ʃɪl]
yellow (adj)	sarı	[sa'rı]
red (adj)	qırmızı	[gırmı'zı]

blue (adj)	göy	['gøj]
light blue (adj)	mavi	[ma'vi]
pink (adj)	çəhrayı	[ʧəhra'jı]
orange (adj)	narıncı	[narın'ʤı]
violet (adj)	bənövşəyi	[bænøvʃæ'jı]
brown (adj)	şabalıdı	[ʃabalı'dı]

golden (adj)	qızıl	[gı'zıl]
silvery (adj)	gümüşü	[gymy'ʃy]

beige (adj)	bej rəngli	[beʒ ræŋ'li]
cream (adj)	krem rəngli	[krem ræŋ'li]
turquoise (adj)	firuzəyi	[firuzæ'jı]
cherry red (adj)	tünd qırmızı	['tynd gırmı'zı]
lilac (adj)	açıq bənövşəyi	[a'ʧıg bænøvʃæ'jı]
crimson (adj)	moruq rəngli	[morug ræŋ'li]

light (adj)	açıq rəngli	[a'ʧıg ræŋ'li]
dark (adj)	tünd	[tynd]
bright (adj)	parlaq	[par'lag]

coloured (pencils)	rəngli	[ræŋ'li]
colour (e.g. ~ film)	rəngli	[ræŋ'li]
black-and-white (adj)	ağ-qara	['aɣ ga'ra]
plain (one colour)	birrəng	[bir'ræŋ]
multicoloured (adj)	müxtəlif rəngli	[myhtæ'lif ræŋ'li]

15. Questions

Who?	Kim?	[kim]
What?	Nə?	[næ]
Where? (at, in)	Harada?	['harada]
Where (to)?	Haraya?	['haraja]
Where ... from?	Haradan?	['haradan]
When?	Nə zaman?	['næ za'man]
Why? (aim)	Niyə?	[ni'jə]
Why? (reason)	Nə üçün?	['næ y'ʧun]

What for?	Nədən ötrü?	[næ'dæn øt'ry]
How? (in what way)	Necə?	[ne'ʤæ]
What? (which?)	Nə cür?	['næ 'ʤyr]
Which?	Hansı?	[han'sı]
To whom?	Kimə?	[ki'mæ]

About whom?	Kimdən?	[kim'dæn]
About what?	Nədən?	[næ'dæn]
With whom?	Kiminlə?	[ki'minlæ]

How many?	Neçə?	[ne'tʃə]
How much?	Nə qədər?	['næ gæ'dær]
Whose?	Kimin?	[ki'min]

16. Prepositions

with (accompanied by)	ilə	[i'læ]
without	...sız	[sɪz]
to (indicating direction)	da	[da]
about (talking ~ ...)	haqqında	[haggɪn'da]
before (in time)	qabaq	[ga'bag]
in front of ...	qarşısında	[garʃɪsɪn'da]

under (beneath, below)	altında	[altɪn'da]
above (over)	üstündə	[ystyn'dæ]
on (atop)	üzərində	[yzerin'dæ]
from (off, out of)	...dan	[dan]
of (made from)	...dan	[dan]

in (e.g. ~ ten minutes)	sonra	[son'ra]
over (across the top of)	üstündən	[ystyn'dæn]

17. Function words. Adverbs. Part 1

Where? (at, in)	Harada?	['harada]
here (adv)	burada	['burada]
there (adv)	orada	['orada]

somewhere (to be)	harada isə	['harada ise]
nowhere (not anywhere)	heç bir yerdə	['hetʃ 'bir er'dæ]

by (near, beside)	yanında	[janɪn'da]
by the window	pəncərənin yanında	[pændʒæræ'nin janɪn'da]

Where (to)?	Haraya?	['haraja]
here (e.g. come ~!)	buraya	['buraja]
there (e.g. to go ~)	oraya	['oraja]
from here (adv)	buradan	['buradan]
from there (adv)	oradan	['oradan]

close (adv)	yaxın	[ja'hɪn]
far (adv)	uzaq	[u'zag]

near (e.g. ~ Paris)	yanaşı	[jana'ʃɪ]
nearby (adv)	yaxında	[jahɪn'da]
not far (adv)	yaxında	[jahɪn'da]
left (adj)	sol	[sol]
on the left	soldan	[sol'dan]

to the left	sola	[so'la]
right (adj)	sağ	[saɣ]
on the right	sağdan	[saɣ'dan]
to the right	sağa	[saɣ'a]

in front (adv)	qabaqdan	[gabag'dan]
front (as adj)	qabaq	[ga'bag]
ahead (in space)	irəli	[iræ'li]

behind (adv)	arxada	[arha'da]
from behind	arxadan	[arha'dan]
back (towards the rear)	arxaya	[arha'ja]

| middle | orta | [or'ta] |
| in the middle | ortada | [orta'da] |

at the side	qıraqdan	[gırag'dan]
everywhere (adv)	hər yerdə	['hær er'dæ]
around (in all directions)	ətrafında	[ætrafın'da]

from inside	içəridən	[itʃəri'dæn]
somewhere (to go)	haraya isə	['haraja i'sæ]
straight (directly)	düzünə	[dyzy'næ]
back (e.g. come ~)	geriyə	[geri'jə]

| from anywhere | haradan olsa | ['haradan ol'sa] |
| from somewhere | haradansa | ['haradansa] |

firstly (adv)	birincisi	[birindʒi'si]
secondly (adv)	ikincisi	[ikintʃi'si]
thirdly (adv)	üçüncüsü	[ytʃundʒy'sy]

suddenly (adv)	qəflətən	['gæflætæn]
at first (adv)	başlanqıcda	[baʃlaŋıdʒ'da]
for the first time	birinci dəfə	[birin'dʒi dæ'fæ]
long before ...	xeyli əvvəl	['hejli æv'væl]
anew (over again)	yenidən	[eni'dæn]
for good (adv)	həmişəlik	[hæmiʃæ'lik]

never (adv)	heç bir zaman	['hetʃ 'bir za'man]
again (adv)	yenə	['enæ]
now (adv)	indi	[in'di]
often (adv)	tez-tez	['tez 'tez]
then (adv)	onda	[on'da]
urgently (quickly)	təcili	[tædʒi'li]
usually (adv)	adətən	['adætæn]

by the way, ...	yeri gəlmişkən	[e'ri gæl'miʃkæn]
possible (that is ~)	ola bilsin	[o'la bil'sin]
probably (adv)	ehtimal ki	[æhti'mal 'ki]
maybe (adv)	ola bilər	[o'la bi'lær]
besides ...	bundan başqa...	[bun'dan baʃ'ga]
that's why ...	buna görə	[bu'na gø'ræ]
in spite of ...	baxmayaraq ki...	['bahmajarag ki]
thanks to ...	sayəsində...	[sajəsin'dæ]
what (pron.)	nə	[næ]

23

that	ki	[ki]
something	nə isə	['næ i'sæ]
anything (something)	bir şey	['bir 'ʃəj]
nothing	heç bir şey	['hetʃ 'bir 'ʃəj]

who (pron.)	kim	[kim]
someone	kim isə	['kim i'sæ]
somebody	birisi	[biri'si]

nobody	heç kim	['hetʃ kim]
nowhere (a voyage to ~)	heç bir yerə	['hetʃ 'bir e'ræ]
nobody's	heç kimin	['hetʃ ki'min]
somebody's	kiminsə	[ki'minsæ]

so (I'm ~ glad)	belə	[be'læ]
also (as well)	habelə	['habelæ]
too (as well)	həmçinin	['hæmtʃinin]

18. Function words. Adverbs. Part 2

Why?	Nə üçün?	['næ y'tʃun]
for some reason	nədənsə	[næ'dænsæ]
because ...	ona görə ki	[o'na gø'ræ 'ki]
for some purpose	nə səbəbə isə	['næ sæbæ'bæ i'sæ]

and	və	[væ]
or	yaxud	['jahud]
but	amma	['amma]
for (e.g. ~ me)	üçün	[y'tʃun]

too (excessively)	həddindən artıq	[hæddin'dæn ar'tıg]
only (exclusively)	yalnız	['jalnız]
exactly (adv)	dəqiq	[dæ'gig]
about (more or less)	təqribən	[tæg'ribæn]

approximately (adv)	təxminən	[tæh'minæn]
approximate (adj)	təxmini	[tæhmi'ni]
almost (adv)	demək olar ki	[de'mæk o'lar 'ki]
the rest	qalanı	[gala'nı]

each (adj)	hər bir	['hær 'bir]
any (no matter which)	hansı olursa olsun	[han'sı o'lursa ol'sun]
many, much (a lot of)	çox	[tʃoh]
many people	çoxları	[tʃohla'rı]
all (everyone)	hamısı	['hamısı]

in exchange for ...	bunun əvəzində	[bu'nun ævæzin'dæ]
in exchange (adv)	əvəzində	[ævæzin'dæ]
by hand (made)	əl ilə	['æl i'læ]
hardly (negative opinion)	çətin ola bilsin	[tʃə'tin o'la bil'sin]

probably (adv)	guman ki	[gy'man 'ki]
on purpose (adv)	bilərək	[bi'læræk]
by accident (adv)	təsadüfən	[tæ'sadyfæn]

very (adv)	çox	[ʧoh]
for example (adv)	məsələn	['mæsælæn]
between	arasında	[arasın'da]
among	ortasında	[ortasın'da]
so much (such a lot)	bu qədər	['bu gæ'dær]
especially (adv)	xüsusilə	[hysu'silæ]

Basic concepts. Part 2

19. Weekdays

Monday	bazar ertəsi	[ba'zar ærtæ'si]
Tuesday	çərşənbə axşamı	[ʧərʃæn'bæ ahʃa'mı]
Wednesday	çərşənbə	[ʧərʃæn'bæ]
Thursday	cümə axşamı	[ʤu'mæ ahʃa'mı]
Friday	cümə	[ʤu'mæ]
Saturday	şənbə	[ʃæn'bæ]
Sunday	bazar	[ba'zar]

today (adv)	bu gün	['bu 'gyn]
tomorrow (adv)	sabah	['sabah]
the day after tomorrow	birigün	[bi'rigyn]
yesterday (adv)	dünən	['dynæn]
the day before yesterday	sıraǧa gün	[sıraɣ'a 'gyn]

day	gündüz	[gyn'dyz]
working day	iş günü	['iʃ gy'ny]
public holiday	bayram günü	[baj'ram gy'ny]
day off	istirahət günü	[istira'hæt gy'ny]
weekend	istirahət günləri	[istira'hæt gynle'ri]

all day long	bütün günü	[by'tyn gy'ny]
next day (adv)	ertəsi gün	[ærtæ'si 'gyn]
two days ago	iki gün qabaq	[i'ki 'gyn ga'bag]
the day before	ərəfəsində	[æræfæsin'dæ]
daily (adj)	gündəlik	[gyndæ'lik]
every day (adv)	hər gün	['hær gyn]

week	həftə	[hæf'tæ]
last week (adv)	keçən həftə	[ke'ʧən hæf'tæ]
next week (adv)	gələn həftə	[gæ'læn hæf'tæ]
weekly (adj)	həftəlik	[hæftæ'lik]
every week (adv)	həftədə bir	[hæftæ'dæ 'bir]
twice a week	həftədə iki dəfə	[hæftæ'dæ i'ki dæ'fæ]
every Tuesday	hər çərşənbə axşamı	['hær ʧərʃæn'bæ ahʃa'mı]

20. Hours. Day and night

morning	səhər	[sæ'hær]
in the morning	səhərçaǧı	[sæ'hær ʧaɣ'ı]
noon, midday	günorta	[gynor'ta]
in the afternoon	nahardan sonra	[nahar'dan son'ra]

evening	axşam	[ah'ʃam]
in the evening	axşam	[ah'ʃam]

night	gecə	[ge'dʒæ]
at night	gecə	[ge'dʒæ]
midnight	gecəyarı	[gedʒæja'rı]
second	saniyə	[sani'jə]
minute	dəqiqə	[dægi'gæ]
hour	saat	[sa'at]
half an hour	yarım saat	[ja'rım sa'at]
quarter of an hour	on beş dəqiqə	['on 'beʃ dægi'gæ]
fifteen minutes	on beş dəqiqə	['on 'beʃ dægi'gæ]
24 hours	gecə-gündüz	[ge'dʒæ gyn'dyz]
sunrise	günəşin doğması	[gynæ'ʃin doɣma'sı]
dawn	şəfəq	[ʃæ'fæg]
early morning	səhər tezdən	[sæ'hær tez'dæn]
sunset	gün batan çağı	['gyn ba'tan tʃaɣ'ı]
early in the morning	erkəndən	[ærkæn'dæn]
this morning	bu gün səhər	['bu 'gyn sæ'hær]
tomorrow morning	sabah səhər	['sabah sæ'hær]
this afternoon	bu gün günorta çağı	['bu 'gyn gynor'ta tʃaɣ'ı]
in the afternoon	nahardan sonra	[nahar'dan son'ra]
tomorrow afternoon	sabah nahardan sonra	['sabah nahar'dan son'ra]
tonight (this evening)	bu gün axşam	['bu 'gyn ah'ʃam]
tomorrow night	sabah axşam	['sabah ah'ʃam]
at 3 o'clock sharp	saat üç tamamda	[sa'at 'ytʃ tamam'da]
about 4 o'clock	təxminən saat dörd radələrində	[tæh'minæn sa'at dørd … radælærin'dæ]
by 12 o'clock	saat on iki üçün	[sa'at 'on i'ki y'tʃun]
in 20 minutes	iyirmi dəqiqədən sonra	[ijır'mi dægigæ'dæn son'ra]
in an hour	bir saatdan sonra	['bir sa:t'dan son'ra]
on time (adv)	vaxtında	[vahtın'da]
a quarter to …	on beş dəqiqə qalmış	['on 'beʃ dægi'gæ gal'mıʃ]
within an hour	bir saat ərzində	['bir sa'at ærzin'dæ]
every 15 minutes	hər on beş dəqiqədən bir	['hær 'on 'beʃ dægigæ'dæn bir]
round the clock	gecə-gündüz	[ge'dʒæ gyn'dyz]

21. Months. Seasons

January	yanvar	[jan'var]
February	fevral	[fev'ral]
March	mart	[mart]
April	aprel	[ap'rel]
May	may	[maj]
June	iyun	[i'yn]
July	iyul	[i'yl]
August	avqust	['avgust]

27

September	sentyabr	[sen't!abr]
October	oktyabr	[ok't!abr]
November	noyabr	[no'jabr]
December	dekabr	[de'kabr]

spring	yaz	[jaz]
in spring	yazda	[jaz'da]
spring (as adj)	yaz	[jaz]

summer	yay	[jaj]
in summer	yayda	[jaj'da]
summer (as adj)	yay	[jaj]

autumn	payız	[pa'jız]
in autumn	payızda	[pajız'da]
autumn (as adj)	payız	[pa'jız]

winter	qış	[gıʃ]
in winter	qışda	[gıʃ'da]
winter (as adj)	qış	[gıʃ]

month	ay	[aj]
this month	bu ay	['bu 'aj]
next month	gələn ay	[gæ'læn 'aj]
last month	keçən ay	[ke'tʃən 'aj]

a month ago	bir ay qabaq	['bir 'aj ga'bag]
in a month	bir aydan sonra	['bir aj'dan son'ra]
in two months	iki aydan sonra	[i'ki aj'dan son'ra]
a whole month	bütün ay	[by'tyn 'aj]
all month long	bütöv ay	[by'tøv 'aj]

monthly (~ magazine)	aylıq	[aj'lıg]
monthly (adv)	ayda bir dəfə	[aj'da 'bir dæfæ]
every month	hər ay	['hær 'aj]
twice a month	ayda iki dəfə	[aj'da i'ki dæ'fæ]

year	il	[il]
this year	bu il	['bu 'il]
next year	gələn il	[gæ'læn 'il]
last year	keçən il	[ke'tʃən 'il]

a year ago	bir il əvvəl	['bir 'il æv'væl]
in a year	bir ildən sonra	['bir il'dæn son'ra]
in two years	iki ildən sonra	[i'ki il'dæn son'ra]
a whole year	il uzunu	['il uzu'nu]
all year long	bütün il boyu	[by'tyn il bo'y]

every year	hər il	['hær 'il]
annual (adj)	illik	[il'lik]
annually (adv)	hər ilki	['hær il'ki]
4 times a year	ildə dörd dəfə	[il'dæ 'dørd dæ'fæ]

date (e.g. today's ~)	gün	[gyn]
date (e.g. ~ of birth)	tarix	[ta'rih]
calendar	təqvim	[tæg'vim]

half a year	yarım il	[ja'rım 'il]
six months	yarım illik	[ja'rım il'lik]
season (summer, etc.)	mövsüm	[møv'sym]
century	əsr	[æsr]

22. Time. Miscellaneous

time	zaman	[za'man]
instant (n)	qırpım	[gır'pım]
moment	an	[an]
instant (adj)	ani	[a'ni]

period (length of time)	müddət	[myd'dæt]
life	həyat	[hæ'jat]
eternity	əbədiyyat	[æbædi'jːat]

epoch	dövr	['døvr]
era	era	['æra]
cycle	silsilə	[silsi'læ]
period	zaman	[za'man]
term (short-~)	müddət	[myd'dæt]

the future	gələcək	[gælæ'dʒæk]
future (as adj)	gələcək	[gælæ'dʒæk]
next time	gələn dəfə	[gæ'læn dæ'fæ]

the past	keçmiş	[ketʃ'miʃ]
past (recent)	keçən	[ke'tʃən]
last time	keçən dəfə	[ke'tʃən dæ'fæ]

later (adv)	daha sonra	[da'ha 'sonra]
after	sonra	[son'ra]
nowadays (adv)	hal hazırda	['hal hazır'da]
now (adv)	indi	[in'di]
immediately (adv)	dərhal	['dærhal]
soon (adv)	tezliklə	[tez'liklæ]
in advance (beforehand)	qabaqcadan	[gabagdʒa'dan]

a long time ago	çoxdan	[tʃoh'dan]
recently (adv)	bir az bundan əvvəl	['bir 'az bun'dan æv'væl]
destiny	qismət	[gis'mæt]
memories (childhood ~)	xatirə	[hati'ræ]
archives	arxiv	[ar'hiv]

during ...	zamanı...	[zama'nı]
long, a long time (adv)	uzun zaman	[u'zun za'man]
not long (adv)	az vaxta	[az vah'ta]
early (in the morning)	erkən	[ærkæ'æn]
late (not early)	gec	[gedʒ]

forever (for good)	əbədi olaraq	[æbæ'di o'larag]
to start (begin)	başlamaq	[baʃla'mag]
to postpone (vt)	keçirmək	[ketʃir'mæk]
at the same time	eyni zamanda	['æjni zaman'da]

29

permanently (adv)	həmişə	['hæmiʃæ]
constant (noise, pain)	daimi	[dai'mi]
temporary (adj)	müvəqqəti	[myvæggæ'ti]

sometimes (adv)	hərdən	[hær'dæn]
rarely (adv)	nadir hallarda	[na'dir hallar'da]
often (adv)	tez-tez	['tez 'tez]

23. Opposites

rich (adj)	varlı	[var'lı]
poor (adj)	kasıb	[ka'sıb]

ill, sick (adj)	xəstə	[hæs'tæ]
healthy (adj)	sağlam	[saɣ'lam]

big (adj)	böyük	[bø'yk]
small (adj)	kiçik	[ki'tʃik]

quickly (adv)	cəld	[dʒæld]
slowly (adv)	asta-asta	[as'ta as'ta]

fast (adj)	cəld	[dʒæld]
slow (adj)	asta	[as'ta]

cheerful (adj)	şən	[ʃæn]
sad (adj)	qəmgin	[gæm'gin]

together (adv)	birlikdə	[birlik'dæ]
separately (adv)	ayrı-ayrı	[aj'rı aj'rı]

aloud (to read)	ucadan	[udʒa'dan]
silently (to oneself)	ürəyində	[yræjın'dæ]

tall (adj)	hündür	[hyn'dyr]
low (adj)	alçaq	[al'tʃag]

deep (adj)	dərin	[dæ'rin]
shallow (adj)	dayaz	[da'jaz]

yes	bəli	['bæli]
no	xeyr	[hejr]

distant (in space)	uzaq	[u'zag]
nearby (adj)	yaxın	[ja'hın]

far (adv)	uzaqda	[uzag'da]
nearby (adv)	yaxında	[jahın'da]

long (adj)	uzun	[u'zun]
short (adj)	qısa	[gı'sa]

good (kindhearted)	xeyirxah	[hejır'hah]
evil (adj)	hirsli	[hirs'li]

married (adj)	evli	[æv'li]
single (adj)	subay	[su'baj]
to forbid (vt)	qadağan etmək	[gaday'an æt'mæk]
to permit (vt)	icazə vermək	[idʒa'zæ ver'mæk]
end	son	[son]
beginning	başlanqıc	[baʃla'ŋıdʒ]
left (adj)	sol	[sol]
right (adj)	sağ	[say]
first (adj)	birinci	[birin'dʒi]
last (adj)	sonuncu	[sonun'dʒu]
crime	cinayət	[dʒina'jət]
punishment	cəza	[dʒæ'za]
to order (vt)	əmr etmək	['æmr æt'mæk]
to obey (vi, vt)	tabe olmaq	[ta'be ol'mag]
straight (adj)	düz	[dyz]
curved (adj)	əyri	[æj'ri]
heaven	cənnət	[dʒæ'ŋæt]
hell	cəhənnəm	[dʒæhæ'ŋæm]
to be born	anadan olmaq	[ana'dan ol'mag]
to die (vi)	ölmək	[øl'mæk]
strong (adj)	güclü	[gydʒ'ly]
weak (adj)	zəif	[zæ'if]
old (adj)	köhnə	[køh'næ]
young (adj)	cavan	[dʒa'van]
old (adj)	köhnə	[køh'næ]
new (adj)	təzə	[tæ'zæ]
hard (adj)	bərk	[bærk]
soft (adj)	yumşaq	[ym'ʃag]
warm (adj)	isti	[is'ti]
cold (adj)	soyuq	[so'yg]
fat (adj)	yoğun	[joy'un]
slim (adj)	arıq	[a'rıg]
narrow (adj)	ensiz	[æn'siz]
wide (adj)	enli	[æn'li]
good (adj)	yaxşı	[jah'ʃı]
bad (adj)	pis	[pis]
brave (adj)	cəsarətli	[dʒæsaræt'li]
cowardly (adj)	qorxaq	[gor'hag]

24. Lines and shapes

square	kvadrat	[kvad'rat]
square (as adj)	kvadrat şəkilli	[kvad'rat ʃækil'li]
circle	dairə	[dai'ræ]
round (adj)	dəyirmi	[dæjır'mi]
triangle	üçbucaq	[ytʃbu'dʒag]
triangular (adj)	üçbucaqlı	[ytʃbudʒag'lı]

oval	oval	[o'val]
oval (as adj)	oval	[o'val]
rectangle	düzbucaqlı dördbucaq	[dyzbudʒag'lı dørdbu'dʒag]
rectangular (adj)	düzbucaqlı	[dyzbudʒag'lı]

pyramid	piramida	[pira'mida]
rhombus	romb	[romb]
trapezium	trapesiya	[tra'pesija]
cube	kub	[kub]
prism	prizma	['prizma]

circumference	çevrə	[tʃev'ræ]
sphere	kürə	[ky'ræ]
globe (sphere)	kürə	[ky'ræ]
diameter	diametr	[di'ametr]
radius	radius	['radius]
perimeter	perimetr	[pe'rimetr]
centre	mərkəz	[mær'kæz]

horizontal (adj)	üfqi	[yf'gi]
vertical (adj)	şaquli	[ʃagu'li]
parallel (n)	paralel	[para'lel]
parallel (as adj)	paralel	[para'lel]

line	xətt	[hætt]
stroke	xətt	[hætt]
straight line	düz	[dyz]
curve (curved line)	əyri	[æj'ri]
thin (line, etc.)	nazik	[na'zik]
contour (outline)	kontur	['kontur]

intersection	kəsişmə	[kæsiʃ'mæ]
right angle	düz bucaq	['dyz bu'dʒag]
segment	seqment	[seg'ment]
sector	bölmə	[bøl'mæ]
side (of triangle)	tərəf	[tæ'ræf]
angle	bucaq	[bu'dʒag]

25. Units of measurement

weight	çəki	[tʃə'ki]
length	uzunluq	[uzun'lug]
width	en	[æn]
height	hündürlük	[hyndyr'lyk]

depth	dərinlik	[dærin'lik]
volume	həcm	[hædʒm]
area	səth	[sæth]

gram	qram	[gram]
milligram	milliqram	[millig'ram]
kilogram	kiloqram	[kilog'ram]
ton	ton	[ton]
pound	girvənkə	[girvæ'ŋkæ]
ounce	unsiya	['unsija]

metre	metr	[metr]
millimetre	millimetr	[milli'metr]
centimetre	santimetr	[santi'metr]
kilometre	kilometr	[kilo'metr]
mile	mil	[mil]

inch	düym	[dyjm]
foot	fut	[fut]
yard	yard	[jard]

square metre	kvadrat metr	[kvad'rat 'metr]
hectare	hektar	[hæk'tar]

litre	litr	[litr]
degree	dərəcə	[dæræ'dʒæ]
volt	volt	[volt]
ampere	amper	[am'per]
horsepower	at gücü	['at gy'dʒy]

quantity	miqdar	[mig'dar]
a little bit of ...	bir az...	['bir 'az]
half	yarım	[ja'rɪm]
dozen	on iki	['on i'ki]
piece (item)	ədəd	[æ'dæd]

size	ölçü	[øl'tʃu]
scale (map ~)	miqyas	[mig'jas]

minimum (adj)	minimal	[mini'mal]
the smallest (adj)	ən kiçik	['æn ki'tʃik]
medium (adj)	orta	[or'ta]
maximum (adj)	maksimal	[maksi'mal]
the largest (adj)	ən böyük	['æn bø'yk]

26. Containers

jar (glass)	şüşə banka	[ʃy'ʃæ ba'ŋka]
tin, can	konserv bankası	[kon'serv baŋka'sɪ]
bucket	vedrə	[ved'ræ]
barrel	çəllək	[tʃəl'læk]

basin (for washing)	ləyən	[læ'jən]
tank (for liquid, gas)	bak	[bak]

33

hip flask	mehtərə	[mehtæ'ræ]
jerrycan	kanistr	[ka'nistr]
cistern (tank)	sistern	[sis'tern]

mug	parç	[partʃ]
cup (of coffee, etc.)	fincan	[fin'dʒan]
saucer	nəlbəki	[nælbæ'ki]
glass (tumbler)	stəkan	[stæ'kan]
glass (~ of vine)	qədəh	[gæ'dæh]
stew pot	qazan	[ga'zan]

bottle (~ of wine)	şüşə	[ʃy'ʃæ]
neck (of the bottle)	boğaz	[bo'gaz]

carafe	qrafin	[gra'fin]
jug (earthenware)	səhənk	[sæ'hæŋk]
vessel (container)	qab	[gab]
pot (crock)	bardaq	[bar'dag]
vase	güldan	[gyʎ'dan]

bottle (~ of perfume)	flakon	[fla'kon]
vial, small bottle	şüşə	[ʃy'ʃæ]
tube (of toothpaste)	tübik	['tybik]

sack (bag)	torba	[tor'ba]
bag (paper ~, plastic ~)	paket	[pa'ket]
packet (of cigarettes, etc.)	paçka	[patʃ'ka]

box (e.g. shoebox)	qutu	[gu'tu]
crate	yeşik	[e'ʃik]
basket	səbət	[sæ'bæt]

27. Materials

material	material	[materi'al]
wood	taxta	[tah'ta]
wooden (adj)	taxta	[tah'ta]

glass (n)	şüşə	[ʃy'ʃæ]
glass (as adj)	şüşə	[ʃy'ʃæ]

stone (n)	daş	[daʃ]
stone (as adj)	daşdan olan	[daʃ'dan o'lan]

plastic (n)	plastik kütlə	[plas'tik kyt'læ]
plastic (as adj)	plastik kütlədən qayrılmış	[plas'tik kytlæ'dæn gajrıl'mıʃ]

rubber (n)	rezin	[re'zin]
rubber (as adj)	rezin	[re'zin]

material, fabric (n)	parça	[par'tʃa]
fabric (as adj)	parçadan	[partʃa'dan]
paper (n)	kağız	[kaʁ'ız]

paper (as adj)	kağız	[kaɣ'ız]
cardboard (n)	karton	[kar'ton]
cardboard (as adj)	karton	[kar'ton]

polythene	polietilen	[poliæti'len]
cellophane	sellofan	[sello'fan]
plywood	faner	[fa'ner]

porcelain (n)	çini qab	['ʧini 'gab]
porcelain (as adj)	çini	['ʧini]
clay (n)	gil	[gil]
clay (as adj)	saxsı	[sah'sı]
ceramics (n)	keramika	[ke'ramika]
ceramic (as adj)	keramik	[kera'mik]

28. Metals

metal (n)	metal	[me'tal]
metal (as adj)	metal	[me'tal]
alloy (n)	xəlitə	[hæli'tæ]

gold (n)	qızıl	[gı'zıl]
gold, golden (adj)	qızıl	[gı'zıl]
silver (n)	gümüş	[gy'myʃ]
silver (as adj)	gümüş	[gy'myʃ]

iron (n)	dəmir	[dæ'mir]
iron (adj), made of iron	dəmir	[dæ'mir]
steel (n)	polad	[po'lad]
steel (as adj)	polad	[po'lad]
copper (n)	mis	[mis]
copper (as adj)	mis	[mis]

aluminium (n)	alümin	[aly'min]
aluminium (as adj)	alümin	[aly'min]
bronze (n)	bürünc	[by'ryndʒ]
bronze (as adj)	bürünc	[by'ryndʒ]

brass	latun	[la'tun]
nickel	nikel	['nikel]
platinum	platin	[pla'tin]
mercury	civə	[dʒi'væ]
tin	qalay	[ga'laj]
lead	qurğuşun	[gurɣu'ʃun]
zinc	sink	[siŋk]

35

HUMAN BEING

Human being. The body

29. Humans. Basic concepts

human being	adam	[a'dam]
man (adult male)	kişi	[ki'ʃi]
woman	qadın	[ga'dın]
child	uşaq	[u'ʃag]

girl	qız	[gız]
boy	oğlan	[oɣ'lan]
teenager	yeniyetmə	[eniet'mæ]
old man	qoca	[go'dʒa]
old woman	qarı	[ga'rı]

30. Human anatomy

organism	orqanizm	[orga'nizm]
heart	ürək	[y'ræk]
blood	qan	[gan]
artery	arteriya	[ar'terija]
vein	vena	['vena]

brain	beyin	[be'jın]
nerve	sinir	[si'nir]
nerves	sinirlər	[sinir'lær]
vertebra	fəqərə	[fægæ'ræ]
spine	onurğa sümüyü	[onurɣ'a symy'y]

stomach (organ)	mədə	[mæ'dæ]
intestines, bowel	bağırsaqlar	[baɣırsag'lar]
intestine (e.g. large ~)	bağırsaq	[baɣır'sag]
liver	qara ciyər	[ga'ra dʒi'jər]
kidney	böyrək	[bøj'ræk]

bone	sümük	[sy'myk]
skeleton	skelet	[ske'let]
rib	qabırqa	[gabır'ga]
skull	kəllə	[kæl'læ]

muscle	əzələ	[æzæ'læ]
biceps	biseps	['biseps]
triceps	triseps	['triseps]
tendon	vətər	[væ'tær]
joint	oynaq	[oj'nag]

lungs	ağ ciyər	[ˈaɣ dʒiˈær]
genitals	cinsiyyət orqanları	[dʒinsiˈjːət ˈorganları]
skin	dəri	[dæˈri]

31. Head

head	baş	[baʃ]
face	üz	[yz]
nose	burun	[buˈrun]
mouth	ağız	[aɣˈız]

eye	göz	[ˈgøz]
eyes	gözlər	[gøzˈlær]
pupil	göz bəbəyi	[ˈgøz bæˈbæjı]
eyebrow	qaş	[gaʃ]
eyelash	kirpik	[kirˈpik]
eyelid	göz qapağı	[ˈgøz gapaɣˈı]

tongue	dil	[dil]
tooth	diş	[diʃ]
lips	dodaq	[doˈdag]
cheekbones	almacıq sümüyü	[almaˈdʒıg symyˈy]
gum	diş əti	[ˈdiʃ æˈti]
palate	damağ	[daˈmaɣ]

nostrils	burun deşikləri	[buˈrun deʃiklæˈri]
chin	çənə	[ʧəˈnæ]
jaw	çənə	[ʧəˈnæ]
cheek	yanaq	[jaˈnag]

forehead	alın	[aˈlın]
temple	gicgah	[gidʒˈgah]
ear	qulaq	[guˈlag]
back of the head	peysər	[pejˈsær]
neck	boyun	[boˈyn]
throat	boğaz	[boˈgaz]

hair	saç	[saʧ]
hairstyle	saç düzümü	[ˈsaʧ dyzyˈmy]
haircut	saç vurdurma	[ˈsaʧ vurdurˈma]
wig	parik	[paˈrik]

moustache	bığ	[bıɣ]
beard	saqqal	[sagˈgal]
to have (a beard, etc.)	qoymaq	[gojˈmag]
plait	hörük	[høˈryk]
sideboards	bakenbard	[bakenˈbard]

red-haired (adj)	kürən	[kyˈræn]
grey (hair)	saçı ağarmış	[saˈʧı aɣarˈmıʃ]
bald (adj)	keçəl	[keˈʧəl]
bald patch	daz	[daz]
ponytail	quyruq	[gujˈrug]
fringe	zülf	[zyʎf]

37

32. Human body

hand	əl	[æl]
arm	qol	[gol]
finger	barmaq	[bar'mag]
thumb	baş barmaq	['baʃ bar'mag]
little finger	çeçələ barmaq	[ʧeʧə'læ bar'mag]
nail	dırnaq	[dır'nag]
fist	yumruq	[ym'rug]
palm	ovuc içi	[o'vudʒ i'ʧi]
wrist	bilək	[bi'læk]
forearm	bazu önü	[ba'zı ø'ny]
elbow	dirsək	[dir'sæk]
shoulder	çiyin	[ʧi'jın]
leg	topuq	[to'pug]
foot	pəncə	[pæn'dʒæ]
knee	diz	[diz]
calf (part of leg)	baldır	[bal'dır]
hip	omba	[om'ba]
heel	daban	[da'ban]
body	bədən	[bæ'dæn]
stomach	qarın	[ga'rın]
chest	sinə	[si'næ]
breast	döş	['døʃ]
flank	böyür	[bø'yr]
back	kürək	[ky'ræk]
lower back	bel	[bel]
waist	bel	[bel]
navel	göbək	[gø'bæk]
buttocks	sağrı	[saγ'rı]
bottom	arxa	[ar'ha]
beauty mark	xal	[hal]
tattoo	tatuirovka	[tatui'rovka]
scar	çapıq	[ʧa'pıg]

Clothing & Accessories

33. Outerwear. Coats

clothes	geyim	[ge'jım]
outer clothing	üst geyim	['yst ge'jım]
winter clothing	qış paltarı	['gıʃ palta'rı]

overcoat	palto	[pal'to]
fur coat	kürk	[kyrk]
fur jacket	yarımkürk	[jarım'kyrk]
down coat	pərğu geyim	[pærɣ'u ge'jım]

jacket (e.g. leather ~)	gödəkcə	[gødæk'tʃə]
raincoat	plaş	[plaʃ]
waterproof (adj)	su buraxmayan	['su bu'rahmajan]

34. Men's & women's clothing

shirt	köynək	[køj'næk]
trousers	şalvar	[ʃal'var]
jeans	cins	[dʒins]
jacket (of man's suit)	pencək	[pen'dʒæk]
suit	kişi üçün kostyum	[ki'ʃi y'tʃun kost'ym]

dress (frock)	don	[don]
skirt	yubka	[yb'ka]
blouse	bluzka	[bluz'ka]
knitted jacket	yun kofta	['yn kof'ta]
jacket (of woman's suit)	jaket	[ʒa'ket]

T-shirt	futbolka	[futbol'ka]
shorts (short trousers)	şort	[ʃort]
tracksuit	idman paltarı	[id'man palta'rı]
bathrobe	hamam xələti	[ha'mam hælæ'ti]
pyjamas	pijama	[pi'ʒama]

sweater	sviter	['sviter]
pullover	pulover	[pulo'ver]

waistcoat	jilet	[ʒi'let]
tailcoat	frak	[frak]
dinner suit	smokinq	['smokiŋ]

uniform	forma	['forma]
workwear	iş paltarı	['iʃ palta'rı]
boiler suit	kombinezon	[kombine'zon]
coat (e.g. doctor's ~)	həkim xələti	[hæ'kim hælæ'ti]

39

35. Clothing. Underwear

underwear	alt paltarı	['alt palta'rı]
vest (singlet)	mayka	[maj'ka]
socks	corab	[dʒo'rab]
nightgown	gecə köynəyi	[ge'dʒæ køjnæ'jı]
bra	büsthalter	[byst'halter]
knee highs	golf corab	['golf dʒo'rab]
tights	kolqotka	[kolgot'ka]
stockings	uzun corab	[u'zun dʒo'rab]
swimsuit, bikini	çimmə paltarı	[tʃim'mæ palta'rı]

36. Headwear

hat	papaq	[pa'pag]
trilby hat	şlyapa	['ʃʎapa]
baseball cap	beysbol papağı	[bejs'bol papaɣ'ı]
flatcap	kepka	[kep'ka]
beret	beret	[be'ret]
hood	kapyuşon	[kapy'ʃon]
panama hat	panama	[pa'nama]
knitted hat	yun papaq	['yn pa'pag]
headscarf	baş örtüyü	['baʃ ørty'y]
women's hat	kiçik şlyapa	[ki'tʃik 'ʃʎapa]
hard hat	kaska	[kas'ka]
forage cap	pilot papağı	[pi'lot papaɣ'ı]
helmet	dəbilqə	[dæbil'gæ]
bowler	kotelok	[kote'lok]
top hat	silindr	[si'lindr]

37. Footwear

footwear	ayaqqabı	[ajagga'bı]
ankle boots	botinka	[boti'ŋka]
shoes (low-heeled ~)	tufli	[tuf'li]
boots (cowboy ~)	uzunboğaz çəkmə	[uzunboɣ'az tʃək'mæ]
slippers	şap-şap	['ʃap 'ʃap]
trainers	krossovka	[kros'sovka]
plimsolls, pumps	ket	[ket]
sandals	səndəl	[sæn'dæl]
cobbler	çəkməçi	[tʃəkmæ'tʃi]
heel	daban	[da'ban]
pair (of shoes)	tay	[taj]
shoelace	qaytan	[gaj'tan]

to lace up (vt)	qaytanlamaq	[gajtanla'mag]
shoehorn	dabançəkən	[dabantʃə'kæn]
shoe polish	ayaqqabı kremi	[ajagga'bı kre'mi]

38. Textile. Fabrics

cotton (n)	pambıq parça	[pam'bıg par'tʃa]
cotton (as adj)	pambıq parçadan	[pam'bıg partʃa'dan]
flax (n)	kətan	[kæ'tan]
flax (as adj)	kətan parçadan	[kæ'tan partʃa'dan]

silk (n)	ipək	[i'pæk]
silk (as adj)	ipək	[i'pæk]
wool (n)	yun	[yn]
woollen (adj)	yun	[yn]

velvet	məxmər	[mæh'mær]
suede	zamşa	['zamʃa]
corduroy	velvet	[vel'vet]

nylon (n)	neylon	[nej'lon]
nylon (as adj)	neylondan	[nejlon'dan]
polyester (n)	poliester	[poli'æster]
polyester (as adj)	poliesterdən hazırlanan	[poli'æsterdæn hazırla'nan]

leather (n)	dəri	[dæ'ri]
leather (as adj)	dəridən	[dæri'dæn]
fur (n)	xəz	[hæz]
fur (e.g. ~ coat)	xəzdən tikilmiş	[hæz'dæn tikil'miʃ]

39. Personal accessories

gloves	əlcək	[æl'dʒæk]
mittens	təkbarmaq əlcək	[tækbar'mag æl'dʒæk]
scarf (long)	şərf	[ʃærf]

glasses	eynək	[æj'næk]
frame (eyeglass ~)	çərçivə	[tʃərtʃi'væ]
umbrella	çətir	[tʃə'tir]
walking stick	əl ağacı	['æl aɣa'dʒı]
hairbrush	şaç şotkası	['satʃ ʃotka'sı]
fan	yelpik	[el'pik]

tie (necktie)	qalstuk	['galstuk]
bow tie	kəpənək qalstuk	[kæpæ'næk 'galstuk]
braces	çiyinbağı	[tʃijınbaɣ'ı]
handkerchief	cib dəsmalı	['dʒib dæsma'lı]

comb	daraq	[da'rag]
hair slide	baş sancağı	['baʃ sandʒaɣ'ı]
hairpin	baş sancağı	['baʃ sandʒaɣ'ı]
buckle	toqqa	[tog'ga]

41

belt	kəmər	[kæ'mær]
shoulder strap	kəmərcik	[kæmær'dʒik]

bag (handbag)	çanta	[ʧan'ta]
handbag	qadın cantası	[ga'dın ʧanta'sı]
rucksack	arxa çantası	[ar'ha ʧanta'sı]

40. Clothing. Miscellaneous

fashion	moda	['moda]
in vogue (adj)	dəbdə olan	[dæb'dæ o'lan]
fashion designer	modelçi	[model'ʧi]

collar	yaxalıq	[jaha'lıg]
pocket	cib	[dʒib]
pocket (as adj)	cib	[dʒib]
sleeve	qol	[gol]
hanging loop	ilmə asqı	[iʎ'mæ as'gı]
flies (on trousers)	miyança	[mijan'ʧa]

zip (fastener)	zəncir-bənd	[zen'dʒir 'bænd]
fastener	bənd	[bænd]
button	düymə	[dyj'mæ]
buttonhole	ilmə	[iʎ'mæ]
to come off (ab. button)	qopmaq	[gop'mag]

to sew (vi, vt)	tikmək	[tik'mæk]
to embroider (vi, vt)	naxış tikmək	[na'hıʃ tik'mæk]
embroidery	naxış	[na'hıʃ]
sewing needle	iynə	[ij'næ]
thread	sap	[sap]
seam	tikiş	[ti'kiʃ]

to get dirty (vi)	çirklənmək	[ʧirklæn'mæk]
stain (mark, spot)	ləkə	[læ'kæ]
to crease, crumple (vi)	əzilmək	[æzil'mæk]
to tear (vt)	cırmaq	[dʒır'mag]
clothes moth	güvə	[gy'væ]

41. Personal care. Cosmetics

toothpaste	diş məcunu	['diʃ mædʒu'nu]
toothbrush	diş fırçası	['diʃ fırʧa'sı]
to clean one's teeth	dişləri fırçalamaq	[diʃlæ'ri fırʧala'mag]

razor	ülgüc	[yʎ'gydʒ]
shaving cream	üz qırxmaq üçün krem	['yz gırh'mag y'ʧun 'krem]
to shave (vi)	üzünü qırxmaq	[yzy'ny gırh'mag]

soap	sabun	[sa'bun]
shampoo	şampun	[ʃam'pun]
scissors	qayçı	[gaj'ʧı]

nail file	dırnaq üçün kiçik bıçqı	[dɪr'nag y'ʧun ki'ʧik bɪʧ'gɪ]
nail clippers	dırnaq üçün kiçik kəlbətin	[dɪr'nag y'ʧun ki'ʧik kælbæ'tin]
tweezers	maqqaş	[mag'gaʃ]

cosmetics	kosmetika	[kos'metika]
face pack	maska	[mas'ka]
manicure	manikür	[mani'kyr]
to have a manicure	manikür etmək	[mani'kyr æt'mæk]
pedicure	pedikür	[pedi'kyr]

make-up bag	kosmetika üçün kiçik çanta	[kos'metika y'ʧun ki'ʧik ʧan'ta]
face powder	pudra	[pud'ra]
powder compact	pudra qabı	[pud'ra ga'bɪ]
blusher	ənlik	[æn'lik]

perfume (bottled)	ətir	[æ'tir]
toilet water	ətirli su	[ætir'li 'su]
lotion	losyon	[los'jon]
cologne	odekolon	[odeko'lon]

eyeshadow	göz ətrafına sürülən boyalar	['gøz ætrafɪ'na syry'læn boja'lar]
eyeliner	göz üçün karandaş	['gøz y'ʧun karan'daʃ]
mascara	kirpik üçün tuş	[kir'pik y'ʧun 'tuʃ]

lipstick	dodaq boyası	[do'dag boja'sɪ]
nail polish	dırnaq üçün lak	[dɪr'nag y'ʧun 'lak]
hair spray	saç üçün lak	['saʧ y'ʧun 'lak]
deodorant	dezodorant	[dezodo'rant]

cream	krem	[krem]
face cream	üz kremi	['yz kre'mi]
hand cream	əl kremi	['æl kre'mi]
anti-wrinkle cream	qırışığa qarşı krem	[gɪrɪʃɪɣ'a gar'ʃɪ 'krem]
day cream	gündüz kremi	[gyn'dyz kre'mi]
night cream	gecə kremi	[ge'ʤæ kre'mi]

tampon	tampon	[tam'pon]
toilet paper	tualet kağızı	[tua'let kʲaɣɪ'zɪ]
hair dryer	fen	[fen]

42. Jewellery

jewellery	cəvahirat	[ʤævahi'rat]
precious (e.g. ~ stone)	qiymətli	[gijmæt'li]
hallmark	damğa	[damɣ'a]

ring	üzük	[y'zyk]
wedding ring	nişan üzüyü	[ni'ʃan yzy'y]
bracelet	qolbağ	[gol'baɣ]

earrings	sırğa	[sɪrɣ'a]
necklace (~ of pearls)	boyunbağı	[boynbaɣ'ɪ]
crown	tac	[taʤ]

43

bead necklace	muncuq	[mun'dʒug]
diamond	brilyant	[bril'jant]
emerald	zümrüd	[zym'ryd]
ruby	yaqut	[ja'gut]
sapphire	sapfir	[sap'fir]
pearl	mirvari	[mirva'ri]
amber	kəhrəba	[kæhræ'ba]

43. Watches. Clocks

watch (wristwatch)	qol saatı	[gol sa:'tı]
dial	siferblat	[siferb'lat]
hand (of clock, watch)	əqrəb	[æg'ræb]
metal bracelet	saat bilərziyi	[sa'at bilærzi'jı]
watch strap	qayış	[ga'jıʃ]
battery	batareya	[bata'reja]
to be flat (battery)	sıradan çıxmaq	[sıra'dan tʃıh'mag]
to change a battery	batareyanı dəyişmək	[bata'rejanı dæjıʃ'mæk]
to run fast	irəli getmək	[iræ'li get'mæk]
to run slow	geri qalmaq	[ge'ri gal'mag]
wall clock	divar saatı	[di'var sa:'tı]
hourglass	qum saatı	['gum sa:'tı]
sundial	günəş saatı	[gy'næʃ sa:'tı]
alarm clock	zəngli saat	[zæŋ'li sa'at]
watchmaker	saatsaz	[sa:'tsaz]
to repair (v)	təmir etmək	[tæ'mir æt'mæk]

Food. Nutricion

44. Food

meat	ət	[æt]
chicken	toyuq	[to'yg]
young chicken	cücə	[dʒy'dʒæ]
duck	ördək	[ør'dæk]
goose	qaz	[gaz]
game	ov quşları və heyvanları	['ov guʃla'rı 'væ hæjvanla'rı]
turkey	hind toyuğu	['hind toyɣ'u]

pork	donuz əti	[do'nuz æ'ti]
veal	dana əti	[da'na æ'ti]
lamb	qoyun əti	[go'yn æ'ti]
beef	mal əti	['mal æ'ti]
rabbit	ev dovşanı	['æv dovʃa'nı]

sausage (salami, etc.)	kolbasa	[kolba'sa]
vienna sausage	sosiska	[sosis'ka]
bacon	bekon	['bekon]
ham	vetçina	[vetʃi'na]
gammon (ham)	donuz budu	[do'nuz bu'du]

pâté	paştet	[paʃ'tet]
liver	qara ciyər	[ga'ra dʒi'jər]
lard	iç yağı	['itʃ jaɣ'ı]
mince	qiymə	[gij'mæ]
tongue	dil	[dil]

egg	yumurta	[ymur'ta]
eggs	yumurtalar	[ymurta'lar]
egg white	zülal	[zy'lal]
egg yolk	yumurtanın sarısı	[ymurta'nın sarı'sı]

fish	balıq	[ba'lıg]
seafood	dəniz məhsulları	[dæ'niz mæhsulla'rı]
caviar	kürü	[ky'ry]

crab	qısaquyruq	[gısaguj'rug]
prawn	krevet	[kre'vet]
oyster	istridyə	[istrid'jə]
spiny lobster	lanqust	[la'ŋust]
octopus	səkkizayaqlı ilbiz	[sækkizajag'lı il'biz]
squid	kalmar	[kal'mar]

sturgeon	nərə balığı	[næ'ræ balıɣ'ı]
salmon	qızılbalıq	[gızılba'lıg]
halibut	paltus	['paltus]
cod	treska	[tres'ka]

mackerel	skumbriya	['skumbrija]
tuna	tunes	[tu'nes]
eel	angvil balığı	[aŋ'vil balıɣ'ı]

trout	alabalıq	[alaba'lıg]
sardine	sardina	[sar'dina]
pike	durnabalığı	[durnabalıɣ'ı]
herring	siyənək	[sijə'næk]

bread	çörək	[ʧo'ræk]
cheese	pendir	[pen'dir]
sugar	şəkər	[ʃæ'kær]
salt	duz	[duz]

rice	düyü	[dy'y]
pasta	makaron	[maka'ron]
noodles	əriştə	[æriʃ'tæ]

butter	kərə yağı	[kæ'ræ jaɣı]
vegetable oil	bitki yağı	[bit'ki jaɣı]
sunflower oil	günəbaxan yağ	[gynæba'han jaɣ]
margarine	marqarin	[marga'rin]

| olives | zeytun | [zej'tun] |
| olive oil | zeytun yağı | [zej'tun jaɣı] |

milk	süd	[syd]
condensed milk	qatılaşdırılmış süd	[gatılaʃdırıl'mıʃ 'syd]
yogurt	yoqurt	['jogurt]
sour cream	xama	[ha'ma]
cream (of milk)	xama	[ha'ma]

| mayonnaise | mayonez | [majo'nez] |
| buttercream | krem | [krem] |

groats	yarma	[jar'ma]
flour	un	[un]
tinned food	konserv	[kon'serv]

cornflakes	qarğıdalı yumağı	[garɣıda'lı ymaɣ'ı]
honey	bal	['bal]
jam	cem	[ʤem]
chewing gum	saqqız	[sag'gız]

45. Drinks

water	su	[su]
drinking water	içməli su	[iʧmæ'li 'su]
mineral water	mineral su	[mine'ral 'su]

still (adj)	qazsız	[gaz'sız]
carbonated (adj)	qazlı	[gaz'lı]
sparkling (adj)	qazlı	[gaz'lı]
ice	buz	[buz]

with ice	buzlu	[buz'lu]
non-alcoholic (adj)	spirtsiz	[spir'tsiz]
soft drink	spirtsiz içki	[spir'tsiz itʃ'ki]
cool soft drink	sərinləşdirici içki	[særinlæʃdiri'dʒi itʃ'ki]
lemonade	limonad	[limo'nad]

spirits	spirtli içkilər	[spirt'li itʃki'lær]
wine	çaxır	[tʃa'hır]
white wine	ağ çaxır	['aɣ tʃa'hır]
red wine	qırmızı çaxır	[gırmı'zı tʃa'hır]

liqueur	likyor	[lik'jor]
champagne	şampan	[ʃam'pan]
vermouth	vermut	['vermut]

whisky	viski	['viski]
vodka	araq	[a'rag]
gin	cin	[dʒin]
cognac	konyak	[ko'nʲak]
rum	rom	[rom]

coffee	qəhvə	[gæh'væ]
black coffee	qara qəhvə	[ga'ra gæh'væ]
white coffee	südlü qəhvə	[syd'ly gæh'væ]
cappuccino	xamalı qəhvə	[hama'lı gæh'væ]
instant coffee	tez həll olunan qəhvə	['tez 'hæll olu'nan gæh'væ]

milk	süd	[syd]
cocktail	kokteyl	[kok'tejl]
milk shake	südlü kokteyl	[syd'ly kok'tejl]

juice	şirə	[ʃi'ræ]
tomato juice	tomat şirəsi	[to'mat ʃiræ'si]
orange juice	portağal şirəsi	[portaɣ'al ʃiræ'si]
freshly squeezed juice	təzə sıxılmış şirə	[tæ'zæ sıhıl'mıʃ ʃi'ræ]

beer	pivə	[pi'væ]
lager	açıq rəngli pivə	[a'tʃıg ræŋ'li pi'væ]
bitter	tünd rəngli pivə	['tynd ræŋ'li pi'væ]

tea	çay	[tʃaj]
black tea	qara çay	[ga'ra 'tʃaj]
green tea	yaşıl çay	[ja'ʃıl 'tʃaj]

46. Vegetables

vegetables	tərəvəz	[tæræ'væz]
greens	göyərti	[gøjər'ti]

tomato	pomidor	[pomi'dor]
cucumber	xiyar	[hi'jar]
carrot	kök	['køk]
potato	kartof	[kar'tof]
onion	soğan	[soɣ'an]

47

garlic	sarımsaq	[sarım'sag]
cabbage	kələm	[kæ'læm]
cauliflower	gül kələm	['gyʎ kæ'læm]
Brussels sprouts	Brüssel kələmi	['bryssel kælæ'mi]
broccoli	brokkoli kələmi	['brokkoli kælæ'mi]

beetroot	çuğundur	[ʧuɣun'dur]
aubergine	badımcan	[badım'dʒan]
marrow	yunan qabağı	[y'nan gabaɣ'ı]
pumpkin	balqabaq	[balga'bag]
turnip	şalğam	[ʃalɣ'am]

parsley	petruşka	[petruʃ'ka]
dill	şüyüt	[ʃy'yt]
lettuce	salat	[sa'lat]
celery	kərəviz	[kæræ'viz]
asparagus	qulançar	[gulan'ʧar]
spinach	ispanaq	[ispa'nag]

pea	noxud	[no'hud]
beans	paxla	[pah'la]
maize	qarğıdalı	[garɣıda'lı]
kidney bean	lobya	[lob'ja]

bell pepper	bibər	[bi'bær]
radish	turp	[turp]
artichoke	ənginar	[æɲi'nar]

47. Fruits. Nuts

fruit	meyvə	[mej'væ]
apple	alma	[al'ma]
pear	armud	[ar'mud]
lemon	limon	[li'mon]
orange	portağal	[portaɣ'al]
strawberry	bağ çiyələyi	['baɣ ʧijəlæ'jı]

tangerine	mandarin	[manda'rin]
plum	gavalı	[gava'lı]
peach	şaftalı	[ʃafta'lı]
apricot	ərik	[æ'rik]
raspberry	moruq	[mo'rug]
pineapple	ananas	[ana'nas]

banana	banan	[ba'nan]
watermelon	qarpız	[gar'pız]
grape	üzüm	[y'zym]
sour cherry	albalı	[alba'lı]
sweet cherry	gilas	[gi'las]
melon	yemiş	[e'miʃ]

grapefruit	qreypfrut	['grejpfrut]
avocado	avokado	[avo'kado]
papaya	papaya	[pa'paja]

mango	manqo	['maŋo]
pomegranate	nar	[nar]
redcurrant	qırmızı qarağat	[gırmı'zı garaɣ'at]
blackcurrant	qara qarağat	[ga'ra garaɣ'at]
gooseberry	krıjovnik	[krı'ʒovnik]
bilberry	qaragilə	[garagi'læ]
blackberry	böyürtkən	[bøyrt'kæn]
raisin	kişmiş	[kiʃ'miʃ]
fig	əncir	[æn'dʒir]
date	xurma	[hur'ma]
peanut	araxis	[a'rahis]
almond	badam	[ba'dam]
walnut	qoz	[goz]
hazelnut	fındıq	[fın'dıg]
coconut	kokos	[ko'kos]
pistachios	püstə	[pys'tæ]

48. Bread. Sweets

confectionery (pastry)	qənnadı məmulatı	[gæŋa'dı mæmula'tı]
bread	çörək	[tʃo'ræk]
biscuits	peçenye	[pe'tʃeɲje]
chocolate (n)	şokolad	[ʃoko'lad]
chocolate (as adj)	şokolad	[ʃoko'lad]
sweet	konfet	[kon'fet]
cake (e.g. cupcake)	pirojna	[piroʒ'na]
cake (e.g. birthday ~)	tort	[tort]
pie (e.g. apple ~)	piroq	[pi'rog]
filling (for cake, pie)	iç	[itʃ]
whole fruit jam	mürəbbə	[myræb'bæ]
marmalade	marmelad	[marme'lad]
waffle	vafli	[vaf'li]
ice-cream	dondurma	[dondur'ma]

49. Cooked dishes

course, dish	yemək	[e'mæk]
cuisine	mətbəx	[mæt'bæh]
recipe	resept	[re'sept]
portion	porsiya	['porsija]
salad	salat	[sa'lat]
soup	şorba	[ʃor'ba]
clear soup (broth)	ətin suyu	[æ'tin su'y]
sandwich (bread)	buterbrod	[buterb'rod]

49

fried eggs	qayqanaq	[gajga'nag]
cutlet	kotlet	[kot'let]
hamburger (beefburger)	hamburqer	['hamburger]
beefsteak	bifşteks	[biʃ'teks]
roast meat	bozartma	[bozart'ma]

garnish	qarnir	[gar'nir]
spaghetti	spaqetti	[spa'getti]
mash	kartof püresi	[kar'tof pyre'si]
pizza	pitsa	['pitsa]
porridge (oatmeal, etc.)	sıyıq	[sı'jıg]
omelette	omlet	[om'let]

boiled (e.g. ~ beef)	bişmiş	[biʃ'miʃ]
smoked (adj)	hisə verilmiş	[hi'sæ veril'miʃ]
fried (adj)	qızardılmış	[gızardıl'mıʃ]
dried (adj)	quru	[gu'ru]
frozen (adj)	dondurulmuş	[dondurul'muʃ]
pickled (adj)	duza qoyulmuş	[du'za goyl'muʃ]

sweet (sugary)	şirin	[ʃi'rin]
salty (adj)	duzlu	[duz'lu]
cold (adj)	soyuq	[so'yg]
hot (adj)	isti	[is'ti]
bitter (adj)	acı	[a'dʒı]
tasty (adj)	dadlı	[dad'lı]

to cook (in boiling water)	bişirmək	[biʃir'mæk]
to cook (dinner)	hazırlamaq	[hazırla'mag]
to fry (vt)	qızartmaq	[gızart'mag]
to heat up (food)	qızdırmaq	[gızdır'mag]

to salt (vt)	duz vurmaq	['duz vur'mag]
to pepper (vt)	istiot vurmaq	[isti'ot vur'mag]
to grate (vt)	sürtkəcdə xırdalamaq	[syrtkæʤ'dæ hırdala'mag]
peel (n)	qabıq	[ga'bıg]
to peel (vt)	qabığını soymaq	[gabıyı'nı soj'mag]

50. Spices

salt	duz	[duz]
salty (adj)	duzlu	[duz'lu]
to salt (vt)	duz vurmaq	['duz vur'mag]

black pepper	qara istiot	[ga'ra isti'ot]
red pepper	qırmızı istiot	[gırmı'zı isti'ot]
mustard	xardal	[har'dal]
horseradish	qıtığotu	[gıtıyo'tu]

condiment	yeməyə dad verən əlavə	[emæ'jə 'dad ve'ræn æla'væ]
spice	ədviyyat	[ædvi'j:at]
sauce	sous	['sous]
vinegar	sirkə	[sir'kæ]
anise	cirə	[dʒi'ræ]

basil	reyhan	[rej'han]
cloves	mixǝk	[mi'hæk]
ginger	zǝncǝfil	[zænʤæ'fil]
coriander	keşniş	[keʃ'niʃ]
cinnamon	darçın	[dar'tʃɪn]

sesame	küncüt	[kyn'ʤyt]
bay leaf	dǝfnǝ yarpağı	[dæf'næ jarpaɣ'ı]
paprika	paprika	['paprika]
caraway	zirǝ	[zi'ræ]
saffron	zǝfǝran	[zæfæ'ran]

51. Meals

| food | yemǝk | [e'mæk] |
| to eat (vi, vt) | yemǝk | [e'mæk] |

breakfast	sǝhǝr yemǝyi	[sæ'hær eme'jı]
to have breakfast	sǝhǝr yemǝyi yemǝk	[sæ'hær emæ'jı e'mæk]
lunch	nahar	[na'har]
to have lunch	nahar etmǝk	[na'har æt'mæk]
dinner	axşam yemǝyi	[ah'ʃam eme'jı]
to have dinner	axşam yemǝyi yemǝk	[ah'ʃam emæ'jı e'mæk]

| appetite | iştaha | [iʃta'ha] |
| Enjoy your meal! | Nuş olsun! | ['nuʃ ol'sun] |

to open (~ a bottle)	açmaq	[atʃ'mag]
to spill (liquid)	tökmǝk	[tøk'mæk]
to spill out (vi)	tökülmǝk	[tøkyl'mæk]

to boil (vi)	qaynamaq	[gajna'mag]
to boil (vt)	qaynatmaq	[gajnat'mag]
boiled (~ water)	qatnamış	[gajna'mıʃ]
to chill (vt)	soyutmaq	[soyt'mag]
to chill (vi)	soyumaq	[soy'mag]

| taste, flavour | dad | [dad] |
| aftertaste | dad | [dad] |

to be on a diet	pǝhriz saxlamaq	[pæh'riz sahla'mag]
diet	pǝhriz	[pæh'riz]
vitamin	vitamin	[vita'min]
calorie	kaloriya	[ka'lorija]

| vegetarian (n) | ǝt yemǝyǝn adam | ['æt 'emæjǝn a'dam] |
| vegetarian (adj) | ǝtsiz xörǝk | [æ'tsiz hø'ræk] |

fats (nutrient)	yağlar	[jaɣ'lar]
proteins	zülallar	[zylal'lar]
carbohydrates	karbohidratlar	[karbohidrat'lar]
slice (of lemon, ham)	dilim	[di'lim]
piece (of cake, pie)	tikǝ	[ti'kæ]
crumb (of bread)	qırıntı	[gırın'tı]

52. Table setting

spoon	qaşıq	[ga'ʃıg]
knife	bıçaq	[bı'tʃag]
fork	çəngəl	[tʃə'ŋæl]

cup (of coffee)	fincan	[fin'dʒan]
plate (dinner ~)	boşqab	[boʃgab]
saucer	nəlbəki	[nælbæ'ki]
serviette	salfetka	[salfet'ka]
toothpick	dişqurdalayan	[diʃgurdala'jan]

53. Restaurant

restaurant	restoran	[resto'ran]
coffee bar	qəhvəxana	[gæhvæha'na]
pub, bar	bar	[bar]
tearoom	çay salonu	['tʃaj salo'nu]

waiter	ofisiant	[ofisi'ant]
waitress	ofisiant qız	[ofisi'ant 'gız]
barman	barmen	['barmen]

menu	menyu	[men'y]
wine list	çaxırlar kartı	[tʃahır'lar kar'tı]
to book a table	masa sifarişi etmək	[ma'sa sifa'riʃ æt'mæk]

course, dish	yemək	[e'mæk]
to order (meal)	yemək sifarişi etmək	[e'mæk sifa'riʃ æt'mæk]
to make an order	sifariş etmək	[sifa'riʃ æt'mæk]

aperitif	aperitiv	[aperi'tiv]
starter	qəlyanaltı	[gæl'janaltı]
dessert, sweet	desert	[de'sert]

bill	hesab	[he'sab]
to pay the bill	hesabı ödəmək	[hesa'bı ødæ'mæk]
to give change	pulun artığını qaytarmaq	[pu'lun artıyı'nı gajtar'mag]
tip	çaypulu	[tʃajpu'lu]

Family, relatives and friends

54. Personal information. Forms

name, first name	ad	[ad]
family name	soyadı	['sojadı]
date of birth	anadan olduğu tarix	[ana'dan olduɣ'u ta'rih]
place of birth	anadan olduğu yer	[ana'dan olduɣ'u 'er]
nationality	milliyəti	[millijə'ti]
place of residence	yaşayış yeri	[jaʃa'jıʃ e'ri]
country	ölkə	[øl'kæ]
profession (occupation)	peşəsi	[peʃæ'si]
gender, sex	cinsi	[dʒin'si]
height	boyu	[bo'y]
weight	çəki	[tʃə'ki]

55. Family members. Relatives

mother	ana	[a'na]
father	ata	[a'ta]
son	oğul	[oɣ'ul]
daughter	qız	[gız]
younger daughter	kiçik qız	[ki'tʃik 'gız]
younger son	kiçik oğul	[kitʃik oɣ'ul]
eldest daughter	böyük qız	[bø'yk 'gız]
eldest son	böyük oğul	['bøyk oɣ'ul]
brother	qardaş	[gar'daʃ]
sister	bacı	[ba'dʒı]
cousin (masc.)	xalaoğlu	[halaoɣ'lu]
cousin (fem.)	xalaqızı	[halagı'zı]
mummy	ana	[a'na]
dad, daddy	ata	[a'ta]
parents	valideynlər	[validejn'lær]
child	uşaq	[u'ʃag]
children	uşaqlar	[uʃag'lar]
grandmother	nənə	[næ'næ]
grandfather	baba	[ba'ba]
grandson	nəvə	[næ'væ]
granddaughter	nəvə	[næ'væ]
grandchildren	nəvələr	[nævæ'lær]
uncle	dayı	[da'jı]
aunt	xala	[ha'la]

53

nephew	bacıoğlu	[badʒıoɣ'lu]
niece	bacıqızı	[badʒıgı'zı]

mother-in-law	qayınana	[gajına'na]
father-in-law	qayınata	[gajna'ta]
son-in-law	yeznə	[ez'næ]
stepmother	analıq	[ana'lıg]
stepfather	atalıq	[ata'lıg]

infant	südəmər uşaq	[sydæ'mær u'ʃag]
baby (infant)	çağa	[ʧaɣ'a]
little boy, kid	körpə	[kør'pæ]

wife	arvad	[ar'vad]
husband	ər	[ær]
spouse (husband)	həyat yoldaşı	[hæ'jat jolda'ʃı]
spouse (wife)	həyat yoldaşı	[hæ'jat jolda'ʃı]

married (masc.)	evli	[æv'li]
married (fem.)	ərli qadın	[ær'li ga'dın]
single (unmarried)	subay	[su'baj]
bachelor	subay	[su'baj]
divorced (masc.)	boşanmış	[boʃan'mıʃ]
widow	dul qadın	['dul ga'dın]
widower	dul kişi	['dul ki'ʃi]

relative	qohum	[go'hum]
close relative	yaxın qohum	[ja'hın go'hum]
distant relative	uzaq qohum	[u'zag go'hum]
relatives	qohumlar	[gohum'lar]

orphan (boy or girl)	yetim	[e'tim]
guardian (of minor)	himayəçi	[himajə'ʧi]
to adopt (a boy)	oğulluğa götürmək	[oɣulluɣ'a gøtyr'mæk]
to adopt (a girl)	qızlığa götürmək	[gızlıɣ'a gøtyr'mæk]

56. Friends. Colleagues

friend (masc.)	dost	[dost]
friend (fem.)	rəfiqə	[ræfi'gæ]
friendship	dostluq	[dost'lug]
to be friends	dostluq etmək	[dost'lug æt'mæk]

pal (masc.)	dost	[dost]
pal (fem.)	rəfiqə	[ræfi'gæ]
partner	partnyor	[partn'jor]

chief (boss)	rəis	[ræ'is]
superior	müdir	[my'dir]
subordinate	tabelikdə olan	[tabelik'dæ o'lan]
colleague	peşə yoldaşı	[pe'ʃæ jolda'ʃı]

acquaintance (person)	tanış	[ta'nıʃ]
fellow traveller	yol yoldaşı	['jol jolda'ʃı]

classmate	sinif yoldaşı	[si'nif jolda'ʃı]
neighbour (masc.)	qonşu	[gon'ʃu]
neighbour (fem.)	qonşu	[gon'ʃu]
neighbours	qonşular	[gonʃu'lar]

57. Man. Woman

woman	qadın	[ga'dın]
girl (young woman)	qız	[gız]
bride	nişanlı	[niʃan'lı]

beautiful (adj)	gözəl	[gø'zæl]
tall (adj)	ucaboylu	[udʒaboj'lu]
slender (adj)	boylu-buxunlu	[boj'lu buhun'lu]
short (adj)	bəstəboylu	[bæstæboj'lu]

blonde (n)	sarıyağız	[sarıjaɣ'ız]
brunette (n)	qarayağız	[garajaɣ'ız]

ladies' (adj)	qadın	[ga'dın]
virgin (girl)	bakirə qız	[baki'ræ 'gız]
pregnant (adj)	hamilə	[hami'læ]

man (adult male)	kişi	[ki'ʃi]
blonde haired man	sarıyağız	[sarıjaɣ'ız]
dark haired man	qarayağız	[garajaɣ'ız]
tall (adj)	hündür	[hyn'dyr]
short (adj)	bəstəboylu	[bæstæboj'lu]

rude (rough)	kobud	[ko'bud]
stocky (adj)	enlikürək	[ænliky'ræk]
robust (adj)	canıbərk	[dʒa'nı 'bærk]
strong (adj)	güclü	[gydʒ'ly]
strength	güc	[gydʒ]

stout, fat (adj)	yoğun	[joɣ'un]
swarthy (adj)	qarabuğdayı	[garabuɣda'jı]
well-built (adj)	boylu-buxunlu	[boj'lu buhun'lu]
elegant (adj)	zövqlü	[zøvg'ly]

58. Age

age	yaş	[jaʃ]
youth (young age)	gənclik	[gændʒ'lik]
young (adj)	cavan	[dʒa'van]

younger (adj)	kiçik	[ki'tʃik]
older (adj)	böyük	[bø'yk]

young man	gənc oğlan	['gændʒ oɣ'lan]
teenager	yeniyetmə	[eniet'mæ]
guy, fellow	oğlan	[oɣ'lan]

old man	qoca	[goˈdʒa]
old woman	qarı	[gaˈrı]

adult	yetişkin	[etiʃˈkin]
middle-aged (adj)	orta yaşlı	[orˈta jaʃˈlı]
elderly (adj)	yaşa dolmuş	[jaˈʃa dolˈmuʃ]
old (adj)	qoca	[goˈdʒa]

retirement	təqaüd	[tægaˈyd]
to retire (from job)	təqaüdə çıxmaq	[tægayˈdæ tʃıhˈmag]
pensioner	təqaüdçü	[tægaydˈtʃu]

59. Children

child	uşaq	[uˈʃag]
children	uşaqlar	[uʃagˈlar]
twins	əkizlər	[ækizˈlær]

cradle	beşik	[beˈʃik]
rattle	şax-şax	[ˈʃah ˈʃah]
nappy	uşaq əskisi	[uˈʃag æskiˈsi]

dummy, comforter	əmzik	[æmˈzik]
pram	uşaq arabası	[uˈʃag arabaˈsı]
nursery	uşaq baxçası	[uˈʃag bahtʃaˈsı]
babysitter	dayə	[daˈjə]

childhood	uşaqlıq	[uʃagˈlıg]
doll	gəlincik	[gelinˈdʒik]
toy	oyuncaq	[oynˈdʒag]
construction set	konstruktor	[konstˈruktor]

well-bred (adj)	tərbiyəli	[tærbijəˈli]
ill-bred (adj)	tərbiyəsiz	[tærbijəˈsiz]
spoilt (adj)	ərköyün	[ærkøˈyn]

to be naughty	dəcəllik etmək	[dædʒælˈlik ætˈmæk]
mischievous (adj)	dəcəl	[dæˈdʒæl]
mischievousness	dəcəllik	[dædʒælˈlik]
mischievous child	dəcəl uşaq	[dæˈdʒæl uˈʃag]

obedient (adj)	sözə baxan	[søˈzæ baˈhan]
disobedient (adj)	sözə baxmayan	[søˈzæ ˈbahmajan]

docile (adj)	düşüncəli	[dyʃyndʒæˈli]
clever (intelligent)	ağıllı	[aɣılˈlı]
child prodigy	vunderkind	[vunderˈkind]

60. Married couples. Family life

to kiss (vt)	öpmək	[øpˈmæk]
to kiss (vi)	öpüşmək	[øpyʃˈmæk]

family (n)	ailə	[ai'læ]
family (as adj)	ailəli	[ailæ'li]
couple	ər-arvad	['ær ar'vad]
marriage (state)	ailə həyatı	[ai'læ hæja'tı]
hearth (home)	ailə ocağı	[ai'læ odʒaɣ'ı]
dynasty	sülalə	[syla'læ]
date	görüş	[gø'ryʃ]
kiss	öpüş	[ø'pyʃ]
love (for sb)	sevqi	[sev'gi]
to love (sb)	sevmək	[sev'mæk]
beloved	sevqili	[sevgi'li]
tenderness	zəriflik	[zærif'lik]
tender (affectionate)	zərif	[zæ'rif]
faithfulness	sədaqət	[sæda'gæt]
faithful (adj)	sadiq	[sa'dig]
care (attention)	qayğı	[gajɣ'ı]
caring (~ father)	qayğıkeş	[gajɣı'keʃ]
newlyweds	yeni evlənənlər	[e'ni ævlænæn'lær]
honeymoon	bal ayı	['bal a'jı]
to get married (ab. woman)	ərə getmək	[æ'ræ get'mæk]
to get married (ab. man)	evlənmək	[ævlæn'mæk]
wedding	toy	[toj]
golden wedding	qızıl toy	[gı'zıl 'toj]
anniversary	ildönümü	[ildøny'my]
lover (masc.)	məşuq	[mæ'ʃug]
mistress	məşuqə	[mæʃu'gæ]
adultery	xəyanət	[hæja'næt]
to commit adultery	xəyanət etmək	[hæja'næt æt'mæk]
jealous (adj)	qısqanc	[gıs'gandʒ]
to be jealous	qısqanmaq	[gısgan'mag]
divorce	boşanma	[boʃan'ma]
to divorce (vi)	boşanmaq	[boʃan'mag]
to quarrel (vi)	dalaşmaq	[dalaʃ'mag]
to be reconciled	barışmaq	[barıʃ'mag]
together (adv)	birlikdə	[birlik'dæ]
sex	seks	[seks]
happiness	xoşbəxtlik	[hoʃbæht'lik]
happy (adj)	xoşbəxt	[hoʃ'bæht]
misfortune (accident)	bədbəxtlik	[bædbæht'lik]
unhappy (adj)	bədbəxt	[bæd'bæht]

Character. Feelings. Emotions

61. Feelings. Emotions

feeling (emotion)	hiss	[hiss]
feelings	hisslər	[hiss'lær]

hunger	aclıq	[adʒ'lıg]
to be hungry	yemək istəmək	[e'mæk iste'mæk]
thirst	susuzluq	[susuz'lug]
to be thirsty	içmək istəmək	[itʃ'mæk istæ'mæk]
sleepiness	yuxululuq	[yhulu'lug]
to feel sleepy	yatmaq istəmək	[jat'mag istæ'mæk]

tiredness	yorğunluq	[jorɣun'lug]
tired (adj)	yorğun	[jorɣ'un]
to get tired	yorulmaq	[jorul'mag]

mood (humour)	əhval-ruhiyyə	[æh'val ruhi'j:ə]
boredom	darıxma	[darıh'ma]
to be bored	darıxmaq	[darıh'mag]
seclusion	tənhalıq	[tænha'lıg]
to seclude oneself	tənha bir yerə çəkilmək	[tæn'ha 'bir e'ræ tʃəkil'mæk]

to worry (make anxious)	narahat etmək	[nara'hat æt'mæk]
to be worried	narahat olmaq	[nara'hat ol'mag]
worrying (n)	narahatçılıq	[narahatʃı'lıg]
anxiety	həyacan	[hæja'dʒan]
preoccupied (adj)	qayğılı	[gajɣı'lı]
to be nervous	əsəbiləşmək	[æsæbilæʃ'mæk]
to panic (vi)	vahiməyə düşmək	[vahimæ'jə dyʃ'mæk]

hope	ümid	[y'mid]
to hope (vi, vt)	ümid etmək	[y'mid æt'mæk]

certainty	əminlik	[æmin'lik]
certain, sure (adj)	əmin	[æ'min]
uncertainty	əmin olmama	[æ'min 'olmama]
uncertain (adj)	əmin olmayan	[æ'min 'olmajan]

drunk (adj)	sərxoş	[sær'hoʃ]
sober (adj)	içki içməyən	[itʃ'ki 'itʃmæjən]
weak (adj)	zəif	[zæ'if]
happy (adj)	bəxti üzdə olan	[bæh'ti yz'dæ o'lan]
to scare (vt)	qorxutmaq	[gorhut'mag]
fury (madness)	quduzluq	[guduz'lug]
rage (fury)	qəzəb	[gæ'zæb]

depression	ruh düşkünlüyü	['ruh dyʃkynly'y]
discomfort	narahatlıq	[narahat'lıg]

comfort	rahatlıq	[rahat'lıg]
to regret (be sorry)	heyfsilənmək	[hejfsilæn'mæk]
regret	heyfsilənmə	[hejfsilæn'mæ]
bad luck	uğursuzluq	[uɣursuz'lug]
sadness	dilxorluq	[dilhor'lug]

shame (feeling)	xəcalət	[hædʒa'læt]
merriment, fun	şənlik	[ʃæn'lik]
enthusiasm	ruh yüksəkliyi	['ruh yksekli'jı]
enthusiast	entuziast	[æntuzi'ast]
to show enthusiasm	ruh yüksəkliyi göstərmək	['ruh yksekli'jı gøstær'mæk]

62. Character. Personality

character	xasiyyət	[hasi'j:ət]
character flaw	nöqsan	[nøg'san]
mind	ağıl	[aɣ'ıl]
reason	dərrakə	[dærra'kæ]

conscience	vicdan	[vidʒ'dan]
habit (custom)	vərdiş	[vær'diʃ]
ability	qabiliyyət	[gabili'j:ət]
can (e.g. ~ swim)	bacarmaq	[badʒar'mag]

patient (adj)	səbir	[sæ'bir]
impatient (adj)	səbirli	[sæbir'li]
curious (inquisitive)	hər şeyi bilməyə çalışan	['hær ʃe'jı bilmæ'jə tʃalı'ʃan]
curiosity	hər şeyi bilmək istəyi	['hær ʃe'jı bil'mæk istæ'jı]

modesty	təvazökarlıq	[tævazøkar'lıg]
modest (adj)	təvazökar	[tævazø'kar]
immodest (adj)	təvazökar olmayan	[tævazø'kar 'olmajan]

laziness	tənbəllik	['tæn'bællik]
lazy (adj)	tənbəl	[tæn'bæl]
lazy person (masc.)	tənbəl	[tæn'bæl]

cunning (n)	hiyləgərlik	[hijlægær'lik]
cunning (as adj)	hiyləgər	[hijlæ'gær]
distrust	inamsızlıq	[inamsız'lıg]
distrustful (adj)	heç kəsə inanmayan	['hetʃ kæ'sæ i'nanmajan]

generosity	səxavət	[sæha'væt]
generous (adj)	səxavətli	[sæhavæt'li]
talented (adj)	istedadlı	[istedad'lı]
talent	istedad	[iste'dad]

courageous (adj)	cəsarətli	[dʒæsaræt'li]
courage	cəsarət	[dʒæsa'ræt]
honest (adj)	namus	[na'mus]
honesty	namuslu	[namus'lu]

| careful (cautious) | ehtiyatlı | [æhtijat'lı] |
| courageous (adj) | cürətli | [dʒyræt'li] |

59

serious (adj)	ciddi	[dʒid'di]
strict (severe, stern)	tələbkar	[tælæb'kar]
decisive (adj)	qətiyyətli	[gætij:ət'li]
indecisive (adj)	qətiyyətsiz	[gætij:ə'tsiz]
shy, timid (adj)	cəsarətsiz	[dʒæsaræ'tsiz]
shyness, timidity	cəsarətsizlik	[dʒæsarætsiz'lik]
confidence (trust)	inam	[i'nam]
to believe (trust)	inanmaq	[inan'mag]
trusting (naïve)	hər kəsə inanan	['hær kæ'sæ ina'nan]
sincerely (adv)	səmimiyyətlə	[sæmimi'j:ətlæ]
sincere (adj)	səmimi	[sæmi'mi]
sincerity	səmimiyyət	[sæmimi'j:ət]
open (person)	səmimi	[sæmi'mi]
calm (adj)	sakit	[sa'kit]
frank (sincere)	səmimi	[sæmi'mi]
naïve (adj)	sadəlövh	[sadæ'løvh]
absent-minded (adj)	fikri dağınıq	[fik'ri dayı'nıg]
funny (amusing)	məzəli	[mæzæ'li]
greed	acgözlük	[adʒgøz'lyk]
greedy (adj)	acgöz	[adʒ'gøz]
stingy (adj)	xəsis	[hæ'sis]
evil (adj)	hirsli	[hirs'li]
stubborn (adj)	inadkar	[inad'kar]
unpleasant (adj)	nifrət oyadan	[nif'ræt oja'dan]
selfish person (masc.)	xudbin adam	[hud'bin a'dam]
selfish (adj)	xudbin	[hud'bin]
coward	qorxaq	[gor'hag]
cowardly (adj)	qorxaq	[gor'hag]

63. Sleep. Dreams

to sleep (vi)	yatmaq	[jat'mag]
sleep, sleeping	yuxu	[y'hu]
dream	röya	[rø'ja]
to dream (in sleep)	yuxu görmək	[y'hu gør'mæk]
sleepy (adj)	yuxulu	[yhu'lu]
bed	çarpayı	[ʧarpa'jı]
mattress	döşək	[dø'ʃæk]
blanket (eiderdown)	yorğan	[jorɣ'an]
pillow	yastıq	[jas'tıg]
sheet	mələfə	[mælæ'fæ]
insomnia	yuxusuzluq	[yhusuz'lug]
sleepless (adj)	yuxusuz	[yhu'suz]
sleeping pill	yuxu dərmanı	[y'hu dærma'nı]
to take a sleeping pill	yuxu dərmanı qəbul etmək	[y'hu dærma'nı gæ'bul æt'mæk]

to feel sleepy	yatmaq istəmək	[jat'mag istæ'mæk]
to yawn (vi)	əsnəmək	[æsnæ'mæk]
to go to bed	yatmağa getmək	[jatmaɣ'a getmæk]
to make up the bed	yorğan-döşək salmaq	[jorɣ'an dø'ʃæk sal'mag]
to fall asleep	yuxulamaq	[yhula'mag]

nightmare	kabus	[ka'bus]
snoring	xorultu	[horul'tu]
to snore (vi)	xoruldamaq	[horulda'mag]

alarm clock	zəngli saat	[zæŋ'li sa'at]
to wake (vt)	oyatmaq	[ojat'mag]
to wake up	oyanmaq	[ojna'mag]
to get up (vi)	qalxmaq	[galh'mag]
to wash oneself	əl-üz yumaq	['æl 'yz y'mag]

64. Humour. Laughter. Gladness

humour (wit, fun)	yumor	['ymor]
sense of humour	hiss	[hiss]
to have fun	şənlənmək	[ʃænlæn'mæk]
cheerful (adj)	şən	[ʃæn]
merriment, fun	şənlik	[ʃæn'lik]

smile	təbəssüm	[tæbæs'sym]
to smile (vi)	gülümsəmək	[gylymsæ'mæk]
to start laughing	gülmək	[gyʎ'mæk]
to laugh (vi)	gülmək	[gyʎ'mæk]
laugh, laughter	gülüş	[gy'lyʃ]

anecdote	lətifə	[læti'fæ]
funny (amusing)	məzəli	[mæzæ'li]
funny (comical)	gülməli	[gylmæ'li]

to joke (vi)	zarafat etmək	[zara'fat æt'mæk]
joke (verbal)	zarafat	[zara'fat]
joy (emotion)	sevinc	[se'vindʒ]
to rejoice (vi)	sevinmək	[sevin'mæk]
glad, cheerful (adj)	sevincli	[sævindʒ'li]

65. Discussion, conversation. Part 1

communication	ünsiyyət	[ynsi'j:ət]
to communicate	ünsiyyət saxlamaq	[ynsi'j:ət sahla'mag]

conversation	danışıq	[danı'ʃıg]
dialogue	dialoq	[dia'log]
discussion (discourse)	müzakirə	[myzaki'ræ]
debate	mübahisə	[mybahi'sæ]
to debate (vi)	mübahisə etmək	[mybahi'sæ æt'mæk]
interlocutor	həmsöhbət	[hæmsøh'bæt]
topic (theme)	mövzu	[møv'zu]

point of view	nöqteyi-nəzər	[nøg'tei næ'zær]
opinion (viewpoint)	mülahizə	[mylahi'zæ]
speech (talk)	nitq	[nitg]

discussion (of report, etc.)	müzakirə	[myzaki'ræ]
to discuss (vt)	müzakirə etmək	[myzaki'ræ æt'mæk]
talk (conversation)	söhbət	[søh'bæt]
to talk (vi)	söhbət etmək	[søh'bæt æt'mæk]
meeting	görüş	[gø'ryʃ]
to meet (vi, vt)	görüşmək	[gøryʃ'mæk]

proverb	atalar sözü	[ata'lar sø'zy]
saying	zərbi-məsəl	['zærbi mæ'sæl]
riddle (poser)	tapmaca	[tapma'dʒa]
to ask a riddle	tapmaca demək	[tapma'dʒa dæ'mæk]
password	parol	[pa'rol]
secret	gizli iş	[giz'li 'iʃ]

oath (vow)	and	[and]
to swear (an oath)	and içmək	['and itʃ'mæk]
promise	vəd	[væd]
to promise (vt)	vəd etmək	['væd æt'mæk]

advice (counsel)	məsləhət	[mæslæ'hæt]
to advise (vt)	məsləhət vermək	[mæslæ'hæt ver'mæk]
to listen (to parents)	məsləhətə	[mæslæhæ'tæ
	əməl etmək	æ'mæl æt'mæk]

news	yenilik	[eni'lik]
sensation (news)	sensasiya	[sen'sasija]
information (facts)	məlumat	[mælu'mat]
conclusion (decision)	nəticə	[næti'dʒæ]
voice	səs	[sæs]
compliment	kompliment	[kompli'ment]
kind (nice)	iltifatlı	[iltifat'lı]

word	söz	['søz]
phrase	ibarə	[iba'ræ]
answer	cavab	[dʒa'vab]

| truth | həqiqət | [hægi'gæt] |
| lie | uydurma | [ujdur'ma] |

thought	düşüncə	[dyʃyn'dʒæ]
idea (inspiration)	fikir	[fi'kir]
fantasy	xülya	[hy'ʎja]

66. Discussion, conversation. Part 2

respected (adj)	hörmət edilən	[hør'mæt ædi'læn]
to respect (vt)	hörmət etmək	[hør'mæt æt'mæk]
respect	hörmət	[hør'mæt]
Dear ...	Hörmətli...	[hørmæt'li]
to introduce (present)	tanış etmək	[ta'nıʃ æt'mæk]

intention	niyyət	[ni'j:ət]
to intend (have in mind)	niyyətində olmaq	[nij:ətin'dæ ol'mag]
wish	arzu	[ar'zu]
to wish (~ good luck)	arzu etmək	[ar'zu æt'mæk]

surprise (astonishment)	təəccüb	[tæ:'ʤyb]
to surprise (amaze)	təəccübləndirmək	[tæ:ʤyblændir'mæk]
to be surprised	təəccüblənmək	[tæ:ʤyblæn'mæk]

to give (vt)	vermək	[ver'mæk]
to take (get hold of)	almaq	[al'mag]
to give back	qaytarmaq	[gajtar'mag]
to return (give back)	qaytarmaq	[gajtar'mag]

to apologize (vi)	üzr istəmək	['yzr istæ'mæk]
apology	bağışlama	[bayɪʃla'ma]
to forgive (vt)	bağışlamaq	[bayɪʃla'mag]

to talk (speak)	danışmaq	[danɪʃ'mag]
to listen (vi)	qulaq asmaq	[gu'lag as'mag]
to hear out	dinləmək	[dinlæ'mæk]
to understand (vt)	başa düşmək	[ba'ʃa dyʃ'mæk]

to show (display)	göstərmək	[gøstær'mæk]
to look at ...	baxmaq	[bah'mag]
to call (with one's voice)	çağırmaq	[ʧayɪr'mag]
to disturb (vt)	mane olmaq	[ma'ne ol'mag]
to pass (to hand sth)	vermək	[ver'mæk]

demand (request)	xahiş	[ha'iʃ]
to request (ask)	xahiş etmək	[ha'iʃ æt'mæk]
demand (firm request)	tələb	[tæ'læb]
to demand (request firmly)	tələb etmək	[tæ'læb æt'mæk]

to tease (nickname)	cırnatmaq	[ʤɪrnat'mag]
to mock (deride)	rişxənd etmək	[riʃ'hænd æt'mæk]
mockery, derision	rişxənd	[riʃ'hænd]
nickname	ayama	[aja'ma]

allusion	eyham	[æj'ham]
to allude (vi)	eyham vurmaq	[æj'ham vur'mag]
to imply (vt)	nəzərdə tutmaq	[næzær'dæ tut'mag]

description	təsvir	[tæs'vir]
to describe (vt)	təsvir etmək	[tæs'vir æt'mæk]
praise (compliments)	tərif	[tæ'rif]
to praise (vt)	tərifləmək	[tæriflæ'mæk]

disappointment	məyusluq	[mæys'lug]
to disappoint (vt)	məyus etmək	[mæ'ys æt'mæk]
to be disappointed	məyus olmaq	[mæ'ys ol'mag]

supposition	fərziyyə	[færzi'j:ə]
to suppose (assume)	fərz etmək	['færz æt'mæk]
warning (caution)	xəbərdarlıq	[hæbærdar'lıg]
to warn (vt)	xəbərdar etmək	[hæbær'dar æt'mæk]

67. Discussion, conversation. Part 3

to talk into (convince)	yola gətirmək	[jo'la gætir'mæk]
to calm down (vt)	sakitləşdirmək	[sakitlæʃdir'mæk]
silence (~ is golden)	susma	[sus'ma]
to keep silent	susmaq	[sus'mag]
to whisper (vi, vt)	pıçıldamaq	[pɪtʃɪlda'mag]
whisper	pıçıltı	[pɪtʃɪl'tɪ]
frankly, sincerely (adv)	açıq	[a'tʃɪg]
in my opinion ...	mənim fikrimcə...	[mæ'nim fik'rimʤæ]
detail (of the story)	təfərrüat	[tæfærry'at]
detailed (adj)	ətraflı	[ætraf'lɪ]
in detail (adv)	təfərrüatı ilə	[tæfærrya'tɪ i'læ]
hint, clue	xəlvətçə söyləmə	[hæl'vætʃæ søjlæ'mæ]
to give a hint	xəlvətçə söyləmək	[hæl'vætʃæ søjlæ'mæk]
look (glance)	baxış	[ba'hɪʃ]
to have a look	baxmaq	[bah'mag]
fixed (look)	durğun	[durɣ'un]
to blink (vi)	göz qırpmaq	['gøz gɪrp'mag]
to wink (vi)	kirpik çalmaq	[kir'pik tʃal'mag]
to nod (in assent)	başı ilə razılıq bildirmək	[ba'ʃɪ i'læ razɪ'lɪg bildir'mæk]
sigh	nəfəs alma	[næ'fæs al'ma]
to sigh (vi)	nəfəs almaq	[næ'fæs al'mag]
to shudder (vi)	diksinmək	[diksin'mæk]
gesture	əl-qol hərəkəti	['æl 'gol hærækæ'ti]
to touch (one's arm, etc.)	toxunmaq	[tohun'mag]
to seize (by the arm)	tutmaq	[tut'mag]
to tap (on the shoulder)	vurmaq	[vur'mag]
Look out!	Diqqətli ol!	[diggæt'li 'ol]
Really?	Mümkünmü?	[mym'kynmy]
Are you sure?	Bundan əminsən?	[bun'dan æ'minsæn]
Good luck!	Uğurlar olsun!	[uɣur'lar ol'sun]
I see!	Aydındır!	[aj'dɪndɪr]
It's a pity!	Heyf!	['hejf]

68. Agreement. Refusal

consent (mutual ~)	razılıq	[razɪ'lɪg]
to agree (say yes)	razı olmaq	[ra'zɪ ol'mag]
approval	təqdir etmə	[tæg'dir æt'mæ]
to approve (vt)	təqdir etmək	[tæg'dir æt'mæk]
refusal	imtina	[imti'na]
to refuse (vi, vt)	imtina etmək	[imti'na æt'mæk]
Great!	Əla!	[æ'la]
All right!	Yaxşı!	['jahʃɪ]

Okay! (I agree)	Oldu!	[ol'du]
forbidden (adj)	qadağan olmuş	[gaday'an ol'muʃ]
it's forbidden	olmaz	[ol'maz]
it's impossible	mümkün deyil	[mym'kyn 'dejıl]
incorrect (adj)	yanlış	[jan'lıʃ]

to reject (~ a demand)	rədd etmək	['rædd æt'mæk]
to support (cause, idea)	dəstəkləmək	[dæstæklæ'mæk]
to accept (~ an apology)	qəbul etmək	[gæ'bul æt'mæk]

to confirm (vt)	təsdiq etmək	[tæs'dig æt'mæk]
confirmation	təsdiq etmə	[tæs'dig æt'mæ]
permission	icazə	[idʒa'zæ]
to permit (vt)	icazə vermək	[idʒa'zæ ver'mæk]
decision	qərar	[gæ'rar]
to say nothing	susmaq	[sus'mag]

condition (term)	şərt	[ʃært]
excuse (pretext)	bəhanə	[bæha'næ]
praise (compliments)	tərif	[tæ'rif]
to praise (vt)	tərifləmək	[tæriflæ'mæk]

69. Success. Good luck. Failure

success	müvəffəqiyyət	[myvæffægi'j:ət]
successfully (adv)	müvəffəqiyyətlə	[myvæffægi'j:ətlæ]
successful (adj)	müvəffəqiyyətli	[myvæffægij:ət'li]
good luck	bəxtin gətirməsi	[bæh'tin gætirmæ'si]
Good luck!	Uğurlar olsun!	[uyur'lar ol'sun]
lucky (e.g. ~ day)	uğurlu	[uyur'lu]
lucky (fortunate)	uğurlu	[uyur'lu]

failure	müvəffəqiyyətsizlik	[myvæffægij:ətsiz'lik]
misfortune	uğursuzluq	[uyursuz'lug]
bad luck	uğursuzluq	[uyursuz'lug]
unsuccessful (adj)	uğursuz	[uyur'suz]
catastrophe	fəlakət	[fæla'kæt]

pride	fəxr	[fæhr]
proud (adj)	məğrur	[mæy'rur]
to be proud	fəxr etmək	['fæhr æt'mæk]
winner	qalib	[ga'lib]
to win (vi)	qalib gəlmək	[ga'lib gæl'mæk]
to lose (not win)	məğlubiyyətə uğramaq	[mæylubij:ə'tæ uyra'mag]
try	təşəbbüs	[tæʃæb'bys]
to try (vi)	cəhd göstərmək	['dʒæhd gøstær'mæk]
chance (opportunity)	şans	[ʃans]

70. Quarrels. Negative emotions

shout (scream)	çığırtı	[tʃıyır'tı]
to shout (vi)	çığırmaq	[tʃıyır'mag]

to start to cry out	çığırmaq	[ʧɪɣɪr'mag]
quarrel	dalaşma	[dalaʃ'ma]
to quarrel (vi)	dalaşmaq	[dalaʃ'mag]
fight (scandal)	qalmaqal	[galma'gal]
to have a fight	qalmaqal salmaq	[galma'gal sal'mag]
conflict	münaqişə	[mynagi'ʃæ]
misunderstanding	anlaşmazlıq	[anlaʃmaz'lıg]

insult	təhkir	[tæh'kir]
to insult (vt)	təhkir etmək	[tæh'kir æt'mæk]
insulted (adj)	təhkir olunmuş	[tæh'kir olun'muʃ]
offence (to take ~)	inciklik	[indʒik'lik]
to offend (vt)	incitmək	[indʒit'mæk]
to take offence	incimək	[indʒi'mæk]

indignation	hiddət	[hid'dæt]
to be indignant	hiddətlənmək	[hiddætlæn'mæk]
complaint	şikayət	[ʃika'jət]
to complain (vi, vt)	şikayət etmək	[ʃika'jət æt'mæk]

apology	bağışlama	[baɣıʃla'ma]
to apologize (vi)	üzr istəmək	['yzr istæ'mæk]
to beg pardon	əfv diləmək	['æfv dilæ'mæk]

criticism	tənqid	[tæ'ŋid]
to criticize (vt)	tənqid etmək	[tæ'ŋid æt'mæk]
accusation	ittiham	[itti'ham]
to accuse (vt)	ittiham etmək	[itti'ham æt'mæk]

revenge	intiqam	[inti'gam]
to avenge (vt)	intiqam almaq	[inti'gam al'mag]
to pay back	əvəzini çıxmaq	[ævæzi'ni ʧıh'mag]

disdain	xor baxılma	['hor bahıl'ma]
to despise (vt)	xor baxmaq	['hor bah'mag]
hatred, hate	nifrət	[nif'ræt]
to hate (vt)	nifrət etmək	[nif'ræt æt'mæk]

nervous (adj)	əsəbi	[æsæ'bi]
to be nervous	əsəbiləşmək	[æsæbilæʃ'mæk]
angry (mad)	hirsli	[hirs'li]
to make angry	hirsləndirmək	[hirslændir'mæk]

humiliation	alçaltma	[alʧalt'ma]
to humiliate (vt)	alçaltmaq	[alʧalt'mag]
to humiliate oneself	alçalmaq	[alʧal'mag]

shock	şok	[ʃok]
to shock (vt)	şok vəziyyətinə salmaq	['ʃok væzij:əti'næ sal'mag]

trouble (annoyance)	xoşagəlməz hadisə	[hoʃagæl'mæz hadi'sæ]
unpleasant (adj)	nifrət oyadan	[nif'ræt oja'dan]

fear (dread)	qorxu	[gor'hu]
terrible (storm, heat)	şiddətli	[ʃiddæt'li]
scary (e.g. ~ story)	qorxulu	[gorhu'lu]

| horror | dəhşət | [dæh'ʃæt] |
| awful (crime, news) | dəhşətli | [dæhʃæt'li] |

to cry (weep)	ağlamaq	[aɣla'mag]
to start crying	ağlamaq	[aɣla'mag]
tear	göz yaşı	['gøz ja'ʃı]

fault	qəbahət	[gæba'hæt]
guilt (feeling)	taqsır	[tag'sır]
dishonour	biabırçılıq	[biabırtʃı'lıg]
protest	etiraz	[æti'raz]
stress	stres	[stres]

to disturb (vt)	mane olmaq	[ma'ne ol'mag]
to be furious	hirslənmək	[hirslæn'mæk]
angry (adj)	hirsli	[hirs'li]
to end (e.g. relationship)	kəsmək	[kæs'mæk]
to swear (at sb)	söyüş söymək	[sø'yʃ søj'mæk]

to be scared	qorxmaq	[gorh'mag]
to hit (strike with hand)	vurmaq	[vur'mag]
to fight (vi)	dalaşmaq	[dalaʃ'mag]

to settle (a conflict)	nizama salmaq	[niza'ma sal'mag]
discontented (adj)	narazı	[nara'zı]
furious (adj)	qəzəbli	[gæzæb'li]

| It's not good! | Bu, heç də yaxşı iş deyil! | ['bu 'hetʃ 'dæ jah'ʃı 'iʃ 'dejıl] |
| It's bad! | Bu, pisdir! | ['bu 'pisdir] |

Medicine

71. Diseases

illness	xəstəlik	[hæstæ'lik]
to be ill	xəstə olmaq	[hæs'tæ ol'mag]
health	sağlamlıq	[saɣlam'lıg]
runny nose (coryza)	zökəm	[zø'kæm]
tonsillitis	angina	[a'ŋina]
cold (illness)	soyuqdəymə	[soygdæj'mæ]
to catch a cold	özünü soyuğa vermək	[øzy'ny soyɣ'a ver'mæk]
bronchitis	bronxit	[bron'hit]
pneumonia	sətəlcəm	[sætæl'dʒæm]
flu, influenza	qrip	[grip]
short-sighted (adj)	uzağı görməyən	[uzaɣ'ı 'gørmæjən]
long-sighted (adj)	uzağı yaxşı görən	[uzaɣ'ı jah'ʃı gø'ræn]
squint	çəpgözlük	[ʧəpgøz'lyk]
squint-eyed (adj)	çəpgöz	[ʧəp'gøz]
cataract	katarakta	[kata'rakta]
glaucoma	qlaukoma	[glau'koma]
stroke	insult	[in'suʌt]
heart attack	infarkt	[in'farkt]
myocardial infarction	miokard infarktı	[mio'kard infark'tı]
paralysis	iflic	[if'lidʒ]
to paralyse (vt)	iflic olmaq	[if'lidʒ ol'mag]
allergy	allergiya	[aller'gija]
asthma	astma	['astma]
diabetes	diabet	[dia'bet]
toothache	diş ağrısı	['diʃ aɣrı'sı]
caries	kariyes	['karies]
diarrhoea	diareya	[dia'reja]
constipation	qəbizlik	[gæbiz'lik]
stomach upset	mədə pozuntusu	[mæ'dæ pozuntu'su]
food poisoning	zəhərlənmə	[zæhærlæn'mæ]
to have a food poisoning	qidadan zəhərlənmək	[gida'dan zæhærlæn'mæk]
arthritis	artrit	[art'rit]
rickets	raxit	[ra'hit]
rheumatism	revmatizm	[revma'tizm]
atherosclerosis	ateroskleroz	[ateroskle'roz]
gastritis	qastrit	[gast'rit]
appendicitis	appendisit	[appendi'sit]

68

| cholecystitis | xolesistit | [holesis'tit] |
| ulcer | xora | [ho'ra] |

measles	qızılca	[gızıl'dʒa]
German measles	məxmərək	[mæhmæ'ræk]
jaundice	sarılıq	[sarı'lıg]
hepatitis	hepatit	[hepa'tit]

schizophrenia	şizofreniya	[ʃizofre'nija]
rabies (hydrophobia)	quduzluq	[guduz'lug]
neurosis	nevroz	[nev'roz]
concussion	beyin sarsıntısı	[be'jın sarsıntı'sı]

cancer	rak	[rak]
sclerosis	skleroz	[skle'roz]
multiple sclerosis	dağınıq skleroz	[dayı'nıg skle'roz]

alcoholism	əyyaşlıq	[æj:aʃ'lıg]
alcoholic (n)	əyyaş	[æ'j:aʃ]
syphilis	sifilis	['sifilis]
AIDS	QİÇS	[gitʃs]

tumour	şiş	[ʃiʃ]
malignant (adj)	bədxassəli	['bædhas'sæli]
benign (adj)	xoşxassəli	[hoʃhas'sæli]

fever	qızdırma	[gızdır'ma]
malaria	malyariya	[maʎa'rija]
gangrene	qanqrena	[gaŋ'rena]
seasickness	dəniz xəstəliyi	[dæ'niz hæstæli'jı]
epilepsy	epilepsiya	[æpi'lepsija]

epidemic	epidemiya	[æpi'demija]
typhus	yatalaq	[jata'lag]
tuberculosis	vərəm	[væ'ræm]
cholera	vəba	[væ'ba]
plague (bubonic ~)	taun	[ta'un]

72. Symptoms. Treatments. Part 1

symptom	əlamət	[æla'mæt]
temperature	qızdırma	[gızdır'ma]
fever	yüksək qızdırma	[yk'sæk gızdır'ma]
pulse	nəbz	[næbz]

giddiness	başgicəllənməsi	[baʃgidʒællænmæ'si]
hot (adj)	isti	[is'ti]
shivering	titrəmə	[titræ'mæ]
pale (e.g. ~ face)	rəngi ağarmış	[ræ'ŋi aɣar'mıʃ]

cough	öskürək	[øsky'ræk]
to cough (vi)	öskürmək	[øskyr'mæk]
to sneeze (vi)	asqırmaq	[asgır'mag]
faint	bihuşluq	[bihuʃ'lug]

to faint (vi)	huşunu itirmək	['huʃunu itir'mæk]
bruise (hématome)	qançır	[gan'tʃɪr]
bump (lump)	şiş	[ʃiʃ]
to bruise oneself	dəymək	[dæj'mæk]
bruise	zədələmə	[zædælæ'mæ]
to get bruised	zədələnmək	[zædælæn'mæk]

to limp (vi)	axsamaq	[ahsa'mag]
dislocation	burxulma	[burhul'ma]
to dislocate (vt)	burxutmaq	[burhut'mag]
fracture	sınıq	[sɪ'nɪg]
to have a fracture	sındırmaq	[sɪndɪr'mag]

cut (e.g. paper ~)	kəsik	[kæ'sik]
to cut oneself	kəsmək	[kæs'mæk]
bleeding	qanaxma	[ganah'ma]

burn (injury)	yanıq	[ja'nɪg]
to burn oneself	yanmaq	[jan'mag]

to prick (vt)	batırmaq	[batɪr'mag]
to prick oneself	batırmaq	[batɪr'mag]
to injure (vt)	zədələmək	[zædælæ'mæk]
injury	zədə	[zæ'dæ]
wound	yara	[ja'ra]
trauma	travma	['travma]

to be delirious	sayıqlamaq	[sajɪgla'mag]
to stutter (vi)	kəkələmək	[kækælæ'mæk]
sunstroke	gün vurması	['gyn vurma'sɪ]

73. Symptoms. Treatments. Part 2

pain	ağrı	[aɣ'rɪ]
splinter (in foot, etc.)	tikan	[ti'kan]

sweat (perspiration)	tər	[tær]
to sweat (perspire)	tərləmək	[tærlæ'mæk]
vomiting	qusma	[gus'ma]
convulsions	qıc	[gɪdʒ]

pregnant (adj)	hamilə	[hami'læ]
to be born	anadan olmaq	[ana'dan ol'mag]
delivery, labour	doğuş	[doɣ'uʃ]
to labour (vi)	doğmaq	[doɣ'mag]
abortion	uşaq saldırma	[u'ʃag saldɪr'ma]

respiration	tənəffüs	[tænæf'fys]
inhalation	nəfəs alma	[næ'fæs al'ma]
exhalation	nəfəs vermə	[næ'fæs ver'mæ]
to breathe out	nəfəs vermək	[næ'fæs ver'mæk]
to breathe in	nəfəs almaq	[næ'fæs al'mag]
disabled person	əlil	[æ'lil]
cripple	şikəst	[ʃi'kæst]

drug addict	narkoman	[narko'man]
deaf (adj)	kar	[kar]
dumb (adj)	lal	[lal]
deaf-and-dumb (adj)	lal-kar	['lal 'kar]

mad, insane (adj)	dəli	[dæ'li]
madman	dəli	[dæ'li]
madwoman	dəli	[dæ'li]
to go insane	dəli olmaq	[dæ'li ol'mag]

gene	gen	[gen]
immunity	immunitet	[immuni'tet]
hereditary (adj)	irsi	[ir'si]
congenital (adj)	anadangəlmə	[anadaŋæl'mæ]

virus	virus	['virus]
microbe	mikrob	[mik'rob]
bacterium	bakteriya	[bak'terija]
infection	infeksiya	[in'feksija]

74. Symptoms. Treatments. Part 3

hospital	xəstəxana	[hæstæha'na]
patient	pasiyent	[pasi'ent]

diagnosis	diaqnoz	[di'agnoz]
cure	müalicə	[myali'dʒæ]
to get treatment	müalicə olunmaq	[myali'dʒæ olun'mag]
to treat (vt)	müalicə etmək	[myali'dʒæ æt'mæk]
to nurse (look after)	xəstəyə qulluq etmək	[hæstæ'je gul'lug æt'mæk]
care	xəstəyə qulluq	[hæstæ'je gul'lug]

operation, surgery	əməliyyat	[æmæli'j:at]
to bandage (head, limb)	sarğı bağlamaq	[sarɣ'ı bayla'mag]
bandaging	sarğı	[sarɣ'ı]

vaccination	peyvənd	[pej'vænd]
to vaccinate (vt)	peyvənd etmək	[pej'vænd æt'mæk]
injection, shot	iynə	[ij'næ]
to give an injection	iynə vurmaq	[ij'næ vur'mag]

amputation	amputasiya	[ampu'tasija]
to amputate (vt)	amputasiya etmək	[ampu'tasija æt'mæk]
coma	koma	['koma]
to be in a coma	komaya düşmək	['komaja dyʃ'mæk]
intensive care	reanimasiya	[reani'masija]

to recover (~ from flu)	sağalmaq	[saɣal'mag]
state (patient's ~)	vəziyyət	[væzi'j:ət]
consciousness	huş	[huʃ]
memory (faculty)	yaddaş	[jad'daʃ]

to extract (tooth)	çəkdirmək	[ʧəkdir'mæk]
filling	plomb	[plomb]

to fill (a tooth)	plomblamaq	[plombla'mag]
hypnosis	hipnoz	[hip'noz]
to hypnotize (vt)	hipnoz etmək	[hip'noz æt'mæk]

75. Doctors

doctor	həkim	[hæ'kim]
nurse	tibb bacısı	['tibb badʒı'sı]
private physician	şəxsi həkim	[ʃæh'si hæ'kim]

dentist	diş həkimi	['diʃ hæki'mi]
ophthalmologist	göz həkimi	['gøz hæki'mi]
general practitioner	terapevt	[tera'pevt]
surgeon	cərrah	[dʒær'rah]

psychiatrist	psixiatr	[psihi'atr]
paediatrician	pediatr	[pedi'atr]
psychologist	psixoloq	[psi'holog]
gynaecologist	ginekoloq	[gine'kolog]
cardiologist	kardioloq	[kardi'olog]

76. Medicine. Drugs. Accessories

medicine, drug	dərman	[dær'man]
remedy	dava	[da'va]
to prescribe (vt)	yazmaq	[jaz'mag]
prescription	resept	[re'sept]

tablet, pill	həb	[hæb]
ointment	məlhəm	[mæl'hæm]
ampoule	ampula	['ampula]
mixture	mikstura	[miks'tura]
syrup	sirop	[si'rop]
pill	həb	[hæb]
powder	toz dərman	['toz dær'man]

bandage	bint	[bint]
cotton wool	pambıq	[pam'bıg]
iodine	yod	[jod]
plaster	yapışan məlhəm	[japı'ʃan mæl'hæm]
eyedropper	damcıtökən	[damdʒıtø'kæn]
thermometer	termometr	[ter'mometr]
syringe	şpris	[ʃpris]

wheelchair	əlil arabası	[æ'lil araba'sı]
crutches	qoltuqağacı	[goltugaɣa'dʒı]

painkiller	ağrıkəsici	[aɣrıkæsi'dʒi]
laxative	işlətmə dərmanı	[iʃlæt'mæ dærma'nı]
spirit (ethanol)	spirt	[spirt]
medicinal herbs	bitki	[bit'ki]
herbal (~ tea)	bitki	[bit'ki]

77. Smoking. Tobacco products

tobacco	tütün	[ty'tyn]
cigarette	siqaret	[siga'ret]
cigar	siqara	[si'gara]
pipe	tənbəki çubuğu	[tænbæ'ki tʃubuɣ'u]
packet (of cigarettes)	paçka	[patʃ'ka]
matches	kibrit	[kib'rit]
matchbox	kibrit qutusu	[kib'rit gutu'su]
lighter	alışqan	[alıʃ'gan]
ashtray	külqabı	['kyʌgabı]
cigarette case	portsiqar	[portsi'gar]
cigarette holder	müştük	[myʃ'tyk]
filter	süzgəc	[syz'gædʒ]
to smoke (vi, vt)	çəkmək	[tʃək'mæk]
to light a cigarette	çəkmək	[tʃək'mæk]
smoking	çəkmə	[tʃək'mæ]
smoker	çəkən	[tʃə'kæn]
cigarette end	siqaret kötüyü	[siga'ret køty'y]
smoke, fumes	tüstü	[tys'ty]
ash	kül	[kyʌ]

HUMAN HABITAT

City

78. City. Life in the city

city, town	şəhər	[ʃæˈhær]
capital	paytaxt	[pajˈtaht]
village	kənd	[kænd]
city map	şəhərin planı	[ʃæhæˈrin plaˈnɪ]
city centre	şəhərin mərkəzi	[ʃæhæˈrin mærkæˈzi]
suburb	şəhərətrafı qəsəbə	[ʃæhærætraˈfɪ gæsæˈbæ]
suburban (adj)	şəhərətrafı	[ʃæhærætraˈfɪ]
outskirts	kənar	[kæˈnar]
environs (suburbs)	ətraf yerlər	[ætˈraf erˈler]
quarter	məhəllə	[mæhælˈlæ]
residential quarter	yaşayış məhəlləsi	[jaʃaˈjɪʃ mæhællæˈsi]
traffic	hərəkət	[hæræˈkæt]
traffic lights	svetofor	[svetoˈfor]
public transport	şəhər nəqliyyatı	[ʃæˈhær næglij:aˈtɪ]
crossroads	dörd yol ağzı	[ˈdørd ˈjol aɣˈzɪ]
zebra crossing	keçid	[keˈtʃid]
pedestrian subway	yeraltı keçid	[eralˈtɪ keˈtʃid]
to cross (vt)	keçmək	[kætʃˈmæk]
pedestrian	piyada gedən	[pijaˈda geˈdæn]
pavement	küçə səkisi	[kyˈtʃə sækiˈsi]
bridge	körpü	[kørˈpy]
embankment	sahil küçəsi	[saˈhil kytʃəˈsi]
fountain	fəvvarə	[ˈfævvaˈræ]
allée	xiyaban	[hijaˈban]
park	park	[park]
boulevard	bulvar	[bulˈvar]
square	meydan	[mejˈdan]
avenue (wide street)	prospekt	[prosˈpekt]
street	küçə	[kyˈtʃə]
lane	döngə	[døˈŋæ]
dead end	dalan	[daˈlan]
house	ev	[æv]
building	bina	[biˈna]
skyscraper	göydələn	[gøjdæˈlæn]
facade	fasad	[faˈsad]
roof	dam	[dam]

window	pəncərə	[pænʤæ'ræ]
arch	arka	['arka]
column	sütun	[sy'tun]
corner	tin	[tin]

shop window	vitrin	[vit'rin]
shop sign	lövhə	[løv'hæ]
poster	afişa	[a'fiʃa]
advertising poster	reklam plakatı	[rek'lam plaka'tı]
hoarding	reklam lövhəsi	[rek'lam løvhæ'si]

rubbish	tullantılar	[tullantı'lar]
rubbish bin	urna	['urna]
to litter (vi)	zibilləmək	[zibillæ'mæk]
rubbish dump	zibil tökülən yer	[zi'bil tøky'læn 'er]

telephone box	telefon budkası	[tele'fon budka'sı]
street light	fənərli dirək	[fænær'li di'ræk]
bench (park ~)	skamya	[skam'ja]

policeman	polis işçisi	[po'lis iʃʧi'si]
police	polis	[po'lis]
beggar	dilənçi	[dilæn'ʧi]
homeless	evsiz-eşiksiz	[æv'siz æʃik'siz]

79. Urban institutions

shop	mağaza	[may'aza]
chemist, pharmacy	aptek	[ap'tek]
optician	optik cihazlar	[op'tik ʤihaz'lar]
shopping centre	ticarət mərkəzi	[tiʤa'ræt mærkæ'zi]
supermarket	supermarket	[super'market]

bakery	çörəkçixana	[ʧorækʧiha'na]
baker	çörəkçi	[ʧoræk'ʧi]
cake shop	şirniyyat mağazası	[ʃirni'jːat may'azası]
grocery shop	bakaleya mağazası	[baka'leja may'azası]
butcher shop	ət dükanı	['æt dyka'nı]

greengrocer	tərəvəz dükanı	[tæræ'væz dyka'nı]
market	bazar	[ba'zar]

coffee bar	kafe	[ka'fe]
restaurant	restoran	[resto'ran]
pub	pivəxana	[pivæha'na]
pizzeria	pitseriya	[pitse'rija]

hairdresser	bərbərxana	[bærbærha'na]
post office	poçt	[poʧt]
dry cleaners	kimyəvi təmizləmə	[kimjə'vi tæmizlæ'mæ]
photo studio	fotoatelye	[fotoate'ʎje]

shoe shop	ayaqqabı mağazası	[ajagga'bı may'azası]
bookshop	kitab mağazası	[ki'tab may'azası]

sports shop	idman malları mağazası	[id'man malla'rı may'azası]
clothing repair	paltarların təmiri	[paltarla'rın tæmi'ri]
formal wear hire	paltarların kirayəsi	[paltarla'rın kirajə'si]
DVD rental shop	filmlərin kirayəsi	[filmlæ'rin kirajə'si]

circus	sirk	[sirk]
zoo	heyvanat parkı	[hæjva'nat par'kı]
cinema	kinoteatr	[kinote'atr]
museum	muzey	[mu'zej]
library	kitabxana	[kitabha'na]

theatre	teatr	[te'atr]
opera	opera	['opera]
nightclub	gecə klubu	[ge'dʒæ klu'bu]
casino	kazino	[kazi'no]

mosque	məsçid	[mæs'tʃid]
synagogue	sinaqoq	[sina'gog]
cathedral	baş kilsə	['baʃ kil'sæ]
temple	məbəd	[mæ'bæd]
church	kilsə	[kil'sæ]

institute	institut	[insti'tut]
university	universitet	[universi'tet]
school	məktəb	[mæk'tæb]

prefecture	prefektura	[prefek'tura]
town hall	bələdiyyə	[bælædi'j:ə]
hotel	mehmanxana	[mehmanha'na]
bank	bank	[baŋk]

embassy	səfirlik	[sæfir'lik]
travel agency	turizm agentliyi	[tu'rizm agentli'jı]
information office	məlumat bürosu	[mælu'mat byro'su]
money exchange	mübadilə məntəqəsi	[mybadi'læ mæntægæ'si]

| underground, tube | metro | [met'ro] |
| hospital | xəstəxana | [hæstæha'na] |

| petrol station | yanacaq doldurma məntəqəsi | [jana'dʒag doldur'ma mæntægæ'si] |
| car park | avtomobil dayanacağı | [avtomo'bil dajanadʒaɣ'ı] |

80. Signs

shop sign	lövhə	[løv'hæ]
notice (written text)	yazı	[ja'zı]
poster	plakat	[pla'kat]
direction sign	göstərici	[gøsteri'dʒi]
arrow (sign)	göstərici əqrəb	[gøsteri'dʒi æg'ræb]

caution	xəbərdarlıq	[hæbærdar'lıg]
warning sign	xəbərdarlıq	[hæbærdar'lıg]
to warn (vt)	xəbərdarlıq etmək	[hæbærdar'lıg æt'mæk]

closing day	istirahət günü	[istira'hæt gy'ny]
timetable (schedule)	cədvəl	[dʒæd'væl]
opening hours	iş saatları	['iʃ sa:tla'rı]

WELCOME!	XOŞ GƏLMİŞSİNİZ!	['hoʃ gæl'miʃsiniz]
ENTRANCE	GİRİŞ	[gi'riʃ]
WAY OUT	ÇIXIŞ	[tʃı'hıʃ]

PUSH	ÖZÜNDƏN	[øzyn'dæn]
PULL	ÖZÜNƏ TƏRƏF	[øzy'næ tæ'ræf]
OPEN	AÇIQDIR	[a'tʃıgdır]
CLOSED	BAĞLIDIR	[baɣ'lıdır]

| WOMEN | QADINLAR ÜÇÜN | [gadın'lar y'tʃun] |
| MEN | KİŞİLƏR ÜÇÜN | [kiʃi'lær y'tʃun] |

DISCOUNTS	ENDİRİMLƏR	[ændirim'lær]
SALE	ENDİRİMLİ SATIŞ	[ændirim'li sa'tıʃ]
NEW!	YENİ MAL!	[e'ni 'mal]
FREE	PULSUZ	[pul'suz]

ATTENTION!	DİQQƏT!	[dig'gæt]
NO VACANCIES	BOŞ YER YOXDUR	['boʃ 'er 'johdur]
RESERVED	SİFARİŞ EDİLİB	[sifa'riʃ ædi'lib]

| ADMINISTRATION | MÜDİRİYYƏT | [mydiri'j:ət] |
| STAFF ONLY | YALNIZ İŞÇİLƏR ÜÇÜN | ['jalnız iʃtʃi'lær y'tʃun] |

BEWARE OF THE DOG!	TUTAĞAN İT	[tutaɣ'an 'it]
NO SMOKING	SİQARET ÇƏKMƏYİN!	[siga'ret 'tʃəkmæjın]
DO NOT TOUCH!	ƏL VURMAYIN!	['æl 'vurmajın]

DANGEROUS	TƏHLÜKƏLİDİR	[tæhlykæ'lidir]
DANGER	TƏHLÜKƏ	[tæhly'kæ]
HIGH TENSION	YÜKSƏK GƏRGİNLİK	[yk'sæk gærgin'lik]
NO SWIMMING!	ÇİMMƏK QADAĞANDIR	[tʃim'mæk gadaɣ'andır]
OUT OF ORDER	İŞLƏMİR	[iʃ'læmir]

FLAMMABLE	ODDAN TƏHLÜKƏLİDİR	[od'dan tæhlykæ'lidir]
FORBIDDEN	QADAĞANDIR	[gadaɣ'andır]
NO TRESPASSING!	KEÇMƏK QADAĞANDIR	[ketʃ'mæk gadaɣ'andır]
WET PAINT	RƏNGLƏNİB	[ræŋlæ'nib]

81. Urban transport

bus, coach	avtobus	[av'tobus]
tram	tramvay	[tram'vaj]
trolleybus	trolleybus	[trol'lejbus]
route (of bus)	marşrut	[marʃ'rut]
number (e.g. bus ~)	nömrə	[nøm'ræ]

to go by ...	getmək	[get'mæk]
to get on (~ the bus)	minmək	[min'mæk]
to get off ...	enmək	[æn'mæk]

stop (e.g. bus ~)	dayanacaq	[dajana'dʒag]
next stop	növbəti dayanacaq	[nøvbæ'ti dajana'dʒag]
terminus	axırıncı dayanacaq	[ahırın'dʒı dajana'dʒag]
timetable	hərəkət cədvəli	[hæræ'kæt dʒædvæ'li]
to wait (vt)	gözləmək	[gøzlæ'mæk]

ticket	bilet	[bi'let]
fare	biletin qiyməti	[bile'tin gijmæ'ti]

cashier	kassir	[kas'sir]
ticket inspection	nəzarət	[næza'ræt]
inspector	nəzarətçi	[næzaræ'tʃi]

to be late (for ...)	gecikmək	[gedʒik'mæk]
to miss (~ the train, etc.)	gecikmək	[gedʒik'mæk]
to be in a hurry	tələsmək	[tælæs'mæk]

taxi, cab	taksi	[tak'si]
taxi driver	taksi sürücüsü	[tak'si syrydʒy'sy]
by taxi	taksi ilə	[tak'si i'læ]
taxi rank	taksi dayanacağı	[tak'si dajanadʒaɣ'ı]
to call a taxi	taksi sifariş etmək	[tak'si sifa'riʃ æt'mæk]
to take a taxi	taksi tutmaq	[tak'si tut'mag]

traffic	küçə hərəkəti	[ky'tʃə hærækæ'ti]
traffic jam	tıxac	[tı'hadʒ]
rush hour	pik saatları	['pik sa:tla'rı]
to park (vi)	park olunmaq	['park olun'mag]
to park (vt)	park etmək	['park æt'mæk]
car park	avtomobil dayanacağı	[avtomo'bil dajanadʒaɣ'ı]

underground, tube	metro	[met'ro]
station	stansiya	['stansija]
to take the tube	metro ilə getmək	[met'ro i'læ get'mæk]
train	qatar	[ga'tar]
train station	dəmiryol vağzalı	[dæ'mirjol vaɣza'lı]

82. Sightseeing

monument	abidə	[abi'dæ]
fortress	qala	[ga'la]
palace	saray	[sa'raj]
castle	qəsr	[gæsr]
tower	qüllə	[gyl'læ]
mausoleum	məqbərə	[mægbæ'ræ]

architecture	memarlıq	[memar'lıg]
medieval (adj)	orta əsrlərə aid	[or'ta æsrlæ'ræ a'id]
ancient (adj)	qədimi	[gædi'mi]
national (adj)	milli	[mil'li]
well-known (adj)	məşhur	[mæʃ'hur]

tourist	turist	[tu'rist]
guide (person)	bələdçi	[bælæd'tʃi]

excursion	gəzinti	[gæzin'ti]
to show (vt)	göstərmək	[gøstær'mæk]
to tell (vt)	söyləmək	[søjlæ'mæk]

to find (vt)	tapmaq	[tap'mag]
to get lost	itmək	[it'mæk]
map (e.g. underground ~)	sxem	[shem]
map (e.g. city ~)	plan	[plan]

souvenir, gift	suvenir	[suve'nir]
gift shop	suvenir mağazası	[suve'nir maɣ'azası]
to take pictures	fotoşəkil çəkmək	[fotoʃæ'kil tʃək'mæk]
to be photographed	fotoşəkil çəkdirmək	[fotoʃæ'kil tʃəkdir'mæk]

83. Shopping

to buy (purchase)	almaq	[al'mag]
purchase	satın alınmış şey	[sa'tın alın'mıʃ 'ʃəj]
to go shopping	alış-veriş etmək	[a'lıʃ ve'riʃ æt'mæk]
shopping	şoppinq	['ʃoppiŋ]

to be open (ab. shop)	işləmək	[iʃlæ'mæk]
to be closed	bağlanmaq	[baɣlan'mag]

footwear	ayaqqabı	[ajagga'bı]
clothes, clothing	geyim	[ge'jim]
cosmetics	kosmetika	[kos'metika]
food products	ərzaq	[ær'zag]
gift, present	hədiyyə	[hædi'jːə]

shop assistant (masc.)	satıcı	[satı'dʒı]
shop assistant (fem.)	satıcı qadın	[satı'dʒı ga'dın]

cash desk	kassa	['kassa]
mirror	güzgü	[gyz'gy]
counter (in shop)	piştaxta	[piʃtah'ta]
fitting room	paltarı ölçüb baxmaq üçün yer	[palta'rı øl'tʃub bah'mag y'tʃun 'er]

to try on	paltarı ölçüb baxmaq	[palta'rı øl'tʃub bah'mag]
to fit (ab. dress, etc.)	münasib olmaq	[myna'sib ol'mag]
to fancy (vt)	xoşuna gəlmək	[hoʃu'na gæl'mæk]

price	qiymət	[gij'mæt]
price tag	qiymət yazılan birka	[gij'mæt jazı'lan 'birka]
to cost (vt)	qiyməti olmaq	[gijmæ'ti ol'mag]
How much?	Neçəyədir?	[netʃə'jədir]
discount	endirim	[ændi'rim]

inexpensive (adj)	baha olmayan	[ba'ha 'olmajan]
cheap (adj)	ucuz	[u'dʒuz]
expensive (adj)	bahalı	[baha'lı]
It's expensive	Bu, bahadır.	['bu ba'hadır]
hire (n)	kirayə	[kira'jə]

to hire (~ a dinner jacket)	kirayəyə götürmək	[kirajə'jə gøtyr'mæk]
credit	kredit	[kre'dit]
on credit (adv)	kreditlə almaq	[kre'ditlæ al'mag]

84. Money

money	pul	[pul]
exchange	mübadilə	[mybadi'læ]
exchange rate	kurs	[kurs]
cashpoint	bankomat	[baŋko'mat]
coin	pul	[pul]

| dollar | dollar | ['dollar] |
| euro | yevro | ['evro] |

lira	lira	['lira]
Deutschmark	marka	[mar'ka]
franc	frank	[fraŋk]
pound sterling	funt sterling	['funt 'sterliŋ]
yen	yena	['jena]

debt	borc	[bordʒ]
debtor	borclu	[bordʒ'lu]
to lend (money)	borc vermək	['bordʒ ver'mæk]
to borrow (vi, vt)	borc almaq	['bordʒ al'mag]

bank	bank	[baŋk]
account	hesab	[he'sab]
to deposit into the account	hesaba yatırmaq	[hesa'ba jatır'mag]
to withdraw (vt)	hesabdan pul götürmək	[hæsab'dan 'pul gøtyr'mæk]

credit card	kredit kartı	[kre'dit kar'tı]
cash	nəqd pul	['nægd 'pul]
cheque	çek	[tʃek]
to write a cheque	çek yazmaq	['tʃek jaz'mag]
chequebook	çek kitabçası	['tʃek kitabtʃa'sı]

wallet	cib kisəsi	['dʒib kisæ'si]
purse	pul kisəsi	['pul kisæ'si]
billfold	portmone	[portmo'ne]
safe	seyf	[sejf]

heir	verəsə	[væræ'sæ]
inheritance	miras	[mi'ras]
fortune (wealth)	var-dövlət	['var døv'læt]

lease, let	icarə	[idʒa'ræ]
rent money	mənzil haqqı	[mæn'zil hag'gı]
to rent (sth from sb)	kirayə etmək	[kira'jə æt'mæk]

price	qiymət	[gij'mæt]
cost	qiymət	[gij'mæt]
sum	məbləğ	[mæb'læɣ]
to spend (vt)	sərf etmək	['særf æt'mæk]

expenses	xərclər	[hærdʒ'lær]
to economize (vi, vt)	qənaət etmək	[gæna'æt æt'mæk]
economical	qənaətcil	[gænaæt'dʒil]

to pay (vi, vt)	pulunu ödəmək	[pulu'nu ødæ'mæk]
payment	ödəniş	[ødæ'niʃ]
change (give the ~)	pulun artığı	[pu'lun artıɣ'ı]

tax	vergi	[ver'gi]
fine	cərimə	[dʒæri'mæ]
to fine (vt)	cərimə etmək	[dʒæri'mæ æt'mæk]

85. Post. Postal service

post office	poçt binası	['potʃt bina'sı]
post (letters, etc.)	poçt	[potʃt]
postman	poçtalyon	[potʃta'ʎon]
opening hours	iş saatları	['iʃ sa:tla'rı]

letter	məktub	[mæk'tub]
registered letter	sifarişli məktub	[sifariʃ'li mæk'tub]
postcard	poçt kartoçkası	['potʃt kartotʃka'sı]
telegram	teleqram	[teleg'ram]
parcel	bağlama	[baɣla'ma]
money transfer	pul köçürməsi	['pul køtʃurmæ'si]

to receive (vt)	almaq	[al'mag]
to send (vt)	göndərmək	[gøndær'mæk]
sending	göndərilmə	[gøndæril'mæ]

address	ünvan	[yn'van]
postcode	indeks	['indeks]
sender	göndərən	[gøndæ'ræn]
receiver, addressee	alan	[a'lan]

name	ad	[ad]
family name	soyadı	['sojadı]

rate (of postage)	tarif	[ta'rif]
standard (adj)	adi	[a'di]
economical (adj)	qənaətə imkan verən	[gænaæ'tæ im'kan ve'ræn]

weight	çəki	[tʃə'ki]
to weigh up (vt)	çəkmək	[tʃək'mæk]
envelope	zərf	[zærf]
postage stamp	marka	[mar'ka]

Dwelling. House. Home

86. House. Dwelling

house	ev	[æv]
at home (adv)	evdə	[æv'dæ]
courtyard	həyət	[hæ'jət]
fence	çəpər	[ʧə'pær]
brick (n)	kərpic	[kær'piʤ]
brick (as adj)	kərpicdən olan	[kærpiʤ'dæn o'lan]
stone (n)	daş	[daʃ]
stone (as adj)	daşdan olan	[daʃ'dan o'lan]
concrete (n)	beton	[be'ton]
concrete (as adj)	betondan olan	[beton'dan o'lan]
new (adj)	təzə	[tæ'zæ]
old (adj)	köhnə	[køh'næ]
decrepit (house)	uçuq-sökük	[u'ʧuq sø'kyk]
modern (adj)	müasir	[mya'sir]
multistorey (adj)	çoxmərtəbəli	[ʧohmærtæbæ'li]
high (adj)	hündür	[hyn'dyr]
floor, storey	mərtəbə	[mærtæ'bæ]
single-storey (adj)	birmərtəbəli	[birmærtæbæ'li]
ground floor	alt mərtəbə	['alt mærtæ'bæ]
top floor	üst mərtəbə	['yst mærtæ'bæ]
roof	dam	[dam]
chimney (stack)	boru	[bo'ru]
roof tiles	kirəmit	[kiræ'mit]
tiled (adj)	kirəmitdən olan	[kiræmit'dæn o'lan]
loft (attic)	çardaq	[ʧar'dag]
window	pəncərə	[pænʤæ'ræ]
glass	şüşə	[ʃy'ʃæ]
window ledge	pəncərə altı	[pænʤæ'ræ al'tı]
shutters	pəncərə qapaqları	[pænʤæ'ræ gapagla'rı]
wall	divar	[di'var]
balcony	balkon	[bal'kon]
downpipe	nov borusu	['nov boru'su]
upstairs (to be ~)	yuxarıda	[yharı'da]
to go upstairs	qalxmaq	[galh'mag]
to come down	aşağı düşmək	[aʃaɣ'ı dyʃ'mæk]
to move (to new premises)	köçmək	[køʧ'mæk]

87. House. Entrance. Lift

entrance	giriş yolu	[gi'riʃ jo'lu]
stairs (stairway)	pilləkən	[pillæ'kæn]
steps	pillələr	[pillæ'lær]
banisters	məhəccər	[mæhæ'ʤær]
lobby (hotel ~)	xoll	[holl]

postbox	poçt qutusu	['potʃt gutu'su]
rubbish container	zibil qabı	[zi'bil ga'bı]
refuse chute	zibil borusu	[zi'bil boru'su]

lift	lift	[lift]
goods lift	yük lifti	['yk lif'ti]
lift cage	kabina	[ka'bina]
to take the lift	liftə minmək	[lif'tæ min'mæk]

flat	mənzil	[mæn'zil]
residents, inhabitants	sakinlər	[sakin'lær]
neighbour (masc.)	qonşu	[gon'ʃu]
neighbour (fem.)	qonşu	[gon'ʃu]
neighbours	qonşular	[gonʃu'lar]

88. House. Electricity

electricity	elektrik	[ælekt'rik]
light bulb	elektrik lampası	[ælekt'rik lampa'sı]
switch	elektrik açarı	[ælekt'rik atʃa'rı]
fuse	elektrik mantarı	[ælekt'rik manta'rı]

cable, wire (electric ~)	məftil	[mæf'til]
wiring	şəbəkə	[ʃæbæ'kæ]
electricity meter	sayğac	[sajɣ'aʤ]
readings	sayğac göstəricisi	[sajɣ'aʤ gøsteriʤi'si]

89. House. Doors. Locks

door	qapı	[ga'pı]
vehicle gate	darvaza	[darva'za]
handle, doorknob	qapı dəstəyi	[ga'pı dæstæ'jı]
to unlock (unbolt)	açmaq	[atʃ'mag]
to open (vt)	açmaq	[atʃ'mag]
to close (vt)	bağlamaq	[baɣla'mag]

key	açar	[a'tʃar]
bunch (of keys)	bağlama	[baɣla'ma]
to creak (door hinge)	cırıldamaq	[ʤırılda'mag]
creak	cırıltı	[ʤırıl'tı]
hinge (of door)	rəzə	[ræ'zæ]
doormat	xalça	[hal'tʃa]
door lock	qıfıl	[gı'fıl]

keyhole	açar yeri	[a'tʃar e'ri]
bolt (sliding bar)	siyirmə	[sijɪr'mæ]
door latch	siyirtmə	[sijɪrt'mæ]
padlock	asma qıfıl	[as'ma gɪ'fɪl]

to ring (~ the door bell)	zəng etmək	['zæŋ æt'mæk]
ringing (sound)	zəng	[zæŋ]
doorbell	zəng	[zæŋ]
button	düymə	[dyj'mæ]
knock (at the door)	taqqıltı	[taggɪl'tɪ]
to knock (vi)	taqqıldatmaq	[taggɪldat'mag]

code	kod	[kod]
code lock	kodlu qıfıl	[kod'lu gɪ'fɪl]
door phone	domofon	[domo'fon]
number (on the door)	nömrə	[nøm'ræ]
doorplate	lövhəcik	[løvhæ'dʒik]
peephole	qapının deşiyi	[gapɪ'nɪn deʃi'jɪ]

90. Country house

village	kənd	[kænd]
vegetable garden	bostan	[bos'tan]
fence	hasar	[ha'sar]
paling	çəpər	[tʃə'pær]
wicket gate	kiçik qapı	[ki'tʃik ga'pɪ]

granary	anbar	[an'bar]
cellar	zirzəmi	[zirzæ'mi]
shed (in garden)	dam	[dam]
well (water)	quyu	[gu'y]

stove (wood-fired ~)	soba	[so'ba]
to heat the stove	qalamaq	[gala'mag]
firewood	odun	[o'dun]
log (firewood)	odun parçası	[o'dun partʃa'sɪ]

veranda	şüşəbənd	[ʃyʃæ'bænd]
terrace (patio)	terras	[ter'ras]
front steps	artırma	[artɪr'ma]
swing (hanging seat)	yellənçək	[ellæn'tʃək]

91. Villa. Mansion

country house	şəhər kənarında olan ev	[ʃæ'hær kænarɪn'da o'lan 'æv]
villa (by sea)	villa	['villa]
wing (of building)	cinah	[dʒi'nah]

garden	bağ	[baɣ]
park	park	[park]
tropical glasshouse	oranjereya	[oranʒe'reja]
to look after (garden, etc.)	baxmaq	[bah'mag]

swimming pool	hovuz	[ho'vuz]
gym	idman zalı	[id'man za'lı]
tennis court	tennis meydançası	['teŋis mejdantʃa'sı]
home cinema room	kinoteatr	[kinote'atr]
garage	qaraj	[ga'raʒ]

| private property | xüsusi mülkiyyət | [hysu'si mylki'j:ət] |
| private land | xüsusi malikanə | [hysu'si malika'næ] |

| warning (caution) | xəbərdarlıq | [hæbæerdar'lıg] |
| warning sign | xəbərdarlıq yazısı | [hæbæerdar'lıg jazı'sı] |

security	mühafizə	[myhafi'zæ]
security guard	mühafizəçi	[myhafizæ'tʃi]
burglar alarm	siqnalizasiya	[signali'zasija]

92. Castle. Palace

castle	qəsr	[gæsr]
palace	saray	[sa'raj]
fortress	qala	[ga'la]
wall (round castle)	divar	[di'var]
tower	güllə	[gyl'læ]
main tower, donjon	əsas güllə	[æ'sas gyl'læ]

portcullis	qaldırılan darvaza	[galdırı'lan darva'za]
subterranean passage	yeraltı yol	[eral'tı 'jol]
moat	xəndək	[hæn'dæk]
chain	zəncir	[zæn'dʒir]
arrow loop	qala bacası	[ga'la badʒa'sı]

magnificent (adj)	təmtəraqlı	[tæmtærag'lı]
majestic (adj)	əzəmətli	[æzæmæt'li]
impregnable (adj)	yenilməz	[enil'mæz]
knightly (adj)	rıtsar	['rıtsar]
medieval (adj)	orta əsrlərə aid	[or'ta æsrlæ'ræ a'id]

93. Flat

flat	mənzil	[mæn'zil]
room	otaq	[o'tag]
bedroom	yataq otağı	[ja'tag otaɣ'ı]
dining room	yemək otağı	[e'mæk otaɣ'ı]
living room	qonaq otağı	[go'nag otaɣ'ı]
study	iş otağı	['iʃ otaɣ'ı]

entry room	dəhliz	[dæh'liz]
bathroom	vanna otağı	[va'ŋa otaɣ'ı]
water closet	tualet	[tua'let]
ceiling	tavan	[ta'van]
floor	döşəmə	[døʃæ'mæ]
corner	künc	[kyndʒ]

94. Flat. Cleaning

to clean (vi, vt)	yığışdırmaq	[jıɣıʃdır'mag]
to put away (to stow)	aparmaq	[apar'mag]
dust	toz	[toz]
dusty (adj)	tozlu	[toz'lu]
to dust (vt)	toz almaq	['toz al'mag]
vacuum cleaner	tozsoran	[tozso'ran]
to vacuum (vt)	tozsoranla toz almaq	[tozso'ranla 'toz al'mag]
to sweep (vi, vt)	süpürmək	[sypyr'mæk]
sweepings	zibil	[zi'bil]
order	səliqə-sahman	[sæli'gæ sah'man]
disorder, mess	səliqəsizlik	[sæligæsiz'lik]
mop	lif süpürgə	['lif sypyr'gæ]
duster	əski	[æs'ki]
broom	süpürgə	[sypyr'gæ]
dustpan	xəkəndaz	[hækæn'daz]

95. Furniture. Interior

furniture	mebel	['mebel]
table	masa	[ma'sa]
chair	stul	[stul]
bed	çarpayı	[ʧarpa'jı]
sofa, settee	divan	[di'van]
armchair	kreslo	['kreslo]
bookcase	kitab şkafı	[ki'tab ʃka'fı]
shelf	kitab rəfi	[ki'tab ræ'fi]
set of shelves	etajer	[æta'ʒer]
wardrobe	paltar üçün şkaf	[pal'tar y'ʧun 'ʃkaf]
coat rack	paltarasan	[paltara'san]
coat stand	dik paltarasan	['dik paltara'san]
chest of drawers	kamod	[ka'mod]
coffee table	jurnal masası	[ʒur'nal masa'sı]
mirror	güzgü	[gyz'gy]
carpet	xalı	[ha'lı]
small carpet	xalça	[hal'ʧa]
fireplace	kamin	[ka'min]
candle	şam	[ʃam]
candlestick	şamdan	[ʃam'dan]
drapes	pərdə	[pær'dæ]
wallpaper	divar kağızı	[di'var kʲaɣı'zı]
blinds (jalousie)	jalyuzi	[ʒaly'zi]
table lamp	stol lampası	['stol lamp'sı]
wall lamp	çıraq	[ʧı'rag]

| standard lamp | torşer | [tor'ʃər] |
| chandelier | çilçıraq | [ʧilʧɪ'rag] |

leg (of chair, table)	ayaq	[a'jag]
armrest	qoltuqaltı	[goltuɣal'tɪ]
back	söykənəcək	[søjkænæ'ʤæk]
drawer	siyirtmə	[sijɪrt'mæ]

96. Bedding

bedclothes	yataq dəyişəyi	[ja'tag dæiʃæ'jɪ]
pillow	yastıq	[jas'tɪg]
pillowslip	yastıqüzü	[jastɪgy'zy]
blanket (eiderdown)	yorğan	[jorɣ'an]
sheet	mələfə	[mælæ'fæ]
bedspread	örtük	[ør'tyk]

97. Kitchen

kitchen	mətbəx	[mæt'bæh]
gas	qaz	[gaz]
gas cooker	qaz plitəsi	['gaz plitæ'si]
electric cooker	elektrik plitəsi	[elekt'rik plitæ'si]
oven	duxovka	[duhov'ka]
microwave oven	mikrodalğalı soba	[mikrodalɣa'lɪ so'ba]

refrigerator	soyuducu	[soydu'ʤu]
freezer	dondurucu kamera	[donduru'ʤu 'kamera]
dishwasher	qabyuyan maşın	[gaby'jan ma'ʃɪn]

mincer	ət çəkən maşın	['æt ʧə'kæn ma'ʃɪn]
juicer	şirə sıxan maşın	[ʃi'ræ ʧɪha'ran ma'ʃɪn]
toaster	toster	['toster]
mixer	mikser	['mikser]

coffee maker	qəhvə hazırlayan maşın	[gæh'væ hazırla'jan ma'ʃɪn]
coffee pot	qəhvədan	[gæhvæ'dan]
coffee grinder	qəhvə üyüdən maşın	[gæh'væ y:'dæn ma'ʃɪn]

kettle	çaydan	[ʧaj'dan]
teapot	dəm çaydanı	['dæm ʧajda'nɪ]
lid	qapaq	[ga'pag]
tea strainer	kiçik ələk	[ki'ʧik æ'læk]

spoon	qaşıq	[ga'ʃɪg]
teaspoon	çay qaşığı	['ʧaj gaʃɪɣ'ɪ]
tablespoon	xörək qaşığı	[hø'ræk gaʃɪɣ'ɪ]
fork	çəngəl	[ʧə'ŋæl]
knife	bıçaq	[bɪ'ʧag]

| tableware (dishes) | qab-qacaq | ['gab ga'ʤag] |
| plate (dinner ~) | boşqab | [boʃ'gab] |

saucer	nəlbəki	[nælbæ'ki]
shot glass	qədəh	[gæ'dæh]
glass (~ of water)	stəkan	[stæ'kan]
cup	fincan	[fin'dʒan]

sugar bowl	qənd qabı	['gænd ga'bı]
salt shaker	duz qabı	['duz ga'bı]
pepper shaker	istiot qabı	[isti'ot ga'bı]
butter dish	yağ qabı	['jaɣ ga'bı]

stew pot	qazan	[ga'zan]
frying pan	tava	[ta'va]
ladle	çömçə	[tʃom'tʃə]
colander	aşsüzən	[aʃsy'zæn]
tray	məcməyi	[mædʒmæ'jı]

bottle	şüşə	[ʃy'ʃæ]
jar (glass)	şüşə banka	[ʃy'ʃæ ba'ŋka]
tin, can	konserv bankası	[kon'serv baŋka'sı]

bottle opener	açan	[a'tʃan]
tin opener	konserv ağzı açan	[kon'serv aɣ'zı a'tʃan]
corkscrew	burğu	[burɣ'u]
filter	süzgəc	[syz'gædʒ]
to filter (vt)	süzgəcdən keçirmək	[syzgædʒ'dæn kætʃir'mæk]

rubbish, refuse	zibil	[zi'bil]
rubbish bin	zibil vedrəsi	[zi'bil vedræ'si]

98. Bathroom

bathroom	vanna otağı	[va'ŋa otaɣ'ı]
water	su	[su]
tap	kran	[kran]
hot water	isti su	[is'ti 'su]
cold water	soyuq su	[so'yg 'su]

toothpaste	diş məcunu	['diʃ mædʒu'nu]
to clean one's teeth	dişləri fırçalamaq	[diʃlæ'ri fırtʃala'mag]

to shave (vi)	üzünü qırxmaq	[yzy'ny gırh'mag]
shaving foam	üz qırxmaq üçün köpük	['yz gırh'mag y'tʃun kø'pyk]
razor	ülgüc	[yʌ'gydʒ]

to wash (clean)	yumaq	[y'mag]
to have a bath	yuyunmaq	[y:n'mag]
shower	duş	[duʃ]
to have a shower	duş qəbul etmək	['duʃ gæ'bul æt'mæk]

bath (tub)	vanna	[va'ŋa]
toilet	unitaz	[uni'taz]
sink (washbasin)	su çanağı	['su tʃanaɣ'ı]
soap	sabun	[sa'bun]
soap dish	sabun qabı	[sa'bun ga'bı]

sponge	hamam süngəri	[ha'mam syŋæ'ri]
shampoo	şampun	[ʃam'pun]
towel	dəsmal	[dæs'mal]
bathrobe	hamam xələti	[ha'mam hælæ'ti]

laundry (process)	paltarın yuyulması	[palta'rın y:lma'sı]
washing machine	paltaryuyan maşın	[paltary'jan ma'ʃın]
to do the laundry	paltar yumaq	[pal'tar y'mag]
washing powder	yuyucu toz	[y:'ʤu 'toz]

99. Household appliances

TV, telly	televizor	[tele'vizor]
tape recorder	maqnitofon	[magnito'fon]
video	videomaqnitofon	[videomagnito'fon]
radio	qəbuledici	[gæbulædi'ʤi]
player (CD, MP3, etc.)	pleyer	['plejer]

video projector	video proyektor	[video pro'ektor]
home cinema	ev kinoteatrı	['æv kinoteat'rı]
DVD player	DVD maqnitofonu	[divi'di magnitofo'nu]
amplifier	səs gücləndiricisi	['sæs gyʤlændiriʤi'si]
video game console	oyun əlavəsi	[o'yn ælavæ'si]

video camera	videokamera	[video'kamera]
camera (photo)	fotoaparat	[fotoapa'rat]
digital camera	rəqəm fotoaparatı	[ræ'gæm fotoapara'tı]

vacuum cleaner	tozsoran	[tozso'ran]
iron (e.g. steam ~)	ütü	[y'ty]
ironing board	ütü taxtası	[y'ty tahta'sı]

telephone	telefon	[tele'fon]
mobile phone	mobil telefon	[mo'bil tele'fon]
typewriter	yazı maşını	[ja'zı maʃı'nı]
sewing machine	tikiş maşını	[ti'kiʃ maʃı'nı]

microphone	mikrofon	[mikro'fon]
headphones	qulaqlıqlar	[gulaglıg'lar]
remote control (TV)	pult	[pult]

CD, compact disc	SD diski	[si'di dis'ki]
cassette	kasset	[kas'set]
vinyl record	val	[val]

100. Repairs. Renovation

renovations	təmir	[tæ'mir]
to renovate (vt)	təmir işləri aparmaq	[tæ'mir iʃlæ'ri apar'mag]
to repair (vt)	təmir etmək	[tæ'mir æt'mæk]
to put in order	qaydaya salmaq	[gajda'ja sal'mag]
to redo (do again)	yenidən düzəltmək	[eni'dæn dyzælt'mæk]

paint	boya	[bo'ja]
to paint (~ a wall)	boyamaq	[boja'mag]
house painter	boyaqçı	[bojag'tʃı]
brush	fırça	[fır'tʃa]

| whitewash | ağartma | [aɣart'ma] |
| to whitewash (vt) | ağartmaq | [aɣart'mag] |

wallpaper	divar kağızı	[di'var kʲaɣı'zı]
to wallpaper (vt)	divar kağızı vurmaq	[di'var kaɣı'zı vur'mag]
varnish	lak	[lak]
to varnish (vt)	lak vurmaq	['lak vur'mag]

101. Plumbing

water	su	[su]
hot water	isti su	[is'ti 'su]
cold water	soyuq su	[so'yg 'su]
tap	kran	[kran]

drop (of water)	damcı	[dam'dʒı]
to drip (vi)	damcılamaq	[damdʒıla'mag]
to leak (ab. pipe)	axmaq	[ah'mag]
leak (pipe ~)	axıb getmək	[a'hıb get'mæk]
puddle	gölməçə	[gølmæ'tʃə]

pipe	boru	[bo'ru]
valve	ventil	['ventil]
to be clogged up	yolu tutulmaq	[jo'lu tutul'mag]

tools	alətlər	[alæt'lær]
adjustable spanner	aralayan açar	[arala'jan a'tʃar]
to unscrew, untwist (vt)	açmaq	[atʃ'mag]
to screw (tighten)	bərkitmək	[bærkit'mæk]

to unclog (vt)	təmizləmək	[tæmizlæ'mæk]
plumber	santexnik	[san'tehnik]
basement	zirzəmi	[zirzæ'mi]
sewerage (system)	kanalizasiya	[kanali'zasija]

102. Fire. Conflagration

fire (to catch ~)	od	[od]
flame	alov	[a'lov]
spark	qığılcım	[gıɣıl'dʒım]
smoke (from fire)	tüstü	[tys'ty]
torch (flaming stick)	məşəl	[mæ'ʃæl]
campfire	tonqal	[to'ŋal]

petrol	benzin	[ben'zin]
paraffin	ağ neft	['aɣ 'neft]
flammable (adj)	alışqan	[alıʃ'gan]

| explosive (adj) | partlama təhlükəsi olan | [partla'ma tæhlykæ'si o'lan] |
| NO SMOKING | SİQARET ÇƏKMƏYİN! | [siga'ret 'tʃəkmæjɪn] |

safety	təhlükəsizlik	[tæhlykæsiz'lik]
danger	təhlükə	[tæhly'kæ]
dangerous (adj)	təhlükəli	[tæhlykæ'li]

to catch fire	alışmaq	[alɪʃ'mag]
explosion	partlayış	[partla'jɪʃ]
to set fire	yandırmaq	[jandır'mag]
incendiary (arsonist)	qəsdən yandıran	['gæsdæn jandı'ran]
arson	od vurma	['od vur'ma]

to blaze (vi)	alışıb yanmaq	[alı'ʃıb jan'mag]
to burn (be on fire)	yanmaq	[jan'mag]
to burn down	yanıb qurtarmaq	[ja'nıb gurtar'mag]

firefighter	yanğınsöndürən	[janɣınsøndy'ræn]
fire engine	yanğın maşını	[janɣ'ın maʃı'nı]
fire brigade	yanğınsöndürmə komandası	[janɣınsøndyr'mæ ko'mandası]
fire engine ladder	yanğın nərdivanı	[janɣın nærdiva'nı]

fire hose	şlanq	[ʃlaŋ]
fire extinguisher	odsöndürən	[odsøndy'ræn]
helmet	kaska	[kas'ka]
siren	sirena	[si'rena]

to call out	çığırmaq	[tʃıɣır'mag]
to call for help	köməyə çağırmaq	[kømæ'jə tʃaɣır'mag]
rescuer	xilas edən	[hi'las æ'dæn]
to rescue (vt)	xilas etmək	[hi'las æt'mæk]

to arrive (vi)	gəlmək	[gæl'mæk]
to extinguish (vt)	söndürmək	[søndyr'mæk]
water	su	[su]
sand	qum	[gum]

ruins (destruction)	xarabalıq	[haraba'lıg]
to collapse (building, etc.)	uçmaq	[utʃ'mag]
to fall down (vi)	uçmaq	[utʃ'mag]
to cave in (ceiling, floor)	dağılmaq	[daɣıl'mag]

| fragment (piece of wall, etc.) | qırıntı | [gırın'tı] |
| ash | kül | [kyʎ] |

| to suffocate (die) | boğulmaq | [boɣul'mag] |
| to be killed (perish) | həlak olmaq | [hæ'lak ol'mag] |

HUMAN ACTIVITIES

Job. Business. Part 1

103. Office. Working in the office

office (of firm)	ofis	['ofis]
office (of director, etc.)	iş otağı	['iʃotaɣ'ı]
reception	resepşn	[re'sepʃn]
secretary	katibə	[kʲati'bæ]
director	direktor	[di'rektor]
manager	menecer	['menedʒer]
accountant	mühasib	[myha'sib]
employee	işçi	[iʃ'tʃi]
furniture	mebel	['mebel]
desk	masa	[ma'sa]
desk chair	kreslo	['kreslo]
chest of drawers	dolabça	[dolab'tʃa]
coat stand	dik paltarasan	['dik paltara'san]
computer	bilgisayar	[bilgisa'jar]
printer	printer	['printer]
fax machine	faks	[faks]
photocopier	surətçıxaran aparat	[suрætʃıha'ran apa'rat]
paper	kağız	[kaɣ'ız]
office supplies	dəftərxana ləvazimatı	[dæftærha'na lævazima'tı]
mouse mat	altlıq	[alt'lıg]
sheet of paper	vərəq	[væ'ræg]
folder, binder	qovluq	[gov'lug]
catalogue	kataloq	[ka'talog]
directory (of addresses)	məlumat kitabçası	[mælu'mat kitabtʃa'sı]
documentation	sənədlər	[sænæd'lær]
brochure	broşür	[bro'ʃyr]
leaflet	vərəqə	[væræ'gæ]
sample	nümunə	[nymu'næ]
training meeting	treninq	['treninŋ]
meeting (of managers)	müşavirə	[myʃavi'ræ]
lunch time	nahar fasiləsi	[na'har fasilæ'si]
to make a copy	surət çıxarmaq	[su'ræt tʃıhar'mag]
to make copies	çoxaltmaq	[tʃohalt'mag]
to receive a fax	faks almaq	['faks al'mag]
to send a fax	faks göndərmək	['faks gøndær'mæk]
to ring (telephone)	zəng etmək	['zæŋ æt'mæk]

| to answer (vt) | cavab vermək | [ʤa'vab ver'mæk] |
| to put through | bağlamaq | [baɣla'mag] |

to arrange, to set up	təyin etmək	[tæ'jɪn æt'mæk]
to demonstrate (vt)	nümayiş etdirmək	[nyma'iʃ ætdir'mæk]
to be absent	olmamaq	['olmamag]
absence	gəlməmə	['gælmæmæ]

104. Business processes. Part 1

occupation	məşğuliyyət	[mæʃɣuli'j:ət]
firm	firma	['firma]
company	şirkət	[ʃir'kæt]
corporation	korporasiya	[korpo'rasija]
enterprise	müəssisə	[myæssi'sæ]
agency	agentlik	[agent'lik]

agreement (contract)	müqavilə	[mygavi'læ]
contract	kontrakt	[kont'rakt]
deal	sövdə	[søv'dæ]
order (to place an ~)	sifariş	[sifa'riʃ]
term (of contract)	şərt	[ʃært]

wholesale (adv)	topdan	[top'dan]
wholesale (adj)	topdan satılan	[top'dan satı'lan]
wholesale (n)	topdan satış	[top'dan sa'tɪʃ]
retail (adj)	pərakəndə	[pærakæn'dæ]
retail (n)	pərakəndə satış	[pærakæn'dæ sa'tɪʃ]

competitor	rəqib	[ræ'gib]
competition	rəqabət	[ræga'bæt]
to compete (vi)	rəqabət aparmaq	[ræga'bæt apar'mag]

| partner (associate) | partnyor | [partn'jor] |
| partnership | partnyorluq | [partnjor'lug] |

crisis	böhran	[bøh'ran]
bankruptcy	müflislik	[myflis'lik]
to go bankrupt	müflis olmaq	[myf'lis ol'mag]
difficulty	çətinlik	[ʧətin'lik]
problem	problem	[prob'lem]
catastrophe	fəlakət	[fæla'kæt]

economy	iqtisadiyyat	[igtisadi'j:at]
economic (~ growth)	iqtisadi	[igtisa'di]
economic recession	iqtisadi zəifləmə	[igtisa'di zæiflæ'mæ]

| goal (aim) | məqsəd | [mæg'sæd] |
| task | vəzifə | [væzi'fæ] |

to trade (vi)	alver etmək	[al'ver æt'mæk]
network (distribution ~)	şəbəkə	[ʃæbæ'kæ]
inventory (stock)	anbar	[an'bar]
assortment	çeşid	[ʧe'ʃid]

leader	lider	['lider]
large (~ company)	iri	[i'ri]
monopoly	inhisar	[inhi'sar]

theory	nəzəriyyə	[næzæ'rij:ə]
practice	praktika	['praktika]
experience (in my ~)	təcrübə	[tædʒry'bæ]
trend (tendency)	təmayül	[tæma'yl]
development	inkişaf	[iŋki'ʃaf]

105. Business processes. Part 2

profitability	mənfəət	[mænfæ'æt]
profitable (adj)	mənfəətli	[mænfæ:t'li]

delegation (group)	nümayəndəlik	[nymajəndæ'lik]
salary	əmək haqqı	[æ'mæk hag'gı]
to correct (an error)	düzəltmək	[dyzælt'mæk]
business trip	iş səyahəti	['iʃ sæjahæ'ti]
commission	komissiya	[ko'missija]

to control (vt)	nəzarət etmək	[næza'ræt æt'mæk]
conference	konfrans	[konf'rans]
licence	lisenziya	[li'senzija]
reliable (~ partner)	etibarlı	[ætibar'lı]

initiative (undertaking)	təşəbbüs	[tæʃæb'bys]
norm (standard)	norma	['norma]
circumstance	hal	[hal]
duty (of employee)	vəzifə	[væzi'fæ]

enterprise	təşkilat	[tæʃki'lat]
organization (process)	təşkil etmə	[tæʃ'kil æt'mæ]
organized (adj)	təşkil edilmiş	[tæʃ'kil ædil'miʃ]
cancellation	ləğv etmə	['læɣv æt'mæ]
to cancel (call off)	ləğv etmək	['læɣv æt'mæk]
report (official ~)	hesabat	[hesa'bat]

patent	patent	[pa'tent]
to patent (obtain patent)	patent vermək	[pa'tent ver'mæk]
to plan (vt)	planlaşdırmaq	[planlaʃdır'mag]

bonus (money)	mükafat	[myka'fat]
professional (adj)	peşəkar	[peʃæ'kar]
procedure	prosedur	[prose'dur]

to examine (contract, etc.)	baxmaq	[bah'mag]
calculation	hesablaşma	[hesablaʃ'ma]
reputation	ad	[ad]
risk	risk	[risk]

to manage, to run	idarə etmək	[ida'ræ æt'mæk]
information	məlumat	[mælu'mat]
property	mülkiyyət	[mylki'j:ət]

union	ittifaq	[itti'fag]
life insurance	həyatın sığortalanması	[hæja'tın sıɣortalanma'sı]
to insure (vt)	sığortalamaq	[sıɣortala'mag]
insurance	sığorta müqaviləsi	[sıɣor'ta mygavilæ'si]

auction	hərrac	[hær'radʒ]
to notify (inform)	bildirmək	[bildir'mæk]
management (process)	idarə etmə	[ida'ræ æt'mæ]
service (~ industry)	xidmət	[hid'mæt]

forum	forum	['forum]
to function (vi)	işləmək	[iʃlæ'mæk]
stage (phase)	mərhələ	[mærhæ'læ]
legal (~ services)	hüquqi	[hygu'gi]
lawyer (legal expert)	hüquqşünas	[hygugʃy'nas]

106. Production. Works

plant	zavod	[za'vod]
factory	fabrik	['fabrik]
workshop	sex	[seh]
production site	istehsalat	[istehsa'lat]

industry	sənaye	[sæna'je]
industrial (adj)	sənaye	[sæna'je]
heavy industry	ağır sənaye	[aɣ'ır sæna'jə]
light industry	yüngül sənaye	[y'ŋyl sæna'je]

products	məhsul	[mæh'sul]
to produce (vt)	istehsal etmək	[isteh'sal æt'mæk]
raw materials	xammal	['hammal]

foreman	briqadir	[briga'dir]
workers team	briqada	[bri'gada]
worker	fəhlə	[fæh'læ]

working day	iş günü	['iʃ gy'ny]
pause	fasilə	[fasi'læ]
meeting	iclas	[idʒ'las]
to discuss (vt)	müzakirə etmək	[myzaki'ræ æt'mæk]

plan	plan	[plan]
to fulfil the plan	planı yerinə yetirmək	[pla'nı eri'næ etir'mæk]
rate of output	norma	['norma]
quality	keyfiyyət	[kejfi'j:ət]
checking (control)	yoxlama	[johla'ma]
quality control	keyfiyyətə nəzarət etmək	[kejfij:ə'tæ næza'ræt æt'mæk]

safety of work	əmək təhlükəsizliyi	[æ'mæk tæhlykæsizli'jı]
discipline	nizam-intizam	[ni'zam inti'zam]
infraction	pozma	[poz'ma]
to violate (rules)	pozmaq	[poz'mag]
strike	tətil	[tæ'til]
striker	tətilçi	[tætil'tʃi]

to be on strike	tətil etmək	[tæ'til æt'mæk]
trade union	həmkarlar ittifaqı	[hæmkar'lar ittifa'gı]

to invent (machine, etc.)	ixtira etmək	[ihti'ra æt'mæk]
invention	ixtira	[ihti'ra]
research	araşdırma	[araʃdır'ma]
to improve (make better)	yaxşılaşdırmaq	[jahʃılaʃdır'mag]
technology	texnoloqiya	[tehno'logija]
technical drawing	cizgi	[dʒiz'gi]

load, cargo	yük	[yk]
loader (person)	malyükləyən	[malyklæ'jən]
to load (vehicle, etc.)	yükləmək	[yklæ'mæk]
loading (process)	yükləmə	[yklæ'mæ]
to unload (vi, vt)	yük boşaltmaq	['yk boʃalt'mag]
unloading	yük boşaltma	['yk boʃalt'ma]

transport	nəqliyyat	[nægli'j:at]
transport company	nəqliyyat şirkəti	[nægli'j:at ʃirkæ'ti]
to transport (vt)	nəql etmək	['nægl æt'mæk]

wagon	vaqon	[va'gon]
cistern	sistern	[sis'tern]
lorry	yük maşını	['yk maʃı'nı]

machine tool	dəzgah	[dæz'g¹ah]
mechanism	mexanizm	[meha'nizm]

industrial waste	tullantılar	[tullantı'lar]
packing (process)	qablaşdırma	[gablaʃdır'ma]
to pack (vt)	qablaşdırmaq	[gablaʃdır'mag]

107. Contract. Agreement

contract	kontrakt	[kont'rakt]
agreement	saziş	[sa'ziʃ]
addendum	əlavə	[æla'væ]

to sign a contract	kontrakt bağlamaq	[kont'rakt baɣla'mag]
signature	imza	[im'za]
to sign (vt)	imzalamaq	[imzala'mag]
stamp (seal)	möhür	[mø'hyr]

subject of contract	müqavilənin predmeti	[mygavilæ'nin predme'ti]
clause	bənd	[bænd]
parties (in contract)	tərəflər	[tæræf'lær]
legal address	hüquqi ünvan	[hygu'gi yn'van]

to break the contract	kontraktı pozmaq	[kontrak'tı poz'mag]
commitment	vəzifə	[væzi'fæ]
responsibility	məsuliyyət	[mæsuli'j:ət]
force majeure	fors-major	['fors ma'ʒor]
dispute	mübahisə	[mybahi'sæ]
penalties	cərimə sanksiyaları	[dʒæri'mæ saŋksijala'rı]

108. Import & Export

import	idxal	[id'hal]
importer	idxalatçı	[idhala'tʃı]
to import (vt)	idxal etmək	[id'hal æt'mæk]
import (e.g. ~ goods)	idxal edilmiş mallar	[id'hal ædil'miʃ mal'lar]

exporter	ixracatçı	[ihraʤa'tʃı]
to export (vi, vt)	ixrac etmək	[ih'raʤ æt'mæk]

goods	mal	[mal]
consignment, lot	partiya	['partija]

weight	çəki	[tʃə'ki]
volume	həcm	[hæʤm]
cubic metre	kub metr	['kub 'metr]

manufacturer	istehsalçı	[istehsal'tʃı]
transport company	nəqliyyat şirkəti	[nægli'jːat ʃirkæ'ti]
container	konteyner	[kon'tejner]

border	sərhəd	[sær'hæd]
customs	gömrük	[gøm'ryk]
customs duty	gömrük rüsumu	[gøm'ryk rysu'mu]
customs officer	gömrük işçisi	[gøm'ryk iʃtʃi'si]
smuggling	qaçaqçılıq	[gatʃagtʃı'lıg]
contraband (goods)	qaçaq mal	[ga'tʃag 'mal]

109. Finances

share, stock	səhm	[sæhm]
bond (certificate)	istiqraz	[istig'raz]
bill of exchange	veksel	['veksel]

stock exchange	birja	['birʒa]
stock price	səhm kursu	['sæhm kur'su]

to become cheaper	ucuzlaşmaq	[uʤuzlaʃ'mag]
to rise in price	bahalanmaq	[bahalan'mag]

controlling interest	kontrol paketi	[kont'rol pake'ti]
investment	investisiyalar	[inves'tisijalar]
to invest (vt)	investisiya qoymaq	[inves'tisija goj'mag]
percent	faiz	[fa'iz]
interest (on investment)	faiz	[fa'iz]

profit	gəlir	[gæ'lir]
profitable (adj)	gəlirli	[gælir'li]
tax	vergi	[ver'gi]

currency (foreign ~)	valyuta	[val'yta]
national (adj)	milli	[mil'li]
exchange (currency ~)	mübadilə	[mybadi'læ]

| accountant | mühasib | [myha'sib] |
| accounting | mühasibat | [myhasi'bat] |

bankruptcy	müflislik	[myflis'lik]
collapse, ruin	iflas	[if'las]
ruin	var-yoxdan çıxma	['var joh'dan ʧıh'ma]
to be ruined	var-yoxdan çıxmaq	['var joh'dan ʧıh'mag]
inflation	inflyasiya	[inf'ʎasija]
devaluation	devalvasiya	[devaʎ'vasija]

capital	kapital	[kapi'tal]
income	gəlir	[gæ'lir]
turnover	tədavül	[tæda'vyl]
resources	ehtiyat	[æhti'jat]
monetary resources	pul vəsaiti	['pul væsai'ti]
to reduce (expenses)	ixtisara salmaq	[ihtisa'ra sal'mag]

110. Marketing

marketing	marketinq	[mar'ketiŋ]
market	bazar	[ba'zar]
market segment	bazarın segmenti	[baza'rın segmen'ti]
product	məhsul	[mæh'sul]
goods	mal	[mal]

trademark	ticarət markası	[tidʒa'ræt marka'sı]
logotype	firma nişanı	['firma niʃa'nı]
logo	loqotip	[logo'tip]

demand	tələb	[tæ'læb]
supply	təklif	[tæk'lif]
need	tələbat	[tælæ'bat]
consumer	istehlakçı	[istehlak'ʧı]

analysis	təhlil	[tæh'lil]
to analyse (vt)	təhlil etmək	[tæh'lil æt'mæk]
positioning	mövqenin təyin edilməsi	[møvge'nin tæ'jın ædilmæ'si]
to position (vt)	mövqeni təyin etmək	[møvge'ni tæ'jın æt'mæk]

price	qiymət	[gij'mæt]
pricing policy	qiymət siyasəti	[gij'mæt sijasæ'ti]
pricing	qiymət qoyulma	[gij'mæt goyl'ma]

111. Advertising

advertising	reklam	[rek'lam]
to advertise (vt)	reklam etmək	[rek'lam æt'mæk]
budget	büdcə	[byd'dʒæ]

ad, advertisement	reklam	[rek'lam]
TV advertising	televiziya reklamı	[tele'vizija rekla'mı]
radio advertising	radio reklamı	['radio rekla'mı]

outdoor advertising	küçə-çöl reklamı	[ky'tʃə 'tʃol rekla'mı]
mass medias	kütləvi informasiya vasitələri	[kytlæ'vi infor'masija vasitælæ'ri]
periodical (n)	vaxtaşırı nəşriyyat	[vahtaʃı'rı næʃri'j:at]
image (public appearance)	imic	['imidʒ]

| slogan | şüar | [ʃy'ar] |
| motto (maxim) | şüar | [ʃy'ar] |

campaign	kampaniya	[kam'panija]
advertising campaign	reklam kampaniyası	[rek'lam kam'panijası]
target group	məqsədli auditoriya	[mæqsæd'li audi'torija]

business card	vizit kartı	[vi'zit kar'tı]
leaflet	vərəqə	[væræ'gæ]
brochure	broşür	[bro'ʃyr]
pamphlet	buklet	[buk'let]
newsletter	bülleten	[bylle'ten]

shop sign	lövhə	[løv'hæ]
poster	plakat	[pla'kat]
hoarding	lövhə	[løv'hæ]

112. Banking

| bank | bank | [baŋk] |
| branch (of bank, etc.) | şöbə | [ʃo'bæ] |

| consultant | məsləhətçi | [mæslæhæ'tʃi] |
| manager (director) | idarə başçısı | [ida'ræ baʃtʃı'sı] |

bank account	hesab	[he'sab]
account number	hesab nömrəsi	[he'sab nømræ'si]
current account	cari hesab	[dʒa'ri he'sab]
deposit account	yığılma hesabı	[jıɣıl'ma hesa'bı]

to open an account	hesab açmaq	[he'sab atʃ'mag]
to close the account	bağlamaq	[baɣla'mag]
to deposit into the account	hesaba yatırmaq	[hesa'ba jatır'mag]
to withdraw (vt)	hesabdan pul götürmək	[hæsab'dan 'pul gøtyr'mæk]

deposit	əmanət	[æma'næt]
to make a deposit	əmanət qoymaq	[æma'næt goj'mag]
wire transfer	köçürmə	[køtʃur'mæ]
to wire (money)	köçürmə etmək	[køtʃur'mæ æt'mæk]

| sum | məbləğ | [mæb'læɣ] |
| How much? | Nə qədər? | ['næ gæ'dær] |

| signature | imza | [im'za] |
| to sign (vt) | imzalamaq | [imzala'mag] |

| credit card | kredit kartı | [kre'dit kar'tı] |
| code | kod | [kod] |

credit card number	kredit kartının nömrəsi	[kre'dit kartı'nın nømræ'si]
cashpoint	bankomat	[baŋko'mat]

cheque	çek	[ʧek]
to write a cheque	çek yazmaq	['ʧek jaz'mag]
chequebook	çek kitabçası	['ʧek kitabʧa'sı]

loan (bank ~)	kredit	[kre'dit]
to apply for a loan	kredit üçün müraciet etmək	[kre'dit y'ʧun myradʒi'æt æt'mæk]
to get a loan	kredit götürmək	[kre'dit gøtyr'mæk]
to give a loan	kredit vermək	[kre'dit ver'mæk]
guarantee	qarantiya	[ga'rantija]

113. Telephone. Phone conversation

telephone	telefon	[tele'fon]
mobile phone	mobil telefon	[mo'bil tele'fon]
answering machine	avtomatik cavab verən	[avtoma'tik dʒa'vab ve'ræn]

to ring (telephone)	zəng etmək	['zæŋ æt'mæk]
call, ring	zəng	[zæŋ]

to dial a number	nömrəni yığmaq	[nømræ'ni jıɣ'mag]
Hello!	allo!	[al'lo]
to ask (vt)	soruşmaq	[soruʃ'mag]
to answer (vi, vt)	cavab vermək	[dʒa'vab ver'mæk]

to hear (vt)	eşitmək	[æʃit'mæk]
well (adv)	yaxşı	[jah'ʃı]
not well (adv)	pis	[pis]
noises (interference)	maneələr	[maneæ'lær]

receiver	dəstək	[dæs'tæk]
to pick up (~ the phone)	dəstəyi götürmək	[dæstæ'jı gøtyr'mæk]
to hang up (~ the phone)	dəstəyi qoymaq	[dæstæ'jı goj'mag]

engaged (adj)	məşğul	[mæʃɣ'ul]
to ring (ab. phone)	zəng etmək	['zæŋ æt'mæk]
telephone book	telefon kitabçası	[tele'fon kitabʧa'sı]

local (adj)	yerli	[er'li]
trunk (e.g. ~ call)	şəhərlərarası	[ʃæhærlærara'sı]
international (adj)	beynəlxalq	[bejnæl'halg]

114. Mobile telephone

mobile phone	mobil telefon	[mo'bil tele'fon]
display	displey	[disp'lej]
button	düymə	[dyj'mæ]
SIM card	SİM kart	['sim 'kart]
battery	batareya	[bata'reja]

to be flat (battery)	boşalmaq	[boʃal'mag]
charger	elektrik doldurucu cihaz	[ælekt'rik dolduru'dʒu dʒi'haz]

menu	menyu	[men'y]
settings	sazlamalar	[sazlama'lar]
tune (melody)	melodiya	[me'lodija]
to select (vt)	seçmək	[setʃ'mæk]

calculator	kalkulyator	[kaʌku'ʌator]
answering machine	avtomatik cavab verən	[avtoma'tik dʒa'vab ve'ræn]
alarm clock	zəngli saat	[zæŋ'li sa'at]
contacts	telefon kitabçası	[tele'fon kitabtʃa'sı]

SMS (text message)	SMS-xəbər	[æsæ'mæs hæ'bær]
subscriber	abunəçi	[abunæ'tʃi]

115. Stationery

ballpoint pen	diyircəkli avtoqələm	[dijırdʒæk'li avtogæ'læm]
fountain pen	ucluğu olan qələm	[udʒuluɣ'u o'lan gæ'læm]

pencil	karandaş	[karan'daʃ]
highlighter	markyor	[mark'jor]
felt-tip pen	flomaster	[flo'master]

notepad	bloknot	[blok'not]
diary	gündəlik	[gyndæ'lik]

ruler	xətkeş	[hæt'keʃ]
calculator	kalkulyator	[kaʌku'ʌator]
rubber	pozan	[po'zan]
drawing pin	basmadüymə	[basmadyj'mæ]
paper clip	qısqac	[gıs'gadʒ]

glue	yapışqan	[japıʃ'gan]
stapler	stepler	['stepler]
hole punch	deşikaçan	[deʃika'tʃan]
pencil sharpener	qələm yonan	[gæ'læm jo'nan]

116. Various kinds of documents

account (report)	hesabat	[hesa'bat]
agreement	saziş	[sa'ziʃ]
application form	tələbnamə	[tælæbna'mæ]
authentic (adj)	əsil	[æ'sil]
badge (identity tag)	bec	[bedʒ]
business card	vizit kartı	[vi'zit kar'tı]

certificate (~ of quality)	sertifikat	[sertifi'kat]
cheque (e.g. draw a ~)	çek	[tʃek]
bill (in restaurant)	hesab	[he'sab]
constitution	konstitusiya	[konsti'tusija]

contract	müqavilə	[mygavi'læ]
copy	surət	[su'ræt]
copy (of contract, etc.)	nüsxə	[nys'hæ]

customs declaration	bəyannamə	[bæjaŋa'mæ]
document	sənəd	[sæ'næd]
driving licence	sürücülük vəsiqəsi	[syrydʒy'lyk væsigæ'si]
addendum	əlavə	[æla'væ]
form	anket	[a'ŋket]

identity card, ID	vəsiqə	[væsi'gæ]
inquiry (request)	sorğu	[sorɣ'u]
invitation card	dəvətnamə	[dævætna'mæ]
invoice	hesablama	[hesabla'ma]

law	qanun	[ga'nun]
letter (mail)	məktub	[mæk'tub]
letterhead	blank	[blaŋk]
list (of names, etc.)	siyahı	[sija'hı]
manuscript	əlyazma	[æljaz'ma]
newsletter	bülleten	[bylle'ten]
note (short message)	kağız	[kaɣ'ız]

pass (for worker, visitor)	buraxılış vərəqəsi	[burahı'lıʃ værægæ'si]
passport	pasport	['pasport]
permit	icazənamə	[idʒazæna'mæ]
curriculum vitae, CV	CV	[si'vi]
debt note, IOU	qeyd etmə	['gejd æt'mæ]
receipt (for purchase)	qəbz	[gæbz]
till receipt	çek	[ʧek]
report	raport	['raport]

to show (ID, etc.)	təqdim etmək	[tæg'dim æt'mæk]
to sign (vt)	imzalamaq	[imzala'mag]
signature	imza	[im'za]
stamp (seal)	möhür	[mø'hyr]
text	mətn	[mætn]
ticket (for entry)	bilet	[bi'let]

to cross out	üstündən xətt çəkmək	[ystyn'dæn 'hætt ʧək'mæk]
to fill in (~ a form)	doldurmaq	[doldur'mag]

waybill	faktura	[fak'tura]
will (testament)	vəsiyyətnamə	[væsij:ətna'mæ]

117. Kinds of business

accounting services	mühasibat xidmətləri	[myhasi'bat hidmætlæ'ri]
advertising	reklam	[rek'lam]
advertising agency	reklam agentliyi	[rek'lam agentli'jı]
air-conditioners	kondisionerlər	[kondisioner'lær]
airline	hava yolu şirkəti	[ha'va jo'lu ʃirkæ'ti]
alcoholic drinks	spirtli içkilər	[spirt'li itʃki'lær]
antiques	qədimi əşyalar	[gædi'mi æʃja'lar]

| art gallery | qalereya | [gale'reja] |
| audit services | auditor xidmətləri | [au'ditor hidmætlæ'ri] |

banks	bank biznesi	['baŋk 'biznesi]
beauty salon	gözəllik salonu	[gøzæl'lik salo'nu]
bookshop	kitab mağazası	[ki'tab maɣ'azası]
brewery	pivə zavodu	[pi'væ zavo'du]
business centre	biznes mərkəzi	['biznes mærkæ'zi]
business school	biznes məktəbi	['biznes mæktæ'bi]

casino	kazino	[kazi'no]
chemist, pharmacy	aptek	[ap'tek]
cinema	kinoteatr	[kinote'atr]
construction	inşaat	[inʃa'at]
consulting	konsaltinq	[kon'saltiŋ]

dentistry	stomatologiya	[stomato'logija]
design	dizayn	[di'zajn]
dry cleaners	kimyavi təmizləmə	[kimjə'vi tæmizlæ'mæ]

employment agency	kadrlar agentliyi	['kadrlar agentli'jı]
financial services	maliyyə xidmətləri	[mali'j:ə hidmætlæ'ri]
food products	ərzaq məhsulları	[ær'zag mæhsulla'rı]
furniture (for house)	mebel	['mebel]
garment	geyim	[ge'jım]
hotel	mehmanxana	[mehmanha'na]

ice-cream	dondurma	[dondur'ma]
industry	sənaye	[sæna'je]
insurance	sığorta	[sıɣor'ta]
Internet	internet	[inter'net]
investment	investisiyalar	[inves'tisijalar]
jeweller	zərgər	[zær'gær]
jewellery	zərgərlik məmulatı	[zærgær'lik mæmula'tı]

laundry (room, shop)	camaşırxana	[dʒamaʃırha'na]
legal adviser	hüquqi xidmətlər	[hygu'gi hidmæt'lær]
light industry	yüngül sənaye	[y'ŋyl sæna'je]

magazine	jurnal	[ʒur'nal]
mail-order selling	kataloq üzrə ticarət	[ka'talog yz'ræ tidʒa'ræt]
medicine	təbabət	[tæba'bæt]
museum	muzey	[mu'zej]

news agency	məlumat agentliyi	[mælu'mat agentli'jı]
newspaper	qəzet	[gæ'zet]
nightclub	gecə klubu	[ge'dʒæ klu'bu]

oil (petroleum)	neft	[neft]
parcels service	kuryer xidməti	[ku'rjer hidmætlæ'ri]
pharmaceuticals	əczaçılıq	[ædʒzatʃı'lıg]
printing (industry)	mətbəə işləri	[mætbæ'æ iʃlæ'ri]
pub	bar	[bar]
publishing house	nəşriyyat	[næʃri'j:at]
radio	radio	['radio]
real estate	mülk	[myʎk]

restaurant	restoran	[resto'ran]
security agency	mühafizə agentliyi	[myhafi'zæ agentli'jı]
shop	mağaza	[maɣ'aza]
sport	idman	[id'man]
stock exchange	birja	['birʒa]
supermarket	supermarket	[super'market]
swimming pool	hovuz	[ho'vuz]

tailors	atelye	[ate'ʎje]
television	televiziya	[tele'vizija]
theatre	teatr	[te'atr]
trade	ticarət	[tidʒa'ræt]
transport companies	daşımalar	[daʃıma'lar]
travel	turizm	[tu'rizm]

undertakers	dəfn etmə bürosu	['dæfn æt'mæ byro'su]
veterinary surgeon	baytar	[baj'tar]
warehouse	anbar	[an'bar]
waste collection	zibilin daşınması	[zibi'lin daʃınma'sı]

Job. Business. Part 2

118. Show. Exhibition

exhibition, show	sərgi	[sær'gi]
trade show	ticarət sərgisi	[tidʒa'ræt særgi'si]
participation	iştirak	[iʃti'rak]
to participate (vi)	iştirak etmək	[iʃti'rak æt'mæk]
participant (exhibitor)	iştirakçı	[iʃtirak'tʃı]
director	direktor	[di'rektor]
organizer's office	müdiriyyət,	[mydiri'j:ət,
	təşkilat komitəsi	tæʃki'lat komitæ'si]
organizer	təşkilatçı	[tæʃkila'tʃı]
to organize (vt)	təşkil etmək	[tæʃ'kil æt'mæk]
participation form	iştirak etmək istəyi	[iʃti'rak æt'mæk istæ'jı]
to fill in (vt)	doldurmaq	[doldur'mag]
details	təfərrüatlar	[tæfærryat'lar]
information	məlumat	[mælu'mat]
price	qiymət	[gij'mæt]
including	daxil olmaqla	[da'hil ol'magla]
to include (vt)	daxil olmaq	[da'hil ol'mag]
to pay (vi, vt)	pulunu ödəmək	[pulu'nu ødæ'mæk]
registration fee	qeydiyyat haqqı	[gejdi'j:at hag'gı]
entrance	giriş	[gi'riʃ]
pavilion, hall	pavilyon	[pavil'jon]
to register (vt)	qeyd etmək	['gejd æt'mæk]
badge (identity tag)	bec	[bedʒ]
stand	sərgi	[sær'gi]
to reserve, to book	sifariş etmək	[sifa'riʃ æt'mæk]
display case	vitrin	[vit'rin]
spotlight	çıraq	[tʃı'rag]
design	dizayn	[di'zajn]
to place (put, set)	yerləşdirmək	[erlæʃdir'mæk]
distributor	distribütor	[distri'bytor]
supplier	tədarükçü	[tædaryk'tʃu]
country	ölkə	[øl'kæ]
foreign (adj)	xarici	[hari'dʒi]
product	məhsul	[mæh'sul]
association	birlik	[bir'lik]
conference hall	konfrans zalı	[konf'rans za'lı]

| congress | konqress | [koŋ'ress] |
| contest (competition) | müsabiqə | [mysabi'gæ] |

visitor	ziyarətçi	[zijaræ'ʧi]
to visit (attend)	ziyarət etmək	[zija'ræt æt'mæk]
customer	sifarişçi	[sifariʃ'ʧi]

119. Mass Media

newspaper	qəzet	[gæ'zet]
magazine	jurnal	[ʒur'nal]
press (printed media)	mətbuat	[mætbu'at]
radio	radio	['radio]
radio station	radio stansiyası	['radio 'stansijası]
television	televiziya	[tele'vizija]

presenter, host	aparıcı	[aparı'ʤı]
newsreader	diktor	['diktor]
commentator	şərhçi	[ʃærh'ʧi]

journalist	jurnalist	[ʒurna'list]
correspondent (reporter)	müxbir	[myh'bir]
press photographer	foto müxbir	['foto myh'bir]
reporter	reportyor	[report'jor]

| editor | redaktor | [re'daktor] |
| editor-in-chief | baş redaktor | ['baʃ re'daktor] |

to subscribe (to …)	abunə olmaq	[abu'næ ol'mag]
subscription	abunə	[abu'næ]
subscriber	abunəçi	[abunæ'ʧi]
to read (vi, vt)	oxumaq	[ohu'mag]
reader	oxucu	[ohu'ʤu]

circulation (of newspaper)	tiraj	[ti'raʒ]
monthly (adj)	aylıq	[aj'lıg]
weekly (adj)	həftəlik	[hæftæ'lik]
issue (edition)	nömrə	[nøm'ræ]
new (~ issue)	təzə	[tæ'zæ]

headline	başlıq	[baʃ'lıg]
short article	kiçik məqalə	[ki'ʧik mæga'læ]
column (regular article)	rubrika	['rubrika]
article	məqalə	[mæga'læ]
page	səhifə	[sæhi'fæ]

reportage, report	reportaj	[repor'taʒ]
event	hadisə	[hadi'sæ]
sensation (news)	sensasiya	[sen'sasija]
scandal	qalmaqal	[galma'gal]
scandalous (adj)	qalmaqallı	[galmagal'lı]
great (~ scandal)	böyük	[bø'yk]
programme	veriliş	[veri'liʃ]
interview	müsahibə	[mysahi'bæ]

| live broadcast | birbaşa translyasiya | [birba'ʃa trans'ʎasija] |
| channel | kanal | [ka'nal] |

120. Agriculture

agriculture	kənd təsərrüfatı	['kænd tæsærryfa'tɪ]
peasant (masc.)	kəndli	[kænd'li]
peasant (fem.)	kəndli qadın	[kænd'li ga'dɪn]
farmer	fermer	['fermer]

| tractor | traktor | ['traktor] |
| combine, harvester | kombayn | [kom'bajn] |

plough	kotan	[ko'tan]
to plough (vi, vt)	şumlamaq	[ʃumla'mag]
ploughland	şum	[ʃum]
furrow (in field)	şırım	[ʃɪ'rɪm]

to sow (vi, vt)	əkmək	[æk'mæk]
seeder	toxumsəpən maşın	[tohumsæ'pæn ma'ʃɪn]
sowing (process)	əkin	[æ'kin]

| scythe | dəryaz | [dær'jaz] |
| to mow, to scythe | ot biçmək | ['ot bitʃ'mæk] |

| shovel (tool) | bel | [bel] |
| to dig (cultivate) | belləmək | [bellæ'mæk] |

hoe	çapacaq	[tʃapa'dʒag]
to hoe, to weed	alaq vurmaq	[a'lag vur'mag]
weed (plant)	alaq otu	[a'lag oty]

watering can	susəpələyən	[susæpælæ'jən]
to water (plants)	suvarmaq	[suvar'mag]
watering (act)	suvarma	[suvar'ma]

| pitchfork | yaba | [ja'ba] |
| rake | dırmıq | [dɪr'mɪg] |

fertilizer	gübrə	[gyb'ræ]
to fertilize (vt)	gübrələmək	[gybræelæ'mæk]
manure (fertilizer)	peyin	[pe'jɪn]

field	tarla	[tar'la]
meadow	çəmən	[tʃə'mæn]
vegetable garden	bostan	[bos'tan]
orchard (e.g. apple ~)	bağ	[baɣ]

to pasture (vt)	otarmaq	[otar'mag]
herdsman	çoban	[tʃo'ban]
pastureland	otlaq	[ot'lag]

| cattle breeding | heyvandarlıq | [hejvandar'lɪg] |
| sheep farming | qoyunçuluq | [goyntʃu'lug] |

plantation	tarla	[tar'la]
row (garden bed ~s)	lək	[læk]
greenhouse (hotbed)	parnik	[par'nik]
drought (lack of rain)	quraqlıq	[gurag'lıg]
dry (~ summer)	quraqlı	[gurag'lı]
cereal plants	dənli	[dæn'li]
to harvest, to gather	yığmaq	[jıɣ'mag]
miller (person)	dəyirmançı	[dæjırman'tʃı]
mill (e.g. gristmill)	dəyirman	[dæjır'man]
to grind (grain)	dən üyütmək	['dæn y:t'mæk]
flour	un	[un]
straw	saman	[sa'man]

121. Building. Building process

building site	inşaat yeri	[inʃa'at e'ri]
to build (vt)	inşa etmək	[in'ʃa æt'mæk]
building worker	inşaatçı	[inʃa:'tʃı]
project	layihə	[lai'hæ]
architect	memar	[me'mar]
worker	fəhlə	[fæh'læ]
foundations (of building)	bünövrə	[bynøv'ræ]
roof	dam	[dam]
foundation pile	dirək	[di'ræk]
wall	divar	[di'var]
reinforcing bars	armatura	[arma'tura]
scaffolding	taxtabənd	[tahta'bænd]
concrete	beton	[be'ton]
granite	qranit	[gra'nit]
stone	daş	[daʃ]
brick	kərpic	[kær'pidʒ]
sand	qum	[gum]
cement	sement	[se'ment]
plaster (for walls)	suvaq	[su'vag]
to plaster (vt)	suvaqlamaq	[suvagla'mag]
paint	boya	[bo'ja]
to paint (~ a wall)	boyamaq	[boja'mag]
barrel	çəllək	[tʃəl'læk]
crane	kran	[kran]
to lift (vt)	qaldırmaq	[galdır'mag]
to lower (vt)	endirmək	[ændir'mæk]
bulldozer	buldozer	[buʎ'dozer]
excavator	ekskavator	[ækska'vator]
scoop, bucket	təknə	[tæk'næ]

| to dig (excavate) | qazmaq | [gaz'mag] |
| hard hat | kaska | [kas'ka] |

122. Science. Research. Scientists

science	elm	[ælm]
scientific (adj)	elmi	[æl'mi]
scientist	alim	[a'lim]
theory	nəzəriyyə	[næzæ'rij:ə]

axiom	aksioma	[aksi'oma]
analysis	təhlil	[tæh'lil]
to analyse (vt)	təhlil etmək	[tæh'lil æt'mæk]
argument (strong ~)	dəlil	[dæ'lil]
substance (matter)	maddə	[mad'dæ]

hypothesis	fərziyyə	[færzi'j:ə]
dilemma	dilemma	[di'lemma]
dissertation	dissertasiya	[disser'tasija]
dogma	doqma	['dogma]

doctrine	doktrina	[dokt'rina]
research	araşdırma	[araʃdɪr'ma]
to do research	araşdırmaq	[araʃdɪr'mag]
testing	yoxlama	[johla'ma]
laboratory	laboratoriya	[labora'torija]

method	metod	['metod]
molecule	molekula	[mo'lekula]
monitoring	monitoring	[moni'toriŋ]
discovery (act, event)	kəşf	[kæʃf]

postulate	postulat	[postu'lat]
principle	prinsip	['prinsip]
forecast	proqnoz	[prog'noz]
to forecast (vt)	proqnozlaşdırmaq	[prognozlaʃdɪr'mag]

synthesis	sintez	['sintez]
trend (tendency)	təmayül	[tæma'yl]
theorem	teorema	[teo'rema]

teachings	nəzəriyyə	[næzæ'rij:ə]
fact	fakt	[fakt]
expedition	ekspedisiya	[ækspe'disija]
experiment	eksperiment	[æksperi'ment]

academician	akademik	[aka'demik]
bachelor (e.g. ~ of Arts)	bakalavr	[baka'lavr]
doctor (PhD)	doktor	['doktor]
Associate Professor	dosent	[do'sent]
Master (e.g. ~ of Arts)	magistr	[ma'gistr]
professor	professor	[pro'fessor]

Professions and occupations

123. Job search. Dismissal

job	iş	[iʃ]
staff (work force)	ştat	[ʃtat]
career	karyera	[kar'jera]
prospect	perspektiv	[perspek'tiv]
skills (mastery)	ustalıq	[usta'lıg]
selection (for job)	seçmə	[setʃ'mæ]
employment agency	kadrlar agentliyi	['kadrlar agentli'jı]
curriculum vitae, CV	CV	[si'vi]
interview (for job)	müsahibə	[mysahi'bæ]
vacancy	vakansiya	[va'kansija]
salary, pay	əmək haqqı	[æ'mæk hag'gı]
fixed salary	maaş	[ma'aʃ]
pay, compensation	haqq	[hagg]
position (job)	vəzifə	[væzi'fæ]
duty (of employee)	vəzifə	[væzi'fæ]
range of duties	dairə	[dai'ræ]
busy (I'm ~)	məşğul	[mæʃɣ'ul]
to fire (dismiss)	azad etmək	[a'zad æt'mæk]
dismissal	azad edilmə	[a'zad ædil'mæ]
unemployment	işsizlik	[iʃsiz'lik]
unemployed (n)	işsiz	[iʃ'siz]
retirement	təqaüd	[tæga'yd]
to retire (from job)	təqaüdə çıxmaq	[tægay'dæ tʃıh'mag]

124. Business people

director	direktor	[di'rektor]
manager (director)	idarə başçısı	[ida'ræ baʃtʃı'sı]
boss	rəhbər	[ræh'bær]
superior	müdir	[my'dir]
superiors	rəhbərlik	[ræhbær'lik]
president	prezident	[prezi'dent]
chairman	sədr	[sædr]
deputy (substitute)	müavin	[mya'vin]
assistant	köməkçi	[kømæk'tʃi]
secretary	katibə	[k'ati'bæ]

personal assistant	şəxsi katib	[ʃæh'si ka'tib]
businessman	biznesmen	['biznesmen]
entrepreneur	sahibkar	[sahib'kᴵar]
founder	təsisçi	[tæsis'ʧi]
to found (vt)	təsis etmək	[tæ'sis æt'mæk]

founding member	təsisçi	[tæsis'ʧi]
partner	partnyor	[partn'jor]
shareholder	səhmdar	[sæhm'dar]

millionaire	milyoner	[miʎjo'ner]
billionaire	milyarder	[miʎjar'der]
owner, proprietor	sahib	[sa'hib]
landowner	torpaq sahibi	[tor'pag sahi'bi]

client	müştəri	[myʃtæ'ri]
regular client	daimi müştəri	[dai'mi myʃtæ'ri]
buyer (customer)	alıcı	[alı'ʤı]
visitor	ziyarətçi	[zijaræ'ʧi]

professional (n)	peşəkar	[peʃæ'kar]
expert	ekspert	[æks'pert]
specialist	mütəxəssis	[mytæhæs'sis]

banker	bank sahibi	['baŋk sahi'bi]
broker	broker	['broker]

cashier	kassir	[kas'sir]
accountant	mühasib	[myha'sib]
security guard	mühafizəçi	[myhafizæ'ʧi]

investor	investor	[in'vestor]
debtor	borclu	[borʤ'lu]
creditor	kreditor	[kredi'tor]
borrower	borc alan	['borʤ a'lan]

importer	idxalatçı	[idhala'ʧı]
exporter	ixracatçı	[ihraʤa'ʧı]

manufacturer	istehsalçı	[istehsal'ʧı]
distributor	distribütor	[distri'bytor]
middleman	vasitəçi	[vasitæ'ʧi]

consultant	məsləhətçi	[mæslæhæ'ʧi]
representative	təmsilçi	[tæmsil'ʧi]
agent	agent	[a'gent]
insurance agent	sığorta agenti	[sıyor'ta agen'ti]

125. Service professions

cook	aşpaz	[aʃ'paz]
chef	baş aşpaz	['baʃ aʃ'paz]
baker	çörəkçi	[ʧøræk'ʧi]
barman	barmen	['barmen]

waiter	ofisiant	[ofisi'ant]
waitress	ofisiant qız	[ofisi'ant 'gız]

lawyer, barrister	vəkil	[væ'kil]
lawyer (legal expert)	hüquqşünas	[hyguɡʃy'nas]
notary	notarius	[no'tarius]

electrician	montyor	[mont'jor]
plumber	santexnik	[san'tehnik]
carpenter	dülgər	[dyʎ'gær]

masseur	masajçı	[masaʒ'ʧı]
masseuse	masajçı qadın	[masaʒ'ʧı ga'dın]
doctor	həkim	[hæ'kim]

taxi driver	taksi sürücüsü	[tak'si syryʤy'sy]
driver	sürücü	[syry'ʤy]
delivery man	kuryer	[ku'rjer]

chambermaid	otaq qulluqçusu	[o'tag gullugʧu'su]
security guard	mühafizəçi	[myhafizæ'ʧi]
stewardess	stüardessa	[styar'dessa]

teacher (in primary school)	müəllim	[myæl'lim]
librarian	kitabxanaçı	[kitabhana'ʧı]
translator	tərcüməçi	[tærʤymæ'ʧi]
interpreter	tərcüməçi	[tærʤymæ'ʧi]
guide	bələdçi	[bælæd'ʧi]

hairdresser	bərbər	[bær'bær]
postman	poçtalyon	[poʧta'ʎon]
shop assistant (masc.)	satıcı	[satı'ʤı]

gardener	bağban	[baɣ'ban]
servant (in household)	nökər	[nø'kær]
maid	ev qulluqçusu	['æv gullugʧu'su]
cleaner (cleaning lady)	xadimə	[hadi'mæ]

126. Military professions and ranks

private	sıravi	[sıra'vi]
sergeant	çavuş	[ʧa'vuʃ]
lieutenant	leytenant	[lejte'nant]
captain	kapitan	[kapi'tan]

major	mayor	[ma'jor]
colonel	polkovnik	[pol'kovnik]
general	general	[gene'ral]
marshal	marşal	['marʃal]
admiral	admiral	[admi'ral]

military man	hərbiçi	[hærbi'ʧi]
soldier	əsgər	[æs'gær]
officer	zabit	[za'bit]

commander	komandir	[koman'dir]
border guard	sərhəd keşikçisi	[sær'hæd keʃiktʃi'si]
radio operator	radist	[ra'dist]
scout (searcher)	kəşfiyyatçı	[kæʃfij:a'tʃɪ]
pioneer (sapper)	istehkamçı	[istehkam'tʃɪ]
marksman	atıcı	[atı'dʒɪ]
navigator	şturman	['ʃturman]

127. Officials. Priests

king	kral	[kral]
queen	kraliçə	[kra'litʃə]
prince	şahzadə	[ʃahza'dæ]
princess	şahzadə xanım	[ʃahza'dæ ha'nım]
tsar, czar	çar	[tʃar]
czarina	çariçə	[tʃa'ritʃə]
president	prezident	[prezi'dent]
Minister	nazir	[na'zir]
prime minister	baş nazir	['baʃ na'zir]
senator	senator	[se'nator]
diplomat	diplomat	[diplo'mat]
consul	konsul	['konsul]
ambassador	səfir	[sæ'fir]
advisor (military ~)	müşavir	[myʃa'vir]
official (civil servant)	məmur	[mæ'mur]
prefect	prefekt	[pre'fekt]
mayor	şəhər icra hakimiyyətinin başçısı	[ʃæ'hær idʒ'ra hakimij:əti'nin baʃtʃı'sı]
judge	hakim	[ha'kim]
prosecutor	prokuror	[proku'ror]
missionary	missioner	[missio'ner]
monk	rahib	[ra'hib]
abbot	abbat	[ab'bat]
rabbi	ravvin	['ravvin]
vizier	vəzir	[væ'zir]
shah	şax	[ʃah]
sheikh	şeyx	[ʃəjh]

128. Agricultural professions

beekeeper	arıçı	[arı'tʃɪ]
herdsman	çoban	[tʃo'ban]
agronomist	aqronom	[agro'nom]
cattle breeder	heyvandar	[hejvan'dar]

veterinary surgeon	baytar	[baj'tar]
farmer	fermer	['fermer]
winemaker	şərabçı	[ʃærab'tʃı]
zoologist	zooloq	[zo'olog]
cowboy	kovboy	[kov'boj]

129. Art professions

actor	aktyor	[akt'jor]
actress	aktrisa	[akt'risa]

singer (masc.)	müğənni	[myɣæ'ŋi]
singer (fem.)	müğənni qadın	[myɣæ'ŋi ga'dın]

dancer (masc.)	rəqqas	[ræg'gas]
dancer (fem.)	rəqqasə	[rægga'sæ]

performing artist (masc.)	artist	[ar'tist]
performing artist (fem.)	artist qadın	[ar'tist ga'dın]

musician	musiqiçi	[musigi'tʃi]
pianist	pianoçu	[pi'anotʃu]
guitar player	qitara çalan	[gi'tara tʃa'lan]

conductor (of musicians)	dirijor	[diri'ʒor]
composer	bəstəkar	[bæstæ'kar]
impresario	impresario	[impre'sario]

film director	rejissor	[reʒis'sor]
producer	prodüser	[pro'dyser]
scriptwriter	ssenarist	[ssena'rist]
critic	tənqidçi	[tæŋid'tʃi]

writer	yazıçı	[jazı'tʃı]
poet	şair	[ʃa'ir]
sculptor	heykəltəraş	[hejkæltæ'raʃ]
artist (painter)	rəssam	[ræs'sam]

juggler	jonqlyor	[ʒoŋl'jor]
clown	təlxək	[tæl'hæk]
acrobat	canbaz	[dʒan'baz]
magician	fokus göstərən	['fokus gøstæ'ræn]

130. Various professions

doctor	həkim	[hæ'kim]
nurse	tibb bacısı	['tibb badʒı'sı]
psychiatrist	psixiatr	[psihi'atr]
stomatologist	stomatoloq	[stoma'tolog]
surgeon	cərrah	[dʒær'rah]
astronaut	astronavt	[astro'navt]
astronomer	astronom	[astro'nom]

driver (of taxi, etc.)	sürücü	[syry'dʒy]
train driver	maşınsürən	[maʃınsy'ræn]
mechanic	mexanik	[me'hanik]

miner	qazmaçı	[gazma'tʃı]
worker	fəhlə	[fæh'læ]
metalworker	çilinğər	[tʃili'ŋær]
joiner (carpenter)	xarrat	[har'rat]
turner	tornaçı	[torna'tʃı]
building worker	inşaatçı	[inʃa:'tʃı]
welder	qaynaqçı	[gajnag'tʃı]

professor (title)	professor	[pro'fessor]
architect	memar	[me'mar]
historian	tarixçi	[tarih'tʃi]
scientist	alim	[a'lim]
physicist	fizik	['fizik]
chemist (scientist)	kimyaçı	[kimja'tʃı]

archaeologist	arxeoloq	[arhe'olog]
geologist	qeoloq	[ge'olog]
researcher	tədqiqatçı	[tædgiga'tʃı]

| babysitter | dayə | [da'jə] |
| teacher, educator | pedaqoq | [peda'gog] |

editor	redaktor	[re'daktor]
editor-in-chief	baş redaktor	['baʃ re'daktor]
correspondent	müxbir	[myh'bir]
typist (fem.)	makinaçı	[ma'kinatʃı]

designer	dizayner	[di'zajner]
computer expert	bilgisayar ustası	[bilgisa'jar usta'sı]
programmer	proqramçı	[program'tʃı]
engineer (designer)	mühəndis	[myhen'dis]

sailor	dənizçi	[dæniz'tʃi]
seaman	matros	[mat'ros]
rescuer	xilas edən	[hi'las æ'dæn]

firefighter	yanğınsöndürən	[janɣınsøndy'ræn]
policeman	polis	[po'lis]
watchman	gözətçi	[gøzæ'tʃi]
detective	xəfiyyə	[hæfi'j:ə]

customs officer	gömrük işçisi	[gøm'ryk iʃtʃi'si]
bodyguard	şəxsi mühafizəçi	[ʃæh'si myhafizæ'tʃi]
prison officer	nəzarətçi	[næzaræ'tʃi]
inspector	inspektor	[ins'pektor]

sportsman	idmançı	[idman'tʃı]
trainer, coach	məşqçi	[mæʃg'tʃi]
butcher	qəssab	[gæs'sab]
cobbler	çəkməçi	[tʃəkmæ'tʃi]
merchant	ticarətçi	[tidʒaræ'tʃi]
loader (person)	malyükləyən	[malyklæ'jən]

fashion designer	modelçi	[model'tʃi]
model (fem.)	model	[mo'del]

131. Occupations. Social status

schoolboy	məktəbli	[mæktæb'li]
student (college ~)	tələbə	[tælæ'bæ]

philosopher	fəlsəfəçi	[fælsæfæ'tʃi]
economist	iqdisadçı	[igtisad'tʃɪ]
inventor	ixtiraçı	[ihtira'tʃɪ]

unemployed (n)	işsiz	[iʃ'siz]
pensioner	təqaüdçü	[tægayd'tʃu]
spy, secret agent	casus	[dʒa'sus]

prisoner	dustaq	[dus'tag]
striker	tətilçi	[tætil'tʃi]
bureaucrat	bürokrat	[byrok'rat]
traveller	səyahətçi	[sæjahæ'tʃi]

homosexual	homoseksualist	[homoseksua'list]
hacker	xaker	['haker]

bandit	quldur	[gul'dur]
hit man, killer	muzdlu qatil	[muzd'lu 'gatil]
drug addict	narkoman	[narko'man]
drug dealer	narkotik alverçisi	[narkotik alvertʃisi]
prostitute (fem.)	fahişə	[fahi'ʃæ]
pimp	qadın alverçisi	[ga'dɪn alvertʃi'si]

sorcerer	caduger	[dʒadu'gær]
sorceress	caduger qadın	[dʒadu'gær ga'dɪn]
pirate	dəniz qulduru	[dæ'niz guldu'ru]
slave	kölə	[kø'læ]
samurai	samuray	[samu'raj]
savage (primitive)	vəhşi adam	[væh'ʃi a'dam]

Sports

132. Kinds of sports. Sportspersons

sportsman	idmançı	[idman'tʃı]
kind of sport	idman növü	[id'man nø'vy]
basketball	basketbol	[basket'bol]
basketball player	basketbolçu	[basketbol'tʃu]
baseball	beysbol	[bejs'bol]
baseball player	beysbolçu	[bejsbol'tʃu]
football	futbol	[fut'bol]
football player	futbolçu	[futbol'tʃu]
goalkeeper	qapıçı	[gapı'tʃı]
ice hockey	xokkey	[hok'kej]
ice hockey player	xokkeyçi	[hokkej'tʃi]
volleyball	voleybol	[volej'bol]
volleyball player	voleybolçu	[volejbol'tʃu]
boxing	boks	[boks]
boxer	boksçu	[boks'tʃu]
wrestling	güləş	[gy'læʃ]
wrestler	güləşçi	[gylæʃ'tʃi]
karate	karate	[kara'te]
karate fighter	karateçi	[karate'tʃi]
judo	dzyudo	[dzy'do]
judo athlete	dzyudoçu	[dzydo'tʃu]
tennis	tennis	['teŋis]
tennis player	tennisçi	[teŋis'tʃi]
swimming	üzmə	[yz'mæ]
swimmer	üzgüçü	[yzgy'tʃu]
fencing	qılınc oynatma	[gı'lındʒ ojnat'ma]
fencer	qılınc oynadan	[gı'lındʒ ojna'dan]
chess	şaxmat	['ʃahmat]
chess player	şaxmatçı	['ʃahmatʃı]
alpinism	alpinizm	[alpi'nizm]
alpinist	alpinist	[alpi'nist]
running	qaçış	[ga'tʃıʃ]

runner	qaçıcı	[gatʃı'ʤı]
athletics	yüngül atletika	[yˈŋyl atˈletika]
athlete	atlet	[atˈlet]

horse riding	atçılıq idmanı	[atʃı'lıg idma'nı]
horse rider	at sürən	['at sy'ræn]

figure skating	fiqurlu konki sürmə	[figur'lu ko'ŋki syr'mæ]
figure skater (masc.)	fiqurist	[figu'rist]
figure skater (fem.)	fiqurist qadın	[figu'rist ga'dın]

weightlifting	ağır atletika	[ay'ır at'letika]
car racing	avtomobil yarışları	[avtomo'bil jarıʃla'rı]
racing driver	avtomobil yarışçısı	[avtomo'bil jarıʃʃı'sı]

cycling	velosiped idmanı	[velosi'ped idma'nı]
cyclist	velosiped sürən	[velosi'ped sy'ræn]

long jump	uzunluğa tullanma	[uzunluy'a tullan'ma]
pole vaulting	çubuqla yüksəyə tullanma	[tʃu'bugla yksæ'jə tullan'ma]
jumper	tullanma üzrə idmanşı	[tullan'ma yz'ræ idman'tʃı]

133. Kinds of sports. Miscellaneous

American football	Amerika futbolu	[a'merika futbo'lu]
badminton	badminton	[badmin'ton]
biathlon	biatlon	[biat'lon]
billiards	bilyard	[bi'ʎjard]

bobsleigh	bobsley	[bobs'lej]
bodybuilding	bodibildinq	[bodi'bildiŋ]
water polo	su polosu	['su 'polosu]
handball	həndbol	[hænd'bol]
golf	qolf	[golf]

rowing	avar çəkmə	[a'var tʃək'mæ]
diving	dayvinq	['dajviŋ]
cross-country skiing	xizək yarışması	[hi'zæk jarıʃma'sı]
ping-pong	stolüstü tennis	[stolys'ty 'teŋis]

sailing	yelkənli qayıq idmanı	[elkæn'li ga'jıg idma'nı]
rally	ralli	['ralli]
rugby	reqbi	['regbi]
snowboarding	snoubord	['snoubord]
archery	kamandan oxatma	[kaman'dan ohat'ma]

134. Gym

barbell	ştanq	['ʃtaŋ]
dumbbells	hantel	[han'tel]
training machine	trenajor	[trena'ʒor]
bicycle trainer	velotrenajor	[velotrena'ʒor]

treadmill	qaçış zolağı	[ga'ʧɪʃ zolaɣ'ı]
horizontal bar	köndələn tir	[køndæ'læn 'tir]
parallel bars	paralel tirlər	[para'lel tir'lær]
vaulting horse	at	[at]
mat (in gym)	həsir	[hæ'sir]

| aerobics | aerobika | [aə'robika] |
| yoga | yoqa | ['joga] |

135. Ice hockey

ice hockey	xokkey	[hok'kej]
ice hockey player	xokkeyçi	[hokkej'ʧi]
to play ice hockey	xokkey oynamaq	[hok'kej ojna'mag]
ice	buz	[buz]

puck	xokkey şaybası	[hok'kej ʃajba'sı]
ice hockey stick	xokkey çubuğu	[hok'kej ʧubuɣ'u]
ice skates	konki	[ko'ŋki]

| board | kənar | [kæ'nar] |
| shot | atış | [a'tıʃ] |

goaltender	qapıçı	[gapı'ʧı]
goal (score)	qol	[gol]
to score a goal	qol vurmaq	['gol vur'mag]

| period | hissə | [his'sæ] |
| substitutes bench | ehtiyat skamyası | [æhti'jat skamja'sı] |

136. Football

football	futbol	[fut'bol]
football player	futbolçu	[futbol'ʧu]
to play football	futbol oynamaq	[fut'bol ojna'mag]

major league	yüksək liqa	[yk'sæk 'liga]
football club	futbol klubu	[fut'bol klu'bu]
coach	məşqçi	[mæʃg'ʧi]
owner, proprietor	sahib	[sa'hib]

team	komanda	[ko'manda]
team captain	komanda kapitanı	[ko'manda kapita'nı]
player	oyunçu	[oyn'ʧu]
substitute	ehtiyat oyunçusu	[æhti'jat oynʧu'su]

forward	hücumçu	[hyʤum'ʧu]
centre forward	mərkəz hücumçusu	[mær'kæz hyʤumʧu'su]
striker, scorer	bombardir	[bombar'dir]
defender, back	müdafiəçi	[mydafiæ'ʧi]
halfback	yarım müdafiəçi	[ja'rım mydafiæ'ʧi]
match	matç	[matʃ]

to meet (vi, vt)	görüşmək	[gøryʃ'mæk]
final	final	[fi'nal]
semi-final	yarım final	[ja'rım fi'nal]
championship	çempionat	[tʃempio'nat]

period, half	taym	[tajm]
first period	birinci taym	[birin'dʒi 'tajm]
half-time	fasilə	[fasi'læ]

goal	qapı	[ga'pı]
goalkeeper	qapıçı	[gapı'tʃı]
goalpost	ştanqa	['ʃtaŋa]
crossbar	köndələn tir	[køndæ'læn 'tir]
net	tor	[tor]
to concede a goal	qol buraxmaq	['gol burah'mag]

ball	top	[top]
pass	pas	[pas]
kick	zərbə	[zær'bæ]
to kick (~ the ball)	zərbə vurmaq	[zær'bæ vur'mag]
free kick	cərimə zərbəsi	[dʒæri'mæ zærbæ'si]
corner kick	küncdən zərbə	[kyndʒ'dæn zær'bæ]

attack	hücum	[hy'dʒum]
counterattack	əks hücum	['æks hy'dʒum]
combination	kombinasiya	[kombi'nasija]

referee	arbitr	[ar'bitr]
to whistle (vi)	fit vermək	['fit ver'mæk]
whistle (sound)	fit	[fit]
foul, misconduct	pozma	[poz'ma]
to commit a foul	pozmaq	[poz'mag]
to send off	meydançadan xaric etmək	[mejdantʃa'dan ha'ridʒ æt'mæk]

yellow card	sarı kart	[sa'rı 'kart]
red card	qlrmızı kart	[gırmı'zı 'kart]
disqualification	iştirakdan məhrum etmə	[iʃtirak'dan mæh'rum æt'mæ]
to disqualify (vt)	iştirakdan məhrum etmək	[iʃtirak'dan mæh'rum æt'mæk]

penalty kick	penalti	[pe'nalti]
wall	divar	[di'var]
to score (vi, vt)	vurmaq	[vur'mag]
goal (score)	qol	[gol]
to score a goal	qol vurmaq	['gol vur'mag]

substitution	dəyişmə	[dæjıʃ'mæ]
to replace (vt)	dəyişmək	[dæiʃ'mæk]
rules	qaydalar	[gajda'lar]
tactics	taktika	['taktika]

stadium	stadion	[stadi'on]
stand (at stadium)	tribuna	[tri'buna]
fan, supporter	azarkeş	[azar'keʃ]
to shout (vi)	çığırmaq	[tʃıɣır'mag]
scoreboard	lövhə	[løv'hæ]

score	hesab	[he'sab]
defeat	məğlubiyyət	[mæɣlubi'jːət]
to lose (not win)	məğlubiyyətə uğramaq	[mæɣlubijːə'tæ uɣra'mag]
draw	heç-heçə oyun	['hetʃ he'tʃə o'yn]
to draw (vi)	heç-heçə oynamaq	['hetʃ he'tʃə ojna'mag]

victory	qələbə	[gælæ'bæ]
to win (vi, vt)	qalib gəlmək	[ga'lib gæl'mæk]
champion	çempion	[tʃempi'on]
best (adj)	ən yaxşı	['æn jah'ʃɪ]
to congratulate (vt)	təbrik etmək	[tæb'rik æt'mæk]

commentator	şərhçi	[ʃærh'tʃi]
to commentate (vt)	şərh etmək	['ʃærh æt'mæk]
broadcast	translyasiya	[trans'ʎasija]

137. Alpine skiing

skis	xizək	[hi'zæk]
to ski (vi)	xizək sürmək	[hi'zæk syr'mæk]
mountain-ski resort	dağ xizəyi kurortu	[daɣ hizæ'jɪ kuror'tu]
ski lift	qaldırıcı mexanizm	[galdɪrɪ'dʒɪ meha'nizm]

ski poles	çubuqlar	[tʃubug'lar]
slope	yamac	[ja'madʒ]
slalom	slalom	['slalom]

138. Tennis. Golf

golf	qolf	[golf]
golf club	qolf klubu	['golf klu'bu]
golfer	qolf oyunçusu	['golf oyntʃu'su]

hole	çuxur	[tʃu'hur]
club	qolf çubuğu	['golf tʃubuɣ'u]
golf trolley	çubuqlar üçün araba	[tʃubug'lar y'tʃun ara'ba]

tennis	tennis	['tenis]
tennis court	tennis meydançası	['tenis mejdantʃa'sɪ]
serve	ötürülmə	[øtyryl'mæ]
to serve (vt)	ötürmək	[øtyr'mæk]
racket	raketka	[raket'ka]
net	tor	[tor]
ball	top	[top]

139. Chess

chess	şahmat	['ʃahmat]
chessmen	figurlar	[figur'lar]
chess player	şahmatçı	['ʃahmatʃɪ]

| chessboard | şahmat taxtası | ['ʃahmat tahta'sı] |
| chessman | figur | [fi'gur] |

| White (white pieces) | ağlar | [aɣ'lar] |
| Black (black pieces) | qaralar | [gara'lar] |

pawn	piyada	[pija'da]
bishop	fil	[fil]
knight	at	[at]
rook (castle)	top	[top]
queen	vəzir	[væ'zir]
king	kral	[kral]

move	oyun	[o'yn]
to move (vi, vt)	oynamaq	[ojna'mag]
to sacrifice (vt)	qurban vermək	[gur'ban ver'mæk]
castling	rokirovka	[roki'rovka]
check	şah	[ʃah]
checkmate	mat	[mat]

chess tournament	şahmat turniri	['ʃahmat turni'ri]
Grand Master	qrossmeyster	[gross'mejster]
combination	kombinasiya	[kombi'nasija]
game (in chess)	partiya	['partija]
draughts	dama	[da'ma]

140. Boxing

boxing	boks	[boks]
fight (bout)	döyüş	[dø'yʃ]
boxing match	döyüş	[dø'yʃ]
round (in boxing)	raund	['raund]

| ring | rinq | [riŋ] |
| gong | qonq | [goŋ] |

punch	zərbə	[zær'bæ]
knock-down	nokdaun	[nok'daun]
knockout	nokaut	[no'kaut]
to knock out	nokaut etmək	[no'kaut æt'mæk]

| boxing glove | boksçu əlcəyi | ['boks ældʒæ'jı] |
| referee | referi | ['referi] |

lightweight	yüngül çəki	[y'ŋyl tʃə'ki]
middleweight	orta çəki	[or'ta tʃə'ki]
heavyweight	ağır çəki	[aɣ'ır tʃə'ki]

141. Sports. Miscellaneous

| Olympic Games | Olimpiya oyunları | [o'limpija oynla'rı] |
| winner | qalib | [ga'lib] |

| to be winning | qalib gəlmək | [ga'lib gæl'mæk] |
| to win (vi) | udmaq | [ud'mag] |

| leader | lider | ['lider] |
| to lead (vi) | irəlidə getmək | [iræli'dæ get'mæk] |

first place	birinci yer	[birin'dʒi 'er]
second place	ikinci yer	[ikin'dʒi 'er]
third place	üçüncü yer	[ytʃun'dʒy 'er]

medal	medal	[me'dal]
trophy	trofey	[tro'fej]
prize cup (trophy)	kubok	['kubok]
prize (in game)	mükafat	[myka'fat]
main prize	baş mükafat	['baʃ myka'fat]

| record | rekord | [re'kord] |
| to set a record | rekord qazanmaq | [re'kord gazan'mag] |

| final | final | [fi'nal] |
| final (adj) | final | [fi'nal] |

| champion | çempion | [tʃempi'on] |
| championship | çempionat | [tʃempio'nat] |

stadium	stadion	[stadi'on]
stand (at stadium)	tribuna	[tri'buna]
fan, supporter	azarkeş	[azar'keʃ]
opponent, rival	rəqib	[ræ'gib]

| start | start | [start] |
| finish line | finiş | ['finiʃ] |

| defeat | məğlubiyyət | [mæɣlubi'jːət] |
| to lose (not win) | məğlubiyyətə uğramaq | [mæɣlubij:ə'tæ uɣra'mag] |

referee	hakim	[ha'kim]
judges	jüri	[ʒy'ri]
score	hesab	[he'sab]
draw	heç-heçə oyun	['hetʃ he'tʃə o'yn]
to draw (vi)	heç-heçə oynamaq	['hetʃ he'tʃə ojna'mag]
point	xal	[hal]
result (final score)	nəticə	[næti'dʒæ]

half-time	fasilə	[fasi'læ]
doping	dopinq	['dopiŋ]
to penalise (vt)	cərimə etmək	[dʒæri'mæ æt'mæk]
to disqualify (vt)	iştirakdan məhrum etmək	[iʃtirak'dan mæh'rum æt'mæk]

apparatus	alət	[a'læt]
javelin	nizə	[ni'zæ]
shot put ball	qumbara	[gumba'ra]
ball (snooker, etc.)	şar	[ʃar]

| aim (target) | hədəf | [hæ'dæf] |
| target | nişan | [ni'ʃan] |

| to shoot (vi) | ateş açmaq | [a'tæʃ atʃ'mag] |
| precise (~ shot) | sərrast | [sær'rast] |

trainer, coach	məşqçi	[mæʃg'tʃi]
to train (sb)	məşq keçmək	['mæʃg ketʃ'mæk]
to train (vi)	məşq etmək	['mæʃg æt'mæk]
training	məşq	[mæʃg]

gym	idman zalı	[id'man za'lı]
exercise (physical)	məşğələ	[mæʃɣæ'læ]
warm-up (of athlete)	isinmə hərəkətləri	[isin'mæ hærækætlæ'ri]

Education

142. School

school	məktəb	[mæk'tæb]
headmaster	məktəb direktoru	[mæk'tæb di'rektoru]
pupil (boy)	şagird	[ʃa'gird]
pupil (girl)	şagird	[ʃa'gird]
schoolboy	məktəbli	[mæktæb'li]
schoolgirl	məktəbli qız	[mæktæb'li 'gız]
to teach (sb)	öyrətmək	[øjræt'mæk]
to learn (language, etc.)	öyrənmək	[øjræn'mæk]
to learn by heart	əzbər öyrənmək	[æz'bær øjræn'mæk]
to study (work to learn)	öyrənmək	[øjræn'mæk]
to be at school	oxumaq	[ohu'mag]
to go to school	məktəbə getmək	[mæktæ'bæ get'mæk]
alphabet	əlifba	[ælif'ba]
subject (at school)	fənn	[fæŋ]
classroom	sinif	[si'nif]
lesson	dərs	[dærs]
playtime, break	tənəffüs	[tænæf'fys]
school bell	zəng	[zæŋ]
desk (for pupil)	parta	['parta]
blackboard	yazı taxtası	[ja'zı tahta'sı]
mark	qiymət	[gij'mæt]
good mark	yaxşı qiymət	[jah'ʃı gij'mæt]
bad mark	pis qiymət	['pis gij'mæt]
to give a mark	qiymət yazmaq	[gij'mæt jaz'mag]
mistake	səhv	[sæhv]
to make mistakes	səhv etmək	['sæhv æt'mæk]
to correct (an error)	düzəltmək	[dyzælt'mæk]
crib	şparqalka	[ʃpar'galka]
homework	ev tapşırığı	['æv tapʃırıɣ'ı]
exercise (in education)	məşğələ	[mæʃɣæ'læ]
to be present	iştirak etmək	[iʃti'rak æt'mæk]
to be absent	iştirak etməmək	[iʃti'rak 'ætmæmæk]
to punish (vt)	cəzalandırmaq	[dʒæzalandır'mag]
punishment	cəza	[dʒæ'za]
conduct (behaviour)	əxlaq	[æh'lag]

school report	gündəlik	[gyndæ'lik]
pencil	karandaş	[karan'daʃ]
rubber	pozan	[po'zan]
chalk	təbaşir	[tæba'ʃir]
pencil case	qələmdan	[gælæm'dan]

schoolbag	portfel	[port'fel]
pen	qələm	[gæ'læm]
exercise book	dəftər	[dæf'tær]
textbook	dərslik	[dærs'lik]
compasses	pərgar	[pær'gıar]

to draw (a blueprint, etc.)	cızmaq	[dʒız'mag]
technical drawing	cizgi	[dʒiz'gi]

poem	şer	[ʃər]
by heart (adv)	əzbərdən	[æzbær'dæn]
to learn by heart	əzbər öyrənmək	[æz'bær øjræn'mæk]

school holidays	tətil	[tæ'til]
to be on holiday	tətilə çıxmaq	[tæti'læ tʃıh'mag]

test (at school)	yoxlama işi	[johla'ma i'ʃi]
essay (composition)	inşa	[in'ʃa]
dictation	imla	[im'la]

exam	imtahan	[imta'han]
to take an exam	imtahan vermək	[imta'han vær'mæk]
experiment (chemical ~)	təcrübə	[tædʒry'bæ]

143. College. University

academy	akademiya	[aka'demija]
university	universitet	[universi'tet]
faculty (section)	fakültə	[fakul'tæ]

student (masc.)	tələbə	[tælæ'bæ]
student (fem.)	tələbə qız	[tælæ'bæ 'gız]
lecturer (teacher)	müəllim	[myæl'lim]

lecture hall, room	auditoriya	[audi'torija]
graduate	məzun	[mæ'zun]

diploma	diplom	[dip'lom]
dissertation	dissertasiya	[disser'tasija]

study (report)	tədqiqat	[tædgi'gat]
laboratory	laboratoriya	[labora'torija]

lecture	leksiya	['leksija]
course mate	kurs yoldaşı	['kurs jolda'ʃı]

scholarship	təqaüd	[tæga'yd]
academic degree	elmi dərəcə	[æl'mi dæræ'dʒæ]

144. Sciences. Disciplines

mathematics	riyaziyyat	[rijazi'j:at]
algebra	cəbr	[dʒæbr]
geometry	həndəsə	[hændæ'sæ]
astronomy	astronomiya	[astro'nomija]
biology	biologiya	[bio'logija]
geography	coğrafiya	[dʒoɣ'rafija]
geology	qeoloqiya	[geo'logija]
history	tarix	[ta'rih]
medicine	təbabət	[tæba'bæt]
pedagogy	pedaqoqika	[peda'gogika]
law	hüquq	[hy'gug]
physics	fizika	['fizika]
chemistry	kimya	['kimja]
philosophy	fəlsəfə	[fælsæ'fæ]
psychology	psixoloqiya	[psiho'logija]

145. Writing system. Orthography

grammar	qrammatika	[gram'matika]
vocabulary	leksika	['leksika]
phonetics	fonetika	[fo'netika]
noun	isim	['isim]
adjective	sifət	[si'fæt]
verb	fel	[fel]
adverb	zərf	[zærf]
pronoun	əvəzlik	[ævæz'lik]
interjection	nida	[ni'da]
preposition	önlük	[øn'lyk]
root	sözün kökü	[sø'zyn kø'ky]
ending	sonluq	[son'lug]
prefix	önşəkilçi	[ønʃækil'tʃi]
syllable	heca	[he'dʒa]
suffix	şəkilçi	[ʃækil'tʃi]
stress mark	vurğu	[vurɣ'u]
apostrophe	apostrof	[apost'rof]
full stop	nöqtə	[nøg'tæ]
comma	verqül	[ver'gyl]
semicolon	nöqtəli verqül	[nøgtæ'li ver'gyl]
colon	iki nöqtə	[i'ki nøg'tæ]
ellipsis	nöqtələr	[nøgtæ'lær]
question mark	sual işarəsi	[su'al iʃaræ'si]
exclamation mark	nida işarəsi	[ni'da iʃaræ'si]

inverted commas	dırnaq	[dır'nag]
in inverted commas	dırnaq arası	[dır'nag ara'sı]
parenthesis	mötərizə	[møtæri'zæ]
in parenthesis	mötərizədə	[møtærizæ'dæ]

hyphen	defis	[de'fis]
dash	tire	[ti're]
space (between words)	ara	[a'ra]

letter	hərf	[hærf]
capital letter	böyük hərf	[bø'yk 'hærf]

vowel (n)	sait səs	[sa'it 'sæs]
consonant (n)	samit səs	[sa'mit 'sæs]

sentence	cümlə	[dʒym'læ]
subject	mübtəda	[mybtæ'da]
predicate	xəbər	[hæ'bær]

line	sətir	[sæ'tir]
on a new line	yeni sətirdən	[e'ni sætir'dæn]
paragraph	abzas	['abzas]

word	söz	['søz]
word group	söz birləşməsi	['søz birlæʃmæ'si]
expression	ifadə	[ifa'dæ]
synonym	sinonim	[si'nonim]
antonym	antonim	[an'tonim]

rule	qayda	[gaj'da]
exception	istisna	[istis'na]
correct (adj)	düzgün	[dyz'gyn]

conjugation	təsrif	[tæs'rif]
declension	hallanma	[hallan'ma]
nominal case	hal	[hal]
question	sual	[su'al]
to underline (vt)	altından xətt çəkmək	[altın'dan 'hætt tʃək'mæk]
dotted line	punktir	[puŋk'tir]

146. Foreign languages

language	dil	[dil]
foreign language	xarici dil	[haridʒi dil]
to study (vt)	öyrənmək	[øjræn'mæk]
to learn (language, etc.)	öyrənmək	[øjræn'mæk]

to read (vi, vt)	oxumaq	[ohu'mag]
to speak (vi, vt)	danışmaq	[danıʃ'mag]
to understand (vt)	başa düşmək	[ba'ʃa dyʃ'mæk]
to write (vt)	yazmaq	[jaz'mag]

fast (adv)	cəld	[dʒæld]
slowly (adv)	yavaş	[ja'vaʃ]

fluently (adv)	sərbəst	[sær'bæst]
rules	qaydalar	[gajda'lar]
grammar	qrammatika	[gram'matika]
vocabulary	leksika	['leksika]
phonetics	fonetika	[fo'netika]

textbook	dərslik	[dærs'lik]
dictionary	lüğət	[lyɣ'æt]
teach-yourself book	rəhbər	[ræh'bær]
phrasebook	danışıq kitabı	[danı'ʃıg kita'bı]

cassette	kasset	[kas'set]
videotape	video kasset	['video kas'set]
CD, compact disc	SD diski	[si'di dis'ki]
DVD	DVD	[divi'di]

alphabet	əlifba	[ælif'ba]
to spell (vt)	hərf-hərf danışmaq	['hærf 'hærf danıʃ'mag]
pronunciation	tələffüz	[tælæf'fyz]

accent	aksent	[ak'sent]
with an accent	aksentlə danışmaq	[ak'sentlæ danıʃ'mag]
without an accent	aksentsiz danışmaq	[aksen'tsiz danıʃ'mag]

| word | söz | ['søz] |
| meaning | məna | [mæ'na] |

course (e.g. a French ~)	kurslar	[kurs'lar]
to sign up	yazılmaq	[jazıl'mag]
teacher	müəllim	[myæl'lim]

translation (process)	tərcümə	[tærdʒy'mæ]
translation (text, etc.)	tərcümə	[tærdʒy'mæ]
translator	tərcüməçi	[tærdʒymæ'tʃi]
interpreter	tərcüməçi	[tærdʒymæ'tʃi]

| polyglot | poliqlot | [polig'lot] |
| memory | yaddaş | [jad'daʃ] |

147. Fairy tale characters

| Santa Claus | Santa Klaus | ['santa 'klaus] |
| mermaid | su pərisi | ['su pæri'si] |

magician, wizard	sehrbaz	[sehr'baz]
fairy	sehrbaz qadın	[sehr'baz ga'dın]
magic (adj)	sehrli	[sehr'li]
magic wand	sehrli çubuq	[sehr'li tʃu'bug]

fairy tale	nağıl	[naɣ'ıl]
miracle	möcüzə	[mødʒy'zæ]
dwarf	qnom	[gnom]
to turn into ...	...dönmək	[døn'mæk]
ghost	qarabasma	[garabas'ma]

phantom	kabus	[ka'bus]
monster	div	[div]
dragon	əjdaha	[æʒda'ha]
giant	nəhənk	[næ'hæŋk]

148. Zodiac Signs

Aries	Qoç	[goʧ]
Taurus	Buğa	[buɣ'a]
Gemini	Əkizlər	[ækiz'lær]
Cancer	Xərçənk	[hær'ʧəŋk]
Leo	Şir	[ʃir]
Virgo	Qız	[gız]

Libra	Tərəzi	[tæræ'zi]
Scorpio	Əqrəb	[æg'ræb]
Sagittarius	Oxatan	[oha'tan]
Capricorn	Oğlağ	[oɣ'laɣ]
Aquarius	Dolça	[dol'ʧa]
Pisces	Balıqlar	[balıg'lar]

character	xasiyyət	[hasi'j:ət]
features of character	xasiyyətin cizgiləri	[hasij:ə'tin ʤizgilæ'ri]
behaviour	əxlaq	[æh'lag]
to tell fortunes	fala baxmaq	[fa'la bah'mag]
fortune-teller	falçı	[fal'ʧı]
horoscope	ulduz falı	[ul'duz fa'lı]

Arts

149. Theatre

theatre	teatr	[te'atr]
opera	opera	['opera]
operetta	operetta	[ope'retta]
ballet	balet	[ba'let]
playbill	afişa	[a'fiʃa]
theatrical company	truppa	['truppa]
tour	qastrol səfəri	[gast'rol sæfæ'ri]
to be on tour	qastrol səfərinə çıxmaq	[gast'rol sæfæri'næ tʃih'mag]
to rehearse (vi, vt)	məşq etmək	['mæʃg æt'mæk]
rehearsal	məşq	[mæʃg]
repertoire	repertuar	[repertu'ar]
performance	oyun	[o'yn]
stage show	teatr tamaşası	[te'atr tamaʃa'sı]
play	pyes	[pjes]
ticket	bilet	[bi'let]
Box office	bilet kassası	[bi'let 'kassası]
lobby, foyer	xoll	[holl]
coat check	qarderob	[garde'rob]
cloakroom ticket	nömrə	[nøm'ræ]
binoculars	binokl	[bi'nokl]
usher	nəzarətçi	[næzaræ'tʃi]
stalls	parter	[par'ter]
balcony	balkon	[bal'kon]
dress circle	beletaj	[belæ'taʒ]
box	loja	['loʒa]
row	sıra	[sı'ra]
seat	yer	[er]
audience	tamaşaçılar	[tamaʃatʃı'lar]
spectator	tamaşaçı	[tamaʃa'tʃı]
to clap (vi, vt)	əl çalmaq	['æl tʃal'mag]
applause	alqışlar	[algıʃ'lar]
ovation	sürəkli alqışlar	[syrek'li algıʃ'lar]
stage	səhnə	[sæh'næ]
curtain	pərdə	[pær'dæ]
scenery	dekorasiya	[deko'rasija]
backstage	səhnə arxası	[sæh'næ arha'sı]
scene (e.g. the last ~)	səhnə	[sæh'næ]
act	akt	[akt]
interval	antrakt	[ant'rakt]

150. Cinema

actor	aktyor	[akt'jor]
actress	aktrisa	[akt'risa]
cinema (industry)	kino	[ki'no]
film	kino	[ki'no]
episode	seriya	['serija]
detective	detektiv	[detek'tiv]
action film	savaş filmi	[sa'vaʃ fil'mi]
adventure film	macəra filmi	[madʒæ'ra fil'mi]
science fiction film	fantastik film	[fantas'tik 'film]
horror film	vahimə filmi	[vahi'mæ fil'mi]
comedy film	kino komediyası	[ki'no ko'medijası]
melodrama	melodram	[melod'ram]
drama	dram	[dram]
fictional film	bədii film	[bædi'i 'film]
documentary	sənədli film	[sænæd'li 'film]
cartoon	cizgi filmi	[dʒiz'gi fil'mi]
silent films	səssiz film	[sæs'siz 'film]
role	rol	[rol]
leading role	baş rol	['baʃ 'rol]
to play (vi, vt)	oynamaq	[ojna'mag]
film star	kino ulduzu	[ki'no uldu'zu]
well-known (adj)	məşhur	[mæʃ'hur]
famous (adj)	məşhur	[mæʃ'hur]
popular (adj)	populyar	[popu'ʎar]
script (screenplay)	ssenari	[sse'nari]
scriptwriter	ssenarist	[ssena'rist]
film director	rejissor	[reʒis'sor]
producer	prodüser	[pro'dyser]
assistant	köməkçi	[kømæk'tʃi]
cameraman	operator	[ope'rator]
stuntman	kaskadyor	[kaskad'jor]
to shoot a film	film çəkmək	['film tʃək'mæk]
audition, screen test	sınaqlar	[sınag'lar]
shooting	çəkiliş	[tʃəki'liʃ]
film crew	çəkiliş qrupu	[tʃəki'liʃ gru'pu]
film set	çəkiliş meydançası	[tʃəki'liʃ mejdantʃa'sı]
camera	kino kamerası	[ki'no 'kamerası]
cinema	kinoteatr	[kinote'atr]
screen (e.g. big ~)	ekran	[æk'ran]
to show a film	film göstərmək	['film gøstær'mæk]
soundtrack	səs zolağı	['sæs zolaɣ'ı]
special effects	xüsusi effektlər	[hysu'si æffekt'lær]
subtitles	subtitrlər	[sub'titrlær]

| credits | titrlər | ['titrlær] |
| translation | tərcümə | [tærʤy'mæ] |

151. Painting

art	incəsənət	[inʤæsæ'næt]
fine arts	incə sənətlər	[in'ʤæ sænæt'lær]
art gallery	qalereya	[gale'reja]
art exhibition	rəsm sərgisi	['ræsm særgi'si]

painting	rəssamlıq	[ræssam'lɪg]
graphic art	qrafika	['grafika]
abstract art	abstraksionizm	[abstraksio'nizm]
impressionism	impressionizm	[impressio'nizm]

picture (painting)	rəsm	[ræsm]
drawing	şəkil	[ʃæ'kil]
poster	plakat	[pla'kat]

illustration (picture)	şəkil	[ʃæ'kil]
miniature	miniatür	[minia'tyr]
copy (of painting, etc.)	surət	[su'ræt]
reproduction	reproduksiya	[repro'duksija]

mosaic	mozaika	[mo'zaika]
stained glass	vitraj	[vit'raʒ]
fresco	freska	['freska]
engraving	qravüra	[gra'vyra]

bust (sculpture)	büst	[byst]
sculpture	heykəl	[hej'kæl]
statue	heykəl	[hej'kæl]
plaster of Paris	qips	[gips]
plaster (as adj)	qipsdən	[gips'dæn]

portrait	portret	[port'ret]
self-portrait	avtoportret	[avtoport'ret]
landscape	mənzərə	[mænzæ'ræ]
still life	natürmort	[natyr'mort]
caricature	karikatura	[karika'tura]
sketch	eskiz	[æs'kiz]

paint	boya	[bo'ja]
watercolour	akvarel	[akva'rel]
oil (paint)	yağ	[jaɣ]
pencil	karandaş	[karan'daʃ]
Indian ink	tuş	[tuʃ]
charcoal	kömür	[kø'myr]

| to draw (vi, vt) | çəkmək | [ʧək'mæk] |
| to paint (vi, vt) | çəkmək | [ʧək'mæk] |

| to pose (vi) | poza almaq | ['poza al'mag] |
| artist's model (masc.) | canlı model | [ʤan'lɪ mo'del] |

133

artist's model (fem.)	canlı model olan qadın	[dʒan'lı mo'del o'lan ga'dın]
artist (painter)	rəssam	[ræs'sam]
work of art	əsər	[æ'sær]
masterpiece	şah əsər	['ʃah æ'sær]
workshop (of artist)	emalatxana	[æmalatha'na]

canvas (cloth)	qalın ketan	[ga'lın kæ'tan]
easel	molbert	[mol'bert]
palette	palitra	[pa'litra]

frame (of picture, etc.)	çərçivə	[ʧərʧi'væ]
restoration	bərpa etmə	[bær'pa æt'mæ]
to restore (vt)	bərpa etmək	[bær'pa æt'mæk]

152. Literature & Poetry

literature	ədəbiyyat	[ædæbi'j:at]
author (writer)	müəllif	[myæl'lif]
pseudonym	təxəllüs	[tæhæl'lys]

book	kitab	[ki'tab]
volume	cild	[dʒild]
table of contents	mündəricat	[mynderi'dʒæt]
page	səhifə	[sæhi'fæ]
main character	baş qəhrəman	['baʃ gæhræ'man]
autograph	avtoqraf	[av'tograf]

short story	hekayə	[heka'jə]
story (novella)	povest	['povest]
novel	roman	[ro'man]
work (writing)	əsər	[æ'sær]
fable	təmsil	[tæm'sil]
detective novel	detektiv	[detek'tiv]

poem (verse)	şer	[ʃər]
poetry	poeziya	[po'æzija]
poem (epic, ballad)	poema	[po'æma]
poet	şair	[ʃa'ir]

fiction	belletristika	[bellet'ristika]
science fiction	elmi fantastika	[æl'mi fan'tastika]
adventures	macəralar	[madʒæra'lar]
educational literature	dərs ədəbiyyatı	['dærs ædæbij:a'tı]
children's literature	uşaq ədəbiyyatı	[u'ʃag ædæbij:a'tı]

153. Circus

circus	sirk	[sirk]
big top (circus)	səyyar sirk	[sæ'j:ar 'sirk]
programme	proqram	[prog'ram]
performance	tamaşa	[tama'ʃa]
act (circus ~)	nömrə	[nøm'ræ]

circus ring	səhnə	[sæh'næ]
pantomime (act)	pantomima	[panto'mima]
clown	təlxək	[tæl'hæk]

acrobat	canbaz	[dʒan'baz]
acrobatics	canbazlıq	[dʒanbaz'lıg]
gymnast	gimnast	[gim'nast]
gymnastics	gimnastika	[gim'nastika]
somersault	salto	['salto]

strongman	atlet	[at'let]
animal-tamer	heyvan təlimçisi	[hej'van tælimtʃi'si]
equestrian	at sürən	['at sy'ræn]
assistant	köməkçi	[kømæk'tʃi]

stunt	kəndirbaz hoqqası	[kændir'baz hogga'sı]
magic trick	fokus	['fokus]
conjurer, magician	fokus göstərən	['fokus gøstæ'ræn]

juggler	jonqlyor	[ʒoŋl'jor]
to juggle (vi, vt)	jonqlyorluq etmək	[ʒoŋljor'lug æt'mæk]
animal trainer	heyvan təlimçisi	[hej'van tælimtʃi'si]
animal training	heyvan təlimi	[hej'van tæli'mi]
to train (animals)	heyvanı təlim etmək	[hejva'nı tæ'lim æt'mæk]

154. Music. Pop music

music	musiqi	[musi'gi]
musician	musiqiçi	[musigi'tʃi]
musical instrument	musiqi aləti	[musi'gi alæ'ti]
to play ...	...çalmaq	[tʃal'mag]

guitar	qitara	[gita'ra]
violin	skripka	['skripka]
cello	violonçel	[violon'tʃel]
double bass	kontrabas	[kontra'bas]
harp	arfa	['arfa]

piano	piano	[pi'ano]
grand piano	royal	[ro'jal]
organ	orqan	[or'gan]

wind instruments	nəfəs alətləri	[næ'fæs alætlæ'ri]
oboe	qoboy	[go'boj]
saxophone	saksofon	[sakso'fon]
clarinet	klarnet	[klar'net]
flute	fleyta	['flejta]
trumpet	truba	[tru'ba]

| accordion | akkordeon | [akkorde'on] |
| drum | təbil | [tæ'bil] |

| duo | duet | [du'æt] |
| trio | trio | ['trio] |

135

quartet	kvartet	[kvar'tet]
choir	xor	[hor]
orchestra	orkestr	[or'kestr]

pop music	pop musiqisi	['pop musigi'si]
rock music	rok musiqisi	['rok musigi'si]
rock group	rok qrupu	['rok gru'pu]
jazz	caz	[dʒaz]

| idol | büt | [byt] |
| admirer, fan | pərəstişkar | [pæræstiʃ'kʲar] |

concert	konsert	[kon'sert]
symphony	simfoniya	[sim'fonija]
composition	əsər	[æ'sær]
to compose (write)	yaratmaq	[jarat'mag]

singing	oxuma	[ohu'ma]
song	mahnı	[mah'nı]
tune (melody)	melodiya	[me'lodija]
rhythm	ritm	[ritm]
blues	blüz	[blyz]

sheet music	notlar	[not'lar]
baton	çubuq	[tʃu'bug]
bow	kaman	[ka'man]
string	sim	[sim]
case (e.g. guitar ~)	qab	[gab]

Rest. Entertainment. Travel

155. Trip. Travel

tourism	turizm	[tu'rizm]
tourist	turist	[tu'rist]
trip, voyage	səyahət	[sæja'hæt]
adventure	macəra	[madʒæ'ra]
trip, journey	səfər	[sæ'fær]
holiday	məzuniyyət	[mæzuni'j:ət]
to be on holiday	məzuniyyətdə olmaq	[mæzunij:ət'dæ ol'mag]
rest	istirahət	[istira'hæt]
train	qatar	[ga'tar]
by train	qatarla	[ga'tarla]
aeroplane	təyyarə	[tæj:a'ræ]
by aeroplane	təyyarə ilə	[tæj:a'ræ i'læ]
by car	maşınla	[ma'ʃınla]
by ship	gəmidə	[gæmi'dæ]
luggage	baqaj	[ba'gaʒ]
suitcase, luggage	çamadan	[tʃama'dan]
luggage trolley	baqaj üçün araba	[ba'gaʒ y'tʃun ara'ba]
passport	pasport	['pasport]
visa	viza	['viza]
ticket	bilet	[bi'let]
air ticket	təyyarə bileti	[tæj:a'ræ bile'ti]
guidebook	soraq kitabçası	[so'rag kitabtʃa'sı]
map	xəritə	[hæri'tæ]
area (rural ~)	yer	[er]
place, site	yer	[er]
exotica	ekzotika	[æk'zotika]
exotic (adj)	ekzotik	[ækzo'tik]
amazing (adj)	təəccüb doğuran	[tæːˈdʒyb doɣu'ran]
group	qrup	[grup]
excursion	ekskursiya	[æks'kursija]
guide (person)	ekskursiya rəhbəri	[æks'kursija ræhbæ'ri]

156. Hotel

hotel	mehmanxana	[mehmanha'na]
motel	motel	[mo'tel]
three-star (adj)	3 ulduzlu	['ytʃ ulduz'lu]

| five-star | 5 ulduzlu | ['beʃ ulduz'lu] |
| to stay (in hotel, etc.) | qalmaq | [gal'mag] |

room	nömrə	[nøm'ræ]
single room	bir nəfərlik nömrə	['bir næfær'lik nøm'ræ]
double room	iki nəfərlik nömrə	[i'ki næfær'lik nøm'ræ]
to book a room	nömrə təxsis etmək	[nøm'ræ tæh'sis æt'mæk]

| half board | yarım pansion | [ja'rım pansi'on] |
| full board | tam pansion | ['tam pansi'on] |

with bath	vannası olan nömrə	[vaŋa'sı o'lan nøm'ræ]
with shower	duşu olan nömrə	[du'ʃu o'lan nøm'ræ]
satellite television	peyk televiziyası	['pejk tele'vizijası]
air-conditioner	kondisioner	[kondisio'ner]
towel	dəsmal	[dæs'mal]
key	açar	[a'ʧar]

administrator	müdir	[my'dir]
chambermaid	otaq qulluqçusu	[o'tag gullugʧu'su]
porter, bellboy	yükdaşıyan	[ykdaʃı'jan]
doorman	qapıçı	[gapı'ʧı]

restaurant	restoran	[resto'ran]
pub, bar	bar	[bar]
breakfast	səhər yeməyi	[sæ'hær eme'jı]
dinner	axşam yeməyi	[ah'ʃam eme'jı]
buffet	İsveç masası	[is'vetʃ masa'sı]

| lobby | vestibül | [vesti'byl] |
| lift | lift | [lift] |

| DO NOT DISTURB | NARAHAT ETMƏYİN! | [nara'hat 'ætmæjın] |
| NO SMOKING | SİQARET ÇƏKMƏYİN! | [siga'ret 'ʧəkmæjın] |

157. Books. Reading

book	kitab	[ki'tab]
author	müəllif	[myæl'lif]
writer	yazıçı	[jazı'ʧı]
to write (~ a book)	yazmaq	[jaz'mag]

reader	oxucu	[ohu'ʤu]
to read (vi, vt)	oxumaq	[ohu'mag]
reading (activity)	oxuma	[ohu'ma]

| silently (to oneself) | ürəyində | [yræjın'dæ] |
| aloud (adv) | ucadan | [uʤa'dan] |

to publish (vt)	nəşr etmək	['næʃr æt'mæk]
publishing (process)	nəşr	[næʃr]
publisher	naşir	[na'ʃir]
publishing house	nəşriyyət	[næʃri'j:ət]
to come out	çıxmaq	[ʧıh'mag]

| release (of a book) | kitabın çıxması | [kita'bın ʧıhma'sı] |
| print run | tiraj | [ti'raʒ] |

| bookshop | kitab mağazası | [ki'tab maɣ'azası] |
| library | kitabxana | [kitabha'na] |

story (novella)	povest	['povesl]
short story	hekayə	[heka'jə]
novel	roman	[ro'man]
detective novel	detektiv	[detek'tiv]

memoirs	xatirələr	[hatiræ'lær]
legend	əfsanə	[æfsa'næ]
myth	əsatir	[æsa'tir]

poetry, poems	şer	[ʃər]
autobiography	tərcümeyi-hal	[tærʤu'mei 'hal]
selected works	seçilmiş əsərlər	[setʃil'miʃ æsær'lær]
science fiction	elmi fantastika	[æl'mi fan'tastika]

title	ad	[ad]
introduction	giriş	[gi'riʃ]
title page	titul vərəqi	['titul væræ'gi]

chapter	fəsil	[fæ'sil]
extract	parça	[par'ʧa]
episode	epizod	[æpi'zod]

plot (storyline)	süjet	[sy'ʒet]
contents	mündəricat	[mynderi'ʤæt]
table of contents	mündəricat	[mynderi'ʤæt]
main character	baş qəhrəman	['baʃ gæhræ'man]

volume	cild	[ʤild]
cover	üz	[yz]
binding	cild	[ʤild]
bookmark	əlfəcin	[ælfæ'ʤin]

page	səhifə	[sæhi'fæ]
to flick through	vərəqləmək	[væræglæ'mæk]
margins	kənarlar	[kænar'lar]
annotation	nişan	[ni'ʃan]
footnote	qeyd	[gejd]

text	mətn	[mætn]
type, fount	şrift	[ʃrift]
misprint, typo	səhv	[sæhv]

translation	tərcümə	[tærʤy'mæ]
to translate (vt)	tərcümə etmək	[tærʤy'mæ æt'mæk]
original (n)	əsil	[æ'sil]

famous (adj)	məşhur	[mæʃ'hur]
unknown (adj)	naməlum	[namæ'lum]
interesting (adj)	maraqlı	[marag'lı]
bestseller	bestseller	[bes'tseller]

dictionary	lüğet	[lyɣ'æt]
textbook	ders kitabı	['dærs kita'bı]
encyclopedia	ensiklopediya	[ænsiklo'pedija]

158. Hunting. Fishing

hunt (of animal)	ov	[ov]
to hunt (vi, vt)	ova çıxmaq	[o'va ʧıh'mag]
hunter	ovçu	[ov'ʧu]
to shoot (vi)	ateş açmaq	[a'tæʃ aʧ'mag]
rifle	tüfeng	[ty'fæn]
bullet (cartridge)	patron	[pat'ron]
shotgun pellets	qırma	[gır'ma]

trap (e.g. bear ~)	tele	[tæ'læ]
snare (for birds, etc.)	tele	[tæ'læ]
to lay a trap	tele qurmaq	[tæ'læ gur'mag]

poacher	brakonyer	[brako'ɲjer]
game (in hunting)	ov quşları ve heyvanları	['ov guʃla'rı 'væ hæjvanla'rı]
hound	ov iti	['ov i'ti]
safari	safari	[sa'fari]
mounted animal	müqevva	[mygæv'va]

fisherman	balıqçı	[balıg'ʧı]
fishing	balıq ovu	[ba'lıg o'vu]
to fish (vi)	balıq tutmaq	[ba'lıg tut'mag]
fishing rod	tilov	[ti'lov]
fishing line	tilov ipi	[ti'lov i'pi]
hook	qarmaq	[gar'mag]
float	qaravul	[gara'vul]
bait	tele yemi	[tæ'læ e'mi]

to cast a line	tilov atmaq	[ti'lov at'mag]
to bite (ab. fish)	tilova gelmek	[tilo'va gæl'mæk]
catch (of fish)	ovlanmış balıq	[ovlan'mıʃ ba'lıg]
ice-hole	buzda açılmış deşik	[buz'da aʧıl'mıʃ de'ʃik]

net	tor	[tor]
boat	qayıq	[ga'jıg]
to net (catch with net)	torla balıq tutmaq	['torla ba'lıg tut'mak]
to cast the net	toru suya atmaq	[to'ru su'ja at'mag]
to haul in the net	toru çıxarmaq	[to'ru ʧıhar'mag]

whaler (person)	balina ovçusu	[ba'lina ovʧu'su]
whaler (vessel)	balina ovlayan gemi	[ba'lina ovla'jan gæ'mi]
harpoon	iri qarmaq	[i'ri gar'mag]

159. Games. Billiards

| billiards | bilyard | [bi'ʎjard] |
| billiard room, hall | bilyard salonu | [bi'ʎjard salo'nu] |

ball	bilyard şarı	[biˈʎjard ʃaˈrɪ]
to pocket a ball	şarı luzaya salmaq	[ʃaˈrɪ ˈluzaja salˈmag]
cue	kiy	[kij]
pocket	luza	[ˈluza]

160. Games. Playing cards

diamonds	kərpicxallı kart	[kærpidʒhalˈlɪ ˈkart]
spades	qaratoxmaq	[garatohˈmag]
hearts	qırmızı toxmaq	[gɪrmɪˈzɪ tohˈmag]
clubs	xaç xallı	[ˈhatʃ halˈlɪ]

ace	tuz	[tuz]
king	kral	[kral]
queen	xanım	[haˈnɪm]
jack, knave	valet	[vaˈlet]

playing card	kart	[kart]
cards	kart	[kart]
trump	kozır	[ˈkozɪr]
pack of cards	bir dəst kart	[ˈbir ˈdæst ˈkart]

to deal (vi, vt)	kart paylamaq	[ˈkart pajlaˈmag]
to shuffle (cards)	kart qarışdırmaq	[ˈkart garɪʃdɪrˈmag]
lead, turn (n)	oyun	[oˈyn]
cardsharp	kart fırıldaqçısı	[ˈkart fɪrɪldagtʃɪˈsɪ]

161. Casino. Roulette

casino	kazino	[kaziˈno]
roulette (game)	ruletka	[ruˈletka]
bet, stake	ortaya qoyulan pul	[ortaˈja goyˈlan ˈpul]
to place bets	ortaya pul qoymaq	[ortaˈja ˈpul gojˈmag]

red	qırmızı	[gɪrmɪˈzɪ]
black	qara	[gaˈra]
to bet on red	qırmızıya pul qoymaq	[gɪrmɪzɪˈja ˈpul gojˈmag]
to bet on black	qaraya pul qoymaq	[garaˈja ˈpul gojˈmag]

croupier (dealer)	krupye	[krupˈje]
to turn the wheel	barabanı fırlatmaq	[barabaˈnɪ fɪrlatˈmag]
rules (of game)	oyun qaydaları	[oˈyn gajdalaˈrɪ]
chip	fişka	[ˈfiʃka]

| to win (vi, vt) | udmaq | [udˈmag] |
| winnings | uduş | [uˈduʃ] |

| to lose (~ 100 dollars) | məğlubiyyətə uğramaq | [mæɣlubij:əˈtæ uɣraˈmag] |
| loss | məğlubiyyət | [mæɣlubiˈj:ət] |

| player | oyunçu | [oynˈtʃu] |
| blackjack (card game) | blek cek | [ˈblæk ˈdʒek] |

| game of dice | zər oyunu | ['zær oy'nu] |
| fruit machine | oyun avtomatı | [o'yn avtoma'tı] |

162. Rest. Games. Miscellaneous

to take a walk	gəzmək	[gæz'mæk]
walk, stroll	gəzinti	[gæzin'ti]
road trip	gəzinti	[gæzin'ti]
adventure	macəra	[madʒæ'ra]
picnic	piknik	[pik'nik]

game (chess, etc.)	oyun	[o'yn]
player	oyunçu	[oyn'tʃu]
game (one ~ of chess)	hissə	[his'sæ]

collector (e.g. philatelist)	kolleksiyaçı	[kol'leksijatʃı]
to collect (vt)	kolleksiya toplamaq	[kol'leksija toplamag]
collection	kolleksiya	[kol'leksija]

crossword puzzle	krossvord	[kross'vord]
racecourse (hippodrome)	cıdır meydanı	[dʒı'dır mejda'nı]
discotheque	diskoteka	[disko'teka]

| sauna | sauna | ['sauna] |
| lottery | lotereya | [lote'reja] |

camping trip	yürüş	[y'ryʃ]
camp	düşərgə	[dyʃær'gæ]
tent (for camping)	çadır	[tʃa'dır]
compass	kompas	['kompas]
camper	turist	[tu'rist]

to watch (film, etc.)	baxmaq	[bah'mag]
viewer	televiziya tamaşaçısı	[tele'vizija tamaʃatʃı'sı]
TV program	televiziya verilişi	[tele'vizija verili'ʃi]

163. Photography

| camera (photo) | fotoaparat | [fotoapa'rat] |
| photo, picture | fotoqrafiya | [fotog'rafija] |

photographer	fotoqrafçı	[fotograf'tʃı]
photo studio	fotostudiya	[fotos'tudija]
photo album	fotoalbom	[fotoal'bom]

camera lens	obyektiv	[objek'tiv]
telephoto lens	teleobyektiv	[teleobjek'tiv]
filter	filtr	[filtr]
lens	linza	['linza]

| optics (high-quality ~) | optika | ['optika] |
| diaphragm (aperture) | diafraqma | [diaf'ragma] |

exposure time	obyektivin açıq qalma müddəti	[objekti'vin a'tʃɪg gal'ma myddæ'ti]
viewfinder	vizir	[vi'zir]

digital camera	rəqəm kamerası	[ræ'gæm 'kamerası]
tripod	üçayaq	[ytʃa'jag]
flash	işartı	[iʃar'tı]

to photograph (vt)	fotoşəkil çəkmək	[fotoʃæ'kil tʃək'mæk]
to take pictures	foto çəkmək	['foto tʃək'mæk]
to be photographed	fotoşəkil çəkdirmək	[fotoʃæ'kil tʃəkdir'mæk]

focus	aydınlıq	[ajdın'lıg]
to adjust the focus	aydınlığa yönəltmək	[ajdınlıɣ'a jonælt'mæk]
sharp, in focus (adj)	aydın	[aj'dın]
sharpness	aydınlıq	[ajdın'lıg]

contrast	təzad	[tæ'zad]
contrasty (adj)	təzadlı	[tæzad'lı]

picture (photo)	fotoşəkil	[fotoʃæ'kil]
negative (n)	neqativ	[nega'tiv]
film (a roll of ~)	fotolent	[foto'lent]
frame (still)	kadr	[kadr]
to print (photos)	şəkil çıxartmaq	[ʃæ'kil tʃıhart'mag]

164. Beach. Swimming

beach	plyaj	[pʎaʒ]
sand	qum	[gum]
deserted (beach)	adamsız	[adam'sız]

suntan	gündən qaralma	[gyn'dæn garal'ma]
to get a tan	qaralmaq	[garal'mag]
tanned (adj)	gündən qaralmış	[gyn'dæn garal'mıʃ]
sunscreen	qaralma kremi	[garal'ma kre'mi]

bikini	bikini	[bi'kini]
swimsuit, bikini	çimmə paltarı	[tʃim'mæ palta'rı]
swim trunks	üzgüçü tumanı	[yzgy'tʃu tuma'nı]

swimming pool	hovuz	[ho'vuz]
to swim (vi)	üzmək	[yz'mæk]
shower	duş	[duʃ]
to change (one's clothes)	əynini dəyişmək	[æjni'ni dæiʃ'mæk]
towel	dəsmal	[dæs'mal]

boat	qayıq	[ga'jıg]
motorboat	kater	['kater]

water ski	su xizəyi	['su hizæ'jı]
pedalo	su velosipedi	['su velosipe'di]
surfing	serfinq	['serfiŋ]
surfer	serfinq idmançısı	['serfiŋ idmantʃı'sı]

scuba set	akvalanq	[akva'laŋ]
flippers (swimfins)	lastlar	[last'lar]
mask	maska	[mas'ka]
diver	dalğıc	[dalɣ'ıʤ]
to dive (vi)	dalmaq	[dal'mag]
underwater (adv)	suyun altında	[su'yn altın'da]

beach umbrella	çətir	[ʧə'tir]
beach chair	şezlonq	[ʃəz'loŋ]
sunglasses	eynək	[æj'næk]
air mattress	üzmək üçün döşək	[yz'mæk y'ʧun dø'ʃæk]

| to play (amuse oneself) | oynamaq | [ojna'mag] |
| to go for a swim | çimmək | [ʧim'mæk] |

beach ball	top	[top]
to inflate (vt)	doldurmak	[doldur'mag]
inflatable, air (adj)	hava ilə doldurulan	[ha'va i'læ dolduru'lan]

wave	dalğa	[dalɣ'a]
buoy	siqnal üzgəci	[sig'nal yzgæ'ʤi]
to drown (ab. person)	boğulub batmaq	[boɣu'lub bat'mag]

to save, to rescue	xilas etmək	[hi'las æt'mæk]
lifejacket	xilas edici jilet	[hi'las ædi'ʤi ʒi'let]
to observe, to watch	müşaidə etmək	[myʃai'dæ æt'mæk]
lifeguard	xilas edən	[hi'las æ'dæn]

TECHNICAL EQUIPMENT. TRANSPORT

Technical equipment

165. Computer

computer	bilgisayar	[bilgisa'jar]
notebook, laptop	noutbuk	['noutbuk]
to switch on	işə salmaq	[i'ʃæ sal'mag]
to turn off	söndürmək	[søndyr'mæk]
keyboard	klaviatura	[klavia'tura]
key	dil	[dil]
mouse	bilgisayar siçanı	[bilgisa'jar sitʃa'nɪ]
mouse mat	altlıq	[alt'lɪg]
button	düymə	[dyj'mæ]
cursor	kursor	[kur'sor]
monitor	monitor	[moni'tor]
screen	ekran	[æk'ran]
hard disk	sərt disk	['sært 'disk]
hard disk volume	sərt diskin həcmi	['sært dis'kin hædʒ'mi]
memory	yaddaş	[jad'daʃ]
random access memory	operativ yaddaş	[opera'tiv jad'daʃ]
file	fayl	[fajl]
folder	qovluq	[gov'lug]
to open (vt)	açmaq	[atʃ'mag]
to close (vt)	bağlamaq	[baɣla'mag]
to save (vt)	saxlamaq	[sahla'mag]
to delete (vt)	silmək	[sil'mæk]
to copy (vt)	kopyalamaq	[kopjala'mag]
to sort (vt)	çeşidləmək	[tʃeʃidlæ'mæk]
to transfer (copy)	yenidən yazmaq	[eni'dæn jaz'mag]
programme	proqram	[prog'ram]
software	proqram təminatı	[prog'ram tæmina'tɪ]
programmer	proqramçı	[program'tʃɪ]
to program (vt)	proqramlaşdırmaq	[programlaʃdɪr'mag]
hacker	xaker	['haker]
password	parol	[pa'rol]
virus	virus	['virus]
to find, to detect	aşkar etmək	[aʃ'kʲar æt'mæk]
byte	bayt	[bajt]

megabyte	meqabayt	[mega'bajt]
data	məlumatlar	[mælumat'lar]
database	məlumatlar bazası	[mælumat'lar 'bazası]

cable (wire)	kabel	['kabel]
to disconnect (vt)	ayırmaq	[ajır'mag]
to connect (sth to sth)	qoşmaq	[goʃ'mag]

166. Internet. E-mail

Internet	internet	[inter'net]
browser	brauzer	['brauzer]
search engine	axtarış mənbəyi	[ahta'rıʃ mænbæ'i]
provider	provayder	[provaj'der]

web master	veb ustası	['veb usta'sı]
website	veb-sayt	['veb 'sajt]
web page	veb-səhifə	['veb sæi'fæ]

address	ünvan	[yn'van]
address book	ünvan kitabı	[yn'van kita'bı]

postbox	poçt qutusu	['potʃt gutu'su]
post	poçt	[potʃt]

message	ismarıc	[isma'rıʤ]
sender	göndərən	[gøndæ'ræn]
to send (vt)	göndərmək	[gøndær'mæk]
sending (of mail)	göndərilmə	[gøndæril'mæ]

receiver	alan	[a'lan]
to receive (vt)	almaq	[al'mag]

correspondence	məktublaşma	[mæktublaʃ'ma]
to correspond (vi)	məktublaşmaq	[mæktublaʃ'mag]

file	fayl	[fajl]
to download (vt)	kopyalamaq	[kopjala'mag]
to create (vt)	yaratmaq	[jarat'mag]
to delete (vt)	silmək	[sil'mæk]
deleted (adj)	silinmiş	[silin'miʃ]

connection (ADSL, etc.)	bağlantı	[baɣlan'tı]
speed	surət	[su'ræt]
modem	modem	[mo'dem]

access	yol	[jol]
port (e.g. input ~)	giriş	[gi'riʃ]

connection (make a ~)	qoşulma	[goʃul'ma]
to connect (vi)	qoşulmaq	[goʃul'mag]

to select (vt)	seçmək	[setʃ'mæk]
to search (for ...)	axtarmaq	[ahtar'mag]

167. Electricity

electricity	elektrik	[ælekt′rik]
electrical (adj)	elektrik	[ælekt′rik]
electric power station	elektrik stansiyası	[ælekt′rik ′stansijası]
energy	enerji	[æner′ʒi]
electric power	elektrik enerjisi	[ælekt′rik ænerʒi′si]
light bulb	lampa	[lam′pa]
torch	əl fənəri	[′æl fænæ′ri]
street light	küçə fənəri	[ky′tʃə fænæ′ri]
light	işıq	[i′ʃıg]
to turn on	qoşmaq	[goʃ′mag]
to turn off	söndürmək	[søndyr′mæk]
to turn off the light	işığı söndürmək	[iʃıɣ′ı søndyr′mæk]
to burn out (vi)	yanmaq	[jan′mag]
short circuit	qısa qapanma	[gı′sa gapan′ma]
broken wire	qırılma	[gırıl′ma]
contact	birləşmə	[birlæʃ′mæ]
light switch	elektrik açarı	[ælekt′rik atʃa′rı]
socket outlet	rozetka	[rozet′ka]
plug	ştepsel	[′ʃtepsel]
extension lead	uzadıcı	[uzadı′dʒı]
fuse	qoruyucu	[goruy′dʒu]
cable, wire	məftil	[mæf′til]
wiring	şəbəkə	[ʃæbæ′kæ]
ampere	amper	[am′per]
amperage	cərəyən gücü	[dʒæræ′jən gy′dʒy]
volt	volt	[volt]
voltage	gərginlik	[gærgin′lik]
electrical device	elektrik cihaz	[ælekt′rik dʒi′haz]
indicator	indikator	[indi′kator]
electrician	elektrik	[æ′lektrik]
to solder (vt)	lehimləmək	[lehimlæ′mæk]
soldering iron	lehim aləti	[le′him alæ′ti]
electric current	cərəyan	[dʒæræ′jən]

168. Tools

tool, instrument	alət	[a′læt]
tools	alətlər	[alæt′lær]
equipment (factory ~)	avadanlıq	[avadan′lıg]
hammer	çəkic	[tʃə′kidʒ]
screwdriver	vintaçan	[vinta′tʃan]
axe	balta	[bal′ta]

saw	mişar	[miˈʃar]
to saw (vt)	mişarlamaq	[miʃarlaˈmag]
plane (tool)	rəndə	[rænˈdæ]
to plane (vt)	rəndələmək	[rændælæˈmæk]
soldering iron	lehim aləti	[leˈhim alæˈti]
to solder (vt)	lehimləmək	[lehimlæˈmæk]

file (for metal)	suvand	[suˈvand]
carpenter pincers	kəlbətin	[kælbæˈtin]
combination pliers	yastıağız kəlbətin	[jastıaɣˈız kælbæˈtin]
chisel	iskənə	[iskæˈnæ]

drill bit	burğu	[burɣˈu]
electric drill	burğu	[burɣˈu]
to drill (vi, vt)	deşmək	[deʃˈmæk]

knife	bıçaq	[bıˈtʃag]
pocket knife	cib bıçağı	[ˈdʒib bıtʃaɣˈı]
folding (knife, etc.)	qatlanan bıçaq	[gatlaˈnan bıˈtʃag]
blade	uc	[udʒ]

sharp (blade, etc.)	iti	[iˈti]
blunt (adj)	küt	[kyt]
to become blunt	kütləşmək	[kytlæʃˈmæk]
to sharpen (vt)	itiləmək	[itilæˈmæk]

bolt	bolt	[bolt]
nut	qayka	[gajˈka]
thread (of a screw)	yiv	[jıv]
wood screw	şurup	[ʃuˈrup]

| nail | mismar | [misˈmar] |
| nailhead | baş | [baʃ] |

ruler (for measuring)	xətkeş	[hætˈkeʃ]
tape measure	ölçü lenti	[ølˈtʃu lenˈti]
spirit level	səviyyə ölçən cihaz	[sæviˈjːə ølˈtʃən dʒiˈhaz]
magnifying glass	zərrəbin	[zærræˈbin]

measuring instrument	ölçü cihazı	[ølˈtʃu dʒihaˈzı]
to measure (vt)	ölçmək	[øltʃˈmæk]
scale (of thermometer, etc.)	şkala	[ʃkaˈla]
readings	göstərici	[gøsteriˈdʒi]

| compressor | kompressor | [kompˈressor] |
| microscope | mikroskop | [mikrosˈkop] |

pump (e.g. water ~)	nasos	[naˈsos]
robot	robot	[roˈbot]
laser	lazer	[ˈlazer]

spanner	qayka açarı	[gajˈka atʃaˈrı]
adhesive tape	lent-skoç	[ˈlent ˈskotʃ]
glue	yapışqan	[japıʃˈgan]
emery paper	sumbata kağızı	[sumbaˈta kaɣıˈzı]
spring	yay	[jaj]

| magnet | maqnit | [mag'nit] |
| gloves | əlçək | [æl'dʒæk] |

rope	kəndir	[kæn'dir]
cord	ip	[ip]
wire (e.g. telephone ~)	məftil	[mæf'til]
cable	kabel	['kabel]

sledgehammer	ağır çəkic	[aɣ'ır tʃə'kidʒ]
crowbar	link	[liŋk]
ladder	nərdivan	[nærdi'van]
stepladder	əl nərdivanı	['æl nærdiva'nı]

to screw (tighten)	bərkitmək	[bærkit'mæk]
to unscrew, untwist (vt)	açmaq	[atʃ'mag]
to tighten (vt)	sıxmaq	[sıh'mag]
to glue, to stick	yapışdırmaq	[japıʃdır'mag]
to cut (vt)	kəsmək	[kæs'mæk]

malfunction (fault)	nasazlıq	[nasaz'lıg]
repair (mending)	təmir	[tæ'mir]
to repair, to mend (vt)	təmir etmək	[tæ'mir æt'mæk]
to adjust (machine, etc.)	sazlamaq	[sazla'mag]

to check (to examine)	yoxlamaq	[johla'mag]
checking	yoxlanış	[johla'nıʃ]
readings	sayğac göstəricisi	[sajɣ'adʒ gøsteridʒi'si]

| reliable (machine) | etibarlı | [ætibar'lı] |
| complicated (adj) | mürəkkəb | [myræk'kæb] |

to rust (vi)	paslanmaq	[paslan'mag]
rusty (adj)	paslı	[pas'lı]
rust	pas	[pas]

Transport

169. Aeroplane

aeroplane	təyyarə	[tæj:a'ræ]
air ticket	təyyarə bileti	[tæj:a'ræ bile'ti]
airline	hava yolu şirkəti	[ha'va jo'lu ʃirkæ'ti]
airport	hava limanı	[ha'va lima'nı]
supersonic (adj)	səsdən sürətli	[sæs'dæn syræt'li]
captain	hava gəmisinin komandiri	[ha'va gæmisi'nin komandi'ri]
crew	heyyət	[he'j:ət]
pilot	pilot	[pi'lot]
stewardess	stüardessa	[styar'dessa]
navigator	şturman	['ʃturman]
wings	qanadlar	[ganad'lar]
tail	arxa	[ar'ha]
cockpit	kabina	[ka'bina]
engine	mühərrik	[myhær'rik]
undercarriage	şassi	[ʃas'si]
turbine	turbina	[tur'bina]
propeller	propeller	[pro'peller]
black box	qara qutu	[ga'ra gu'tu]
control column	sükan çarxı	[sy'kʲan ʧar'hı]
fuel	yanacaq	[jana'ʤag]
safety card	təlimat	[tæli'mat]
oxygen mask	oksigen maskası	[oksi'gen maska'sı]
uniform	rəsmi paltar	[ræs'mi pal'tar]
lifejacket	xilas edici jilet	[hi'las ædi'ʤi ʒi'let]
parachute	paraşüt	[para'ʃyt]
takeoff	havaya qalxma	[hava'ja galh'ma]
to take off (vi)	havaya qalxmaq	[hava'ja galh'mag]
runway	qalxma-enmə zolağı	[galh'ma æn'mæ zolaɣ'ı]
visibility	görünmə dərəcəsi	[gøryn'mæ dærædʒæ'si]
flight (act of flying)	uçuş	[u'ʧuʃ]
altitude	hündürlük	[hyndyr'lyk]
air pocket	hava boşluğu	[ha'va boʃluɣ'u]
seat	yer	[er]
headphones	qulaqlıqlar	[gulaglıɣ'lar]
folding tray	qatlanan masa	[gatla'nan ma'sa]
airplane window	illüminator	[illymi'nator]
aisle	keçid	[ke'ʧid]

170. Train

train	qatar	[ga'tar]
suburban train	elektrik qatarı	[ælekt'rik gata'rı]
fast train	süret qatarı	[sy'ræt gata'rı]
diesel locomotive	teplovoz	[teplo'voz]
steam engine	parovoz	[paro'voz]
coach, carriage	vaqon	[va'gon]
restaurant car	vaqon-restoran	[va'gon resto'ran]
rails	relsler	[rels'lær]
railway	demiryolu	[dæmirjo'lu]
sleeper (track support)	şpal	['ʃpal]
platform (railway ~)	platforma	[plat'forma]
platform (~ 1, 2, etc.)	yol	[jol]
semaphore	semafor	[sema'for]
station	stansiya	['stansija]
train driver	maşınsüren	[maʃınsy'ræn]
porter (of luggage)	yükdaşıyan	[ykdaʃı'jan]
train steward	beledçi	[bælæd'tʃi]
passenger	sernişin	[særni'ʃin]
ticket inspector	nezaretçi	[næzaræ'tʃi]
corridor (in train)	dehliz	[dæh'liz]
emergency break	stop-kran	['stop 'kran]
compartment	kupe	[ku'pe]
berth	yataq yeri	[ja'tag e'ri]
upper berth	yuxarı yer	[yha'rı 'er]
lower berth	aşağı yer	[aʃaɣ'ı 'er]
linen	yataq deyişeyi	[ja'tag dæiʃæ'jı]
ticket	bilet	[bi'let]
timetable	cedvel	[dʒæd'væl]
information display	lövhe	[løv'hæ]
to leave, to depart	yola düşmek	[jo'la dyʃ'mæk]
departure (of train)	yola düşme	[jo'la dyʃ'mæ]
to arrive (ab. train)	gelmek	[gæl'mæk]
arrival	gelme	[gæl'mæ]
to arrive by train	qatarla gelmek	[ga'tarla gæl'mæk]
to get on the train	qatara minmek	[gata'ra min'mæk]
to get off the train	qatardan düşmek	[gatar'dan dyʃ'mæk]
train crash	qeza	[gæ'za]
steam engine	parovoz	[paro'voz]
stoker, fireman	ocaqçı	[odʒag'tʃı]
firebox	odluq	[od'lug]
coal	kömür	[kø'myr]

171. Ship

ship	gəmi	[gæ'mi]
vessel	gəmi	[gæ'mi]
steamship	paroxod	[paro'hod]
riverboat	teploxod	[teplo'hod]
ocean liner	layner	['lajner]
cruiser	kreyser	['krejser]
yacht	yaxta	['jahta]
tugboat	yedək	[e'dæk]
barge	barja	['barʒa]
ferry	bərə	[bæ'ræ]
sailing ship	yelkənli qayıq	[elkæn'li ga'jıg]
brigantine	briqantina	[brigan'tina]
ice breaker	buzqıran	[buzgı'ran]
submarine	sualtı qayıq	[sual'tı ga'jıg]
boat (flat-bottomed ~)	qayıq	[ga'jıg]
dinghy	şlyupka	['ʃlypka]
lifeboat	xilasetmə şlyupkaı	[hilasæt'mæ ʃlypka'sı]
motorboat	kater	['kater]
captain	kapitan	[kapi'tan]
seaman	matros	[mat'ros]
sailor	dənizçi	[dæniz'ʧi]
crew	heyyət	[he'jːət]
boatswain	bosman	['bosman]
ship's boy	gəmi şagirdi	[gæ'mi ʃagir'di]
cook	gəmi aşpazı	[gæ'mi aʃpa'zı]
ship's doctor	gəmi həkimi	[gæ'mi hæki'mi]
deck	göyərtə	[gøjər'tæ]
mast	dirək	[di'ræk]
sail	yelkən	[el'kæn]
hold	anbar	[an'bar]
bow (prow)	gəminin qabaq tərəfi	[gæmi'nin ga'bag tæræ'fi]
stern	gəminin arxa tərəfi	[gæmi'nin ar'ha tæræ'fi]
oar	avar	[a'var]
propeller	pərvanə	[pærva'næ]
cabin	kayuta	[ka'yta]
wardroom	kayut-kompaniya	[ka'yt kom'panija]
engine room	maşın bölməsi	[ma'ʃın bølmæ'si]
bridge	kapitan körpüsü	[kapi'tan kørpy'sy]
radio room	radio-rubka	['radio 'rubka]
wave (radio)	radio dalğası	['radio dalɣa'sı]
logbook	gəmi jurnalı	[gæ'mi ʒurna'lı]
spyglass	müşahidə borusu	[myʃai'dæ boru'su]
bell	zəng	[zæŋ]

flag	bayraq	[baj'rag]
rope (mooring ~)	kanat	[ka'nat]
knot (bowline, etc.)	dənizçi düyünü	[dæniz'ʧi dy:'ny]

| handrail | məhəccər | [mæhæ'ʤær] |
| gangway | pilləkən | [pillæ'kæn] |

anchor	lövbər	[løv'bær]
to weigh anchor	lövbəri qaldırmaq	[løvbæ'ri galdır'mag]
to drop anchor	lövbər salmaq	[løv'bær sal'mag]
anchor chain	lövbər zənciri	[løv'bær zænʤi'ri]

port (harbour)	liman	[li'man]
wharf, quay	körpü	[kør'py]
to berth (moor)	sahilə yaxınlaşmaq	[sahi'læ jahınlaʃ'mag]
to cast off	sahildən ayrılmaq	[sahil'dæn ajrıl'mag]

trip, voyage	səyahət	[sæja'hæt]
cruise (sea trip)	kruiz	[kru'iz]
course (route)	istiqamət	[istiga'mæt]
route (itinerary)	marşrut	[marʃ'rut]

fairway	farvater	[far'vater]
shallows (shoal)	say	[saj]
to run aground	saya oturmaq	[sa'ja otur'mag]

storm	fırtına	[fırtı'na]
signal	siqnal	[sig'nal]
to sink (vi)	batmaq	[bat'mag]
SOS	SOS	[sos]
ring buoy	xilas edici dairə	[hilas ædi'ʤi dai'ræ]

172. Airport

airport	hava limanı	[ha'va lima'nı]
aeroplane	təyyarə	[tæj:a'ræ]
airline	hava yolu şirkəti	[ha'va jo'lu ʃirkæ'ti]
air-traffic controller	dispetçer	[dis'petʃer]

departure	uçub getmə	[u'ʧub get'mæ]
arrival	uçub gəlmə	[u'ʧub gæl'mæ]
to arrive (by plane)	uçub gəlmək	[u'ʧub gæl'mæk]

| departure time | yola düşmə vaxtı | [jo'la dyʃmæ vah'tı] |
| arrival time | gəlmə vaxtı | [gæl'mæ vah'tı] |

| to be delayed | gecikmək | [geʤik'mæk] |
| flight delay | uçuşun gecikməsi | [uʧu'ʃun geʤikmæ'si] |

information board	məlumat lövhəsi	[mælu'mat løvhæ'si]
information	məlumat	[mælu'mat]
to announce (vt)	elan etmək	[æ'lan æt'mæk]
flight (e.g. next ~)	reys	[rejs]
customs	gömrük	[gøm'ryk]

153

customs officer	gömrük işçisi	[gøm'ryk iʃtʃi'si]
customs declaration	bəyannamə	[bæjaŋa'mæ]
to fill in the declaration	bəyannaməni doldurmaq	[bæjaŋamæ'ni doldur'mag]
passport control	pasport nəzarəti	['pasport næzaræ'ti]

luggage	baqaj	[ba'gaʒ]
hand luggage	əl yükü	['æl y'ky]
Lost Luggage Desk	baqajın axtarılması	[baga'ʒɪn ahtarılma'sı]
luggage trolley	araba	[ara'ba]

landing	enmə	[æn'mæ]
landing strip	enmə zolağı	[æn'mæ zolaɣ'ı]
to land (vi)	enmək	[æn'mæk]
airstairs	pilləkən	[pillæ'kæn]

check-in	qeydiyyat	[gejdi'j:at]
check-in desk	qeydiyyat yeri	[gejdi'j:at e'ri]
to check-in (vi)	qeydiyyatdan keçmək	[gejdij:at'dan ketʃ'mæk]
boarding pass	minik talonu	[mi'nik talo'nu]
departure gate	çıxış	[tʃɪ'hɪʃ]

transit	tranzit	[tran'zit]
to wait (vt)	gözləmək	[gøzlæ'mæk]
departure lounge	gözləmə zalı	[gøzlæ'mæ za'lı]
to see off	yola salmaq	[jo'la sal'mag]
to say goodbye	vidalaşmaq	[vidalaʃ'mag]

173. Bicycle. Motorcycle

bicycle	velosiped	[velosi'ped]
scooter	motoroller	[moto'roller]
motorbike	motosiklet	[motosik'let]

to go by bicycle	velosipedlə getmək	[velosi'pedlæ get'mæk]
handlebars	sükan	[sy'kan]
pedal	pedal	[pe'dal]
brakes	tormoz	['tormoz]
saddle	oturmaq yeri	[otur'mag e'ri]

pump	nasos	[na'sos]
luggage rack	baqaj yeri	[ba'gaʒ e'ri]
front lamp	fənər	[fæ'nær]
helmet	dəbilqə	[dæbil'gæ]

wheel	təkər	[tæ'kær]
mudguard	qanad	[ga'nad]
rim	çənbər	[tʃən'bær]
spoke	mil	[mil]

Cars

174. Types of cars

car	avtomobil	[avtomo'bil]
sports car	idman avtomobili	[id'man avtomobi'li]
limousine	limuzin	[limu'zin]
convertible	kabriolet	[kabrio'let]
minibus	mikroavtobus	[mikroav'tobus]
ambulance	təcili yardım maşını	[tæʤi'li jar'dım maʃı'nı]
snowplough	qar təmizləyən maşın	['gar tæmizlæ'jən ma'ʃın]
lorry	yük maşını	['yk maʃı'nı]
road tanker	benzin daşıyan maşın	[ben'zin daʃı'jan ma'ʃın]
van (small truck)	furqon	[fur'gon]
road tractor	yedəkçi	[edæk'ʧi]
trailer	qoşulma araba	[goʃul'ma ara'ba]
comfortable (adj)	komfortlu	[komfort'lu]
second hand (adj)	işlənmiş	[iʃlæn'miʃ]

175. Cars. Bodywork

bonnet	kapot	[ka'pot]
wing	qanad	[ga'nad]
roof	üst	[yst]
windscreen	qabaq şüşəsi	[ga'bag ʃyʃæ'si]
rear-view mirror	arxa görünüş güzgüsü	[ar'ha gøry'nyʃ gyzgy'sy]
windscreen washer	şüşəyuyanlar	[ʃyʃæyjan'lar]
windscreen wipers	şüşə silgəcləri	[ʃy'ʃæ silgæʤlæ'ri]
side window	yan şüşə	['jan ʃy'ʃæ]
window lift	şüşə qaldırıcı mexanizm	[ʃy'ʃæ galdırı'ʤı meha'nizm]
aerial	antenna	[an'teŋa]
sun roof	lyuk	[lyk]
bumper	bamper	['bamper]
boot	baqaj yeri	[ba'gaʒ e'ri]
door	qapı	[ga'pı]
door handle	qapı dəstəyi	[ga'pı dæstæ'jı]
door lock	qıfıl	[gı'fıl]
number plate	nömrə	[nøm'ræ]
silencer	səsboğan	[sæsboɣ'an]

| petrol tank | benzin bakı | [ben'zin ba'kı] |
| exhaust pipe | işlənmiş qaz borusu | [iʃlæn'miʃ 'gaz boru'su] |

accelerator	qaz	[gaz]
pedal	pedal	[pe'dal]
accelerator pedal	qaz pedalı	['gaz peda'lı]

brake	tormoz	['tormoz]
brake pedal	tormoz pedalı	['tormoz peda'lı]
to slow down (to brake)	tormozlamaq	[tormozla'mag]
handbrake	dayanacaq tormozu	[dajana'dʒag 'tormozu]

clutch	ilişmə	[iliʃ'mæ]
clutch pedal	ilişmə pedalı	[iliʃ'mæ peda'lı]
clutch plate	ilişmə diski	[iliʃ'mæ dis'ki]
shock absorber	amortizator	[amorti'zator]

wheel	təkər	[tæ'kær]
spare tyre	ehtiyat təkəri	[æhti'jat tækæ'ri]
tyre	şin	[ʃin]
wheel cover (hubcap)	qapaq	[ga'pag]

driving wheels	aparıcı təkərlər	[aparı'dʒı tækær'lær]
front-wheel drive (as adj)	qabaq ötürücü	[ga'bag øtyry'dʒy]
rear-wheel drive (as adj)	arxa ötürücü	[ar'ha øtyry'dʒy]
all-wheel drive (as adj)	tam ötürücü	['tam øtyry'dʒy]

gearbox	ötürücü qutusu	[øtyry'dʒy gutu'su]
automatic (adj)	avtomat	[avto'mat]
mechanical (adj)	mexaniki	[mehani'ki]
gear lever	ötürücü qutusunun qolu	[øtyry'dʒy gutusu'nun go'lu]

| headlight | fara | ['fara] |
| headlights | faralar | ['faralar] |

dipped headlights	faranın yaxın işığı	['faranın ja'hın iʃıɣ'ı]
full headlights	faranın uzaq işığı	['faranın u'zag iʃıɣ'ı]
brake light	stop-siqnal	['stop sig'nal]

sidelights	qabarit işıqları	[gaba'rit iʃıgla'rı]
hazard lights	qəza işıq siqnalı	[gæ'za i'ʃıg signa'lı]
fog lights	dumana qarşı faralar	[duma'na gar'ʃı 'faralar]
turn indicator	dönmə işığı	[døn'mæ iʃıɣ'ı]
reversing light	arxaya hərəkət	[arha'ja hæræ'kæt]

176. Cars. Passenger compartment

car inside	salon	[sa'lon]
leather (as adj)	dəri	[dæ'ri]
velour (as adj)	velyur	[vel'yr]
upholstery	üz	[yz]

| instrument (gage) | cihaz | [dʒi'haz] |
| dashboard | cizaz lövhəciyi | [dʒi'haz løvhædʒi'jı] |

| speedometer | spidometr | [spi'dometr] |
| needle (pointer) | ox işarəsi | ['oh iʃaræ'si] |

mileometer	sayğac	[sajɣ'adʒ]
indicator (sensor)	göstərici	[gøsteri'dʒi]
level	səviyyə	[sævi'j:ə]
warning light	lampa	[lam'pa]

steering wheel	sükan	[sy'kan]
horn	siqnal	[sig'nal]
button	düymə	[dyj'mæ]
switch	sürətləri dəyişən mexanizm	[syrætlæ'ri dæi'ʃæn meha'nizm]

seat	oturacaq	[otura'dʒag]
seat back	söykənəcək	[søjkænæ'dʒæk]
headrest	başaltı	[baʃal'tı]
seat belt	təhlükəsizlik kəməri	[tæhlykæsiz'lik kæmæ'ri]
to fasten the belt	kəməri bağlamaq	[kæmæ'ri baɣla'mag]
adjustment (of seats)	sazlama	[sazla'ma]

| airbag | təhlükəsizlik yastığı | [tæhlykæsiz'lik jastıɣ'ı] |
| air-conditioner | kondisioner | [kondisio'ner] |

radio	radio	['radio]
CD player	CD səsləndiricisi	[si'di sæslændiridʒi'si]
to turn on	qoşmaq	[goʃ'mag]
aerial	antenna	[an'teŋa]
glove box	qutu	[gu'tu]
ashtray	külqabı	['kyʎgabı]

177. Cars. Engine

engine	mühərrik	[myhær'rik]
motor	motor	[mo'tor]
diesel (as adj)	dizel	['dizel]
petrol (as adj)	benzin	[ben'zin]

engine volume	mühərriyin həcmi	[myhærri'jın hædʒ'mi]
power	güc	[gydʒ]
horsepower	at gücü	['at gy'dʒy]
piston	porşen	['porʃen]
cylinder	silindr	[si'lindr]
valve	qapaq	[ga'pag]

injector	injektor	[in'ʒektor]
generator	generator	[gene'rator]
carburettor	karbyurator	[karby'rator]
engine oil	motor yağı	[mo'tor jaɣ'ı]

radiator	radiator	[radi'ator]
coolant	soyuducu maye	[soydu'dʒu ma'je]
cooling fan	ventilyator	[venti'ʎator]
battery (accumulator)	akkumulyator	[akkumu'ʎator]

starter	starter düyməsi	['starter dyjmæ'si]
ignition	yanma	[jan'ma]
sparking plug	yanma şamı	[jan'ma ʃa'mı]

terminal (of battery)	klemma	['klemma]
positive terminal	plyus	['plys]
negative terminal	minus	['minus]
fuse	qoruyucu	[goruy'dʒu]

air filter	hava filtri	[ha'va filt'ri]
oil filter	yağ filtri	['jaɣ filt'ri]
fuel filter	yanacaq filtri	[jana'dʒag filt'ri]

178. Cars. Crash. Repair

car accident	qəza	[gæ'za]
road accident	yol qəzası	['jol gæza'sı]
to run into ...	toqquşmaq	[togguʃ'mag]
to have an accident	əzilmək	[æzil'mæk]
damage	xarab etmə	[ha'rab æt'mæ]
intact (adj)	salamat	[sala'mat]

to break down (vi)	qırılmaq	[gırıl'mag]
towrope	yedək ipi	[e'dæk i'pi]

puncture	deşilmə	[deʃil'mæ]
to have a puncture	buraxmaq	[burah'mag]
to pump up	doldurmaq	[doldur'mag]
pressure	təzyiq	[tæz'jıg]
to check (to examine)	yoxlamaq	[johla'mag]

repair	təmir	[tæ'mir]
auto repair shop	təmir emalatxanası	[tæ'mir æmalathana'sı]
spare part	ehtiyat hissəsi	[æhti'jat hissæ'si]
part	detal	[de'tal]

bolt	bolt	[bolt]
screw bolt	vint	[vint]
nut	qayka	[gaj'ka]
washer	şayba	['ʃajba]
bearing	podşipnik	[pod'ʃipnik]

tube	borucuq	[boru'dʒug]
gasket, washer	aralıq qat	[ara'lıg 'gat]
cable, wire	məftil	[mæf'til]

jack	domkrat	[domk'rat]
spanner	qayka açarı	[gaj'ka atʃa'rı]
hammer	çəkic	[tʃə'kidʒ]
pump	nasos	[na'sos]
screwdriver	vintaçan	[vinta'tʃan]

fire extinguisher	odsöndürən	[odsøndy'ræn]
warning triangle	Qəza üçbucağı nişanı	[gæ'za ytʃbudʒaɣ'ı niʃa'nı]

to stall (vi)	yatmaq	[jat'mag]
stalling	dayanma	[dajan'ma]
to be broken	qırılmaq	[gırıl'mag]

to overheat (vi)	həddindən artıq qızmaq	[hæddin'dæn ar'tıg gız'mag]
to be clogged up	yolu tutulmaq	[jo'lu tutul'mag]
to freeze up (pipes, etc.)	donmaq	[don'mag]
to burst (vi, ab. tube)	partlamaq	[partla'mag]

pressure	təzyiq	[tæz'jıg]
level	səviyyə	[sævi'j:ə]
slack (~ belt)	zəif	[zæ'if]

dent	batıq	[ba'tıg]
abnormal noise (motor)	səs	[sæs]
crack	çat	[ʧat]
scratch	cızıq	[dʒı'zıg]

179. Cars. Road

road	yol	[jol]
motorway	avtomobil magistralı	[avtomo'bil magistra'lı]
highway	şose	[ʃo'se]
direction (way)	istiqamət	[istiga'mæt]
distance	məsafə	[mæsa'fæ]

bridge	körpü	[kør'py]
car park	park yeri	['park e'ri]
square	meydan	[mej'dan]
road junction	qovşaq	[gov'ʃag]
tunnel	tunel	[tu'nel]

petrol station	yanacaq doldurma məntəqəsi	[jana'dʒag doldur'ma mæntægæ'si]
car park	avtomobil duracağı	[avtomo'bil duradʒaɣ'ı]
petrol pump	benzin kolonkası	[ben'zin kolonka'sı]
auto repair shop	maşın təmiri	[ma'ʃın tæmi'ri]
to fill up	yanacaq doldurmaq	[jana'dʒag doldur'mag]
fuel	yanacaq	[jana'dʒag]
jerrycan	kanistr	[ka'nistr]

asphalt	asfalt	[as'falt]
road markings	nişan vurma	[ni'ʃan vur'ma]
kerb	haşiyə	[haʃi'jə]
guardrail	hasarlama	[hasarla'ma]
ditch	küvet	[ky'vet]
roadside	yolun qırağı	[jo'lun gıraɣ'ı]
lamppost	dirək	[di'ræk]

to drive (a car)	sürmək	[syr'mæk]
to turn (~ to the left)	döndərmək	[døndær'mæk]
to make a U-turn	dönmək	[døn'mæk]
reverse	arxaya hərəkət	[arha'ja hæræ'kæt]
to honk (vi)	siqnal vermək	[sig'nal ver'mæk]

honk (sound)	səs siqnalı	['sæs signa'lı]
to get stuck	ilişib qalmaq	[ili'ʃib gal'mag]
to spin (in mud)	yerində fırlanmaq	[erin'dæ fırlan'mag]
to cut, to turn off	söndürmək	[søndyr'mæk]

speed	sürət	[sy'ræt]
to exceed the speed limit	sürəti aşmaq	[syræ'ti aʃ'mag]
to give a ticket	cərimə etmək	[dʒæri'mæ æt'mæk]
traffic lights	svetofor	[sveto'for]
driving licence	sürücülük vəsiqəsi	[syrydʒy'lyk væsigæ'si]

level crossing	keçid	[ke'ʧid]
crossroads	dörd yol ağzı	['dørd 'jol aɣ'zı]
zebra crossing	piyadalar üçün keçid	[pijada'lar y'ʧun ke'ʧid]
bend, curve	dönmə yeri	[døn'mæ e'ri]
pedestrian precinct	piyadalar zonası	[pijada'lar 'zonası]

180. Signs

Highway Code	yol hərəkət qaydaları	['jol hæræ'kæt gajdala'rı]
traffic sign	işarə	[iʃa'ræ]
overtaking	ötüb keçmə	[ø'tyb keʧ'mæ]
curve	dönmə	[døn'mæ]
U-turn	döndərmə	[døndær'mæ]
roundabout	dairəvi hərəkət	[dairæ'vi hæræ'kæt]

No entry	giriş qadağandır	[gi'riʃ gadaɣ'andır]
All vehicles prohibited	hərəkət qadağandır	[hæræ'kæt gadaɣ'andır]
No overtaking	ötüb keçmə qadağandır	[ø'tyb keʧ'mæ gadaɣ'andır]
No parking	durmaq qadağandır	[dur'mag gadaɣ'andır]
No stopping	dayanmaq qadağandır	[dajan'mag gadaɣ'andır]

dangerous curve	sərt dönmə	['sært døn'mæ]
steep descent	sərt eniş	['sært æ'niʃ]
one-way traffic	birtərəfli yol	[birtæræf'li 'jol]
zebra crossing	piyadalar üçün keçid	[pijada'lar y'ʧun ke'ʧid]
slippery road	sürüşkən yol	[syryʃ'kæn 'jol]
GIVE WAY	başqasına yol ver	[baʃgası'na 'jol 'ver]

PEOPLE. LIFE EVENTS

Life events

181. Holidays. Event

celebration, holiday	bayram	[baj'ram]
national day	milli bayram	[mil'li baj'ram]
public holiday	bayram günü	[baj'ram gy'ny]
to fete (celebrate)	bayram etmək	[baj'ram æt'mæk]
event (happening)	hadisə	[hadi'sæ]
event (organized activity)	tədbir	[tæd'bir]
banquet (party)	banket	[ba'ŋket]
reception (formal party)	ziyafət	[zija'fæt]
feast	böyük qonaqlıq	[bø'yk gonag'lıg]
anniversary	ildönümü	[ildøny'my]
jubilee	yubiley	[ybi'lej]
to celebrate (vt)	qeyd etmək	['gejd æt'mæk]
New Year	Yeni il	[e'ni 'il]
Happy New Year!	Yeni iliniz mübarək!	[e'ni ili'niz myba'ræk]
Christmas	Milad	[mi'lad]
Merry Christmas!	Milad bayramınız şən keçsin!	[mi'lad bajramı'nız 'ʃæn ketʃ'sin]
Christmas tree	Yeni il yolkası	[e'ni 'il jolka'sı]
fireworks	salam atəşi	[sa'lam atæ'ʃi]
wedding	toy	[toj]
groom	bəy	[bæj]
bride	nişanlı	[niʃan'lı]
to invite (vt)	dəvət etmək	[dæ'væt æt'mæk]
invitation card	dəvətnamə	[dævætna'mæ]
guest	qonaq	[go'nag]
to visit (go to see)	qonaq getmək	[go'nag get'mæk]
to greet the guests	qonaq qarşılamaq	[go'nag garʃıla'mag]
gift, present	hədiyyə	[hædi'j:ə]
to give (sth as present)	hədiyyə vermək	[hædi'j:ə ver'mæk]
to receive gifts	hədiyyə almaq	[hædi'j:ə al'mag]
bouquet (of flowers)	gül dəstəsi	['gyʎ dæstæ'si]
greetings (New Year ~)	təbrik	[tæb'rik]
to congratulate (vt)	təbrik etmək	[tæb'rik æt'mæk]
greetings card	təbrik açıqçası	[tæb'rik atʃıgtʃa'sı]

| to send a postcard | açıqça göndərmək | [atʃɪg'tʃa gøndær'mæk] |
| to get a postcard | açıqça almaq | [atʃɪg'tʃa al'mag] |

toast	tost	[tost]
to offer (a drink, etc.)	qonaq etmək	[go'nag æt'mæk]
champagne	şampan şərabı	[ʃam'pan ʃæra'bı]

to have fun	şənlənmək	[ʃænlæn'mæk]
fun, merriment	şənlik	[ʃæn'lik]
joy (emotion)	sevinc	[se'vindʒ]

| dance | rəqs | [rægs] |
| to dance (vi, vt) | rəqs etmək | ['rægs æt'mæk] |

| waltz | vals | [vals] |
| tango | tanqo | ['taŋo] |

182. Funerals. Burial

cemetery	qəbristanlıq	[gæbristan'lıg]
grave, tomb	qəbir	[gæ'bir]
gravestone	qəbir daşı	[gæ'bir da'ʃı]
fence	hasar	[ha'sar]
chapel	kiçik kilsə	[ki'tʃik kil'sæ]

death	ölüm	[ø'lym]
to die (vi)	ölmək	[øl'mæk]
the deceased	ölü	[ø'ly]
mourning	matəm	[ma'tæm]

to bury (vt)	dəfn etmək	['dæfn æt'mæk]
undertakers	dəfn etmə bürosu	['dæfn æt'mæ byro'su]
funeral	dəfn etmə mərasimi	['dæfn æt'mæ mærasi'mi]

wreath	əklil	[æk'lil]
coffin	tabut	[ta'but]
hearse	cənazə arabası	[dʒæna'zæ araba'sı]
shroud	kəfən	[kæ'fæn]

| cremation urn | urna | ['urna] |
| crematorium | meyit yandırılan bina | [me'it jandırı'lan bi'na] |

obituary	nekroloq	[nekro'log]
to cry (weep)	ağlamaq	[ayla'mag]
to sob (vi)	hönkür-hönkür ağlamaq	[hø'ŋkyr hø'ŋkyr ayla'mag]

183. War. Soldiers

platoon	vzvod	[vzvod]
company	rota	['rota]
regiment	alay	[a'laj]
army	ordu	[or'du]

division	diviziya	[di'vizija]
detachment	dəstə	[dæs'tæ]
host (army)	qoşun	[go'ʃun]

| soldier | əsgər | [æs'gær] |
| officer | zabit | [za'bit] |

private	sıravi	[sıra'vi]
sergeant	çavuş	[ʧa'vuʃ]
lieutenant	leytenant	[lejte'nant]
captain	kapitan	[kapi'tan]
major	mayor	[ma'jor]
colonel	polkovnik	[pol'kovnik]
general	general	[gene'ral]

sailor	dənizçi	[dæniz'ʧi]
captain	kapitan	[kapi'tan]
boatswain	bosman	['bosman]

artilleryman	topçu	[top'ʧu]
paratrooper	desantçı	[desan'ʧı]
pilot	təyyarəçi	[tæj:aræ'ʧi]
navigator	şturman	['ʃturman]
mechanic	mexanik	[me'hanik]

pioneer (sapper)	istehkamçı	[istehkam'ʧı]
parachutist	paraşütçü	[paraʃy'ʧy]
scout	kəşfiyyatçı	[kæʃfij:a'ʧı]
sniper	snayper	['snajper]
patrol (group)	patrul	[pat'rul]
to patrol (vt)	patrul çəkmək	[pat'rul ʧæk'mæk]
sentry, guard	keşikçi	[keʃik'ʧi]

warrior	döyüşçü	[døyʃ'ʧu]
hero	qəhrəman	[gæhræ'man]
heroine	qəhrəman qadın	[gæhræ'man ga'dın]
patriot	vətənpərvər	[vætænpær'vær]

traitor	satqın	[sat'gın]
deserter	fərari	[færa'ri]
to desert (vi)	fərarilik etmək	[færari'lik æt'mæk]

mercenary	muzdla tutulan əsgər	['muzdla tutu'lan æs'gær]
recruit	yeni əsgər	[e'ni æs'gær]
volunteer	könüllü	[kønyl'ly]

dead	öldürülən	[øldyry'læn]
wounded (n)	yaralı	[jara'lı]
prisoner of war	əsir	[æ'sir]

184. War. Military actions. Part 1

| war | müharibə | [myhari'bæ] |
| to be at war | müharibə etmək | [myhari'bæ æt'mæk] |

civil war	vətəndaş müharibəsi	[vætæn'daʃ myharibæ'si]
treacherously (adv)	xaincəsinə	[ha'indʒæsinæ]
declaration of war	elan edilmə	[æ'lan ædil'mæ]
to declare (~ war)	elan etmək	[æ'lan æt'mæk]
aggression	təcavüz	[tædʒa'vyz]
to attack (invade)	hücum etmək	[hy'dʒum æt'mæk]

to invade (vt)	işğal etmək	[iʃɣ'al æt'mæk]
invader	işğalçı	[iʃɣal'tʃı]
conqueror	istilaçı	[istila'tʃı]

defence	müdafiyə	[mydafi'jə]
to defend (a country, etc.)	müdafiyə etmək	[mydafi'jə æt'mæk]
to defend oneself	müdafiyə olunmaq	[mydafi'jə olun'mag]

enemy	düşmən	[dyʃ'mæn]
foe, adversary	eleyhdar	[ælejh'dar]
enemy (as adj)	düşmən	[dyʃ'mæn]

| strategy | strategiya | [stra'tegija] |
| tactics | taktika | ['taktika] |

order	əmr	[æmr]
command (order)	əmr	[æmr]
to order (vt)	əmr etmək	['æmr æt'mæk]
mission	tapşırıq	[tapʃı'rıg]
secret (adj)	məxfi	[mæh'fi]

| battle | vuruşma | [vuruʃ'ma] |
| combat | döyüş | [dø'yʃ] |

attack	hücum	[hy'dʒum]
storming (assault)	hücum	[hy'dʒum]
to storm (vt)	hücum etmək	[hy'dʒum æt'mæk]
siege (to be under ~)	mühasirə	[myhasi'ræ]

| offensive (n) | hücum | [hy'dʒum] |
| to go on the offensive | hücum etmək | [hy'dʒum æt'mæk] |

| retreat | geri çəkilmə | [ge'ri tʃəkil'mæ] |
| to retreat (vi) | geri çəkilmək | [ge'ri tʃəkil'mæk] |

| encirclement | mühasirə | [myhasi'ræ] |
| to encircle (vt) | mühasirəyə almaq | [myhasiræ'jə al'mag] |

bombing (by aircraft)	bombalama	[bombala'ma]
to drop a bomb	bomba atmaq	[bom'ba at'mag]
to bomb (vt)	bombalamaq	[bombala'mag]
explosion	partlayış	[partla'jıʃ]

shot	atəş	[a'tæʃ]
to fire a shot	güllə atmaq	[gyl'læ at'mag]
shooting	atəş	[a'tæʃ]

| to take aim (at …) | nişan almaq | [ni'ʃan al'mag] |
| to point (a gun) | tuşlamaq | [tuʃla'mag] |

to hit (the target)	sərrast vurmaq	[sær'rast vur'mag]
to sink (~ a ship)	batırmaq	[batır'mag]
hole (in a ship)	deşik	[de'ʃik]
to founder, to sink (vi)	batmaq	[bat'mag]

front (at war)	cəbhə	[dʒæb'hæ]
rear (homefront)	cəbhə arxası	[dʒæb'hæ arha'sı]
evacuation	təxliyə	[tæhli'jə]
to evacuate (vt)	təxliyə etmək	[tæhli'jə æt'mæk]

trench	səngər	[sæ'ŋær]
barbed wire	tikanlı məftil	[tik'an'lı mæf'til]
barrier (anti tank ~)	çəpərləmə	[ʧəpærlæ'mæ]
watchtower	qüllə	[gyl'læ]

hospital	hospital	['hospital]
to wound (vt)	yaralamaq	[jarala'mag]
wound	yara	[ja'ra]
wounded (n)	yaralı	[jara'lı]
to be injured	yara almaq	[ja'ra al'mag]
serious (wound)	ağır	[aɣ'ır]

185. War. Military actions. Part 2

captivity	əsirlik	[æsir'lik]
to take captive	əsir almaq	[æ'sir al'mag]
to be in captivity	əsirlikdə olmaq	[æsirlik'dæ ol'mag]
to be taken prisoner	əsir düşmək	[æ'sir dyʃ'mæk]

concentration camp	həbs düşərgəsi	['hæbs dyʃærgæ'si]
prisoner of war	əsir	[æ'sir]
to escape (vi)	qaçmaq	[gaʧ'mag]

to betray (vt)	satmaq	[sat'mag]
betrayer	satqın	[sat'gın]
betrayal	satqınlıq	[satgın'lıg]

| to execute (shoot) | güllələmək | [gyllælæ'mæk] |
| execution (shooting) | güllə cəzası | [gyl'læ dʒæza'sı] |

equipment (uniform, etc.)	rəsmi geyim	[ræs'mi ge'jım]
shoulder board	poqon	[po'gon]
gas mask	əleyhqaz	[ælejh'gaz]

radio transmitter	ratsiya	['ratsija]
cipher, code	şifr	[ʃifr]
conspiracy	konspirasiya	[konspi'rasija]
password	parol	[pa'rol]

land mine	mina	['mina]
to mine (road, etc.)	minalamaq	['minalamag]
minefield	minalanmış sahə	['minalanmıʃ sa'hæ]
air-raid warning	hava həyacanı	[ha'va hæjadʒa'nı]
alarm (warning)	həyacan	[hæja'dʒan]

signal	signal	[sig'nal]
signal flare	signal raketi	[sig'nal rake'ti]

headquarters	qərargah	[gærar'g'ah]
reconnaissance	kəsfiyyat	[kæʃfi'j:at]
situation	şərait	[ʃæra'it]
report	raport	['raport]
ambush	pusqu	[pus'gu]
reinforcement (of army)	yardım	[jar'dım]

target	hədəf	[hæ'dæf]
training area	poliqon	[poli'gon]
military exercise	manevrlər	[ma'nevrlær]

panic	panika	['panika]
devastation	xarabalıq	[haraba'lıg]
destruction, ruins	dağıntı	[dayın'tı]
to destroy (vt)	dağıtmaq	[dayıt'mag]

to survive (vi, vt)	sağ qalmaq	['say gal'mag]
to disarm (vt)	tərksilah etmək	[tærksi'lah æt'mæk]
to handle (~ a gun)	işlətmək	[iʃlæt'mæk]

Attention!	Farağat!	[faray'at]
At ease!	Azad!	[a'zad]

feat (of courage)	hünər	[hy'nær]
oath (vow)	and	[and]
to swear (an oath)	and içmək	['and itʃ'mæk]

decoration (medal, etc.)	mükafat	[myka'fat]
to award (give medal to)	təltif etmək	[tæl'tif æt'mæk]
medal	medal	[me'dal]
order (e.g. ~ of Merit)	orden	['orden]

victory	qələbə	[gælæ'bæ]
defeat	məğlubiyyət	[mæylubi'j:ət]
armistice	atəşkəs	[atæʃ'kæs]

banner (standard)	bayraq	[baj'rag]
glory (honour, fame)	şərəf	[ʃæ'ræf]
parade	parad	[pa'rad]
to march (on parade)	addımlamaq	[addımla'mag]

186. Weapons

weapons	silah	[si'lah]
firearm	odlu silah	[od'lu si'lah]
cold weapons (knives, etc.)	soyuq silah	[so'yg si'lah]

chemical weapons	kimyəvi silah	[kimjə'vi si'lah]
nuclear (adj)	nüvə	[ny'væ]
nuclear weapons	nüvə silahı	[ny'væ sila'hı]
bomb	bomba	[bom'ba]

atomic bomb	atom bombası	['atom bomba'sı]
pistol (gun)	tapança	[tapan'tʃa]
rifle	tüfeng	[ty'fæŋ]
submachine gun	avtomat	[avto'mat]
machine gun	pulemyot	[pulem'jot]

muzzle	ağız	[aɣ'ız]
barrel	lülə	[ly'læ]
calibre	kalibr	[ka'libr]

trigger	çaxmaq	[tʃah'mag]
sight (aiming device)	nişangah	[niʃa'ɲ̩ah]
magazine	sandıq	[san'dıg]
butt (of rifle)	qundaq	[gun'dag]

| hand grenade | qumbara | [gumba'ra] |
| explosive | partlayıcı maddə | [partlajı'dʒı mad'dæ] |

bullet	güllə	[gyl'læ]
cartridge	patron	[pat'ron]
charge	güllə	[gyl'læ]
ammunition	döyüş sursatı	[dø'yʃ sursa'tı]

bomber (aircraft)	bombardmançı təyyarə	[bombardman'tʃı tæj:a'ræ]
fighter	qırıcı təyyarə	[gırı'dʒı tæj:a'ræ]
helicopter	vertolyot	[vertol'jot]

anti-aircraft gun	zenit topu	[ze'nit to'pu]
tank	tank	[taŋk]
tank gun	top	[top]

| artillery | top | [top] |
| to lay (a gun) | tuşlamaq | [tuʃla'mag] |

shell (projectile)	mərmi	[mær'mi]
mortar bomb	mina	['mina]
mortar	minaatan	['mina:tan]
splinter (of shell)	qəlpə	[gæl'pæ]

submarine	sualtı qayıq	[sual'tı ga'jıg]
torpedo	torpeda	[tor'peda]
missile	raket	[ra'ket]

to load (gun)	doldurmaq	[doldur'mag]
to shoot (vi)	atəş açmaq	[a'tæʃ atʃ'mag]
to take aim (at ...)	nişan almaq	[ni'ʃan al'mag]
bayonet	süngü	[sy'ŋy]

epee	qılınc	[gı'lındʒ]
sabre (e.g. cavalry ~)	qılınc	[gı'lındʒ]
spear (weapon)	nizə	[ni'zæ]

bow	yay	[jaj]
arrow	ox	[oh]
musket	muşket	[muʃ'ket]
crossbow	arbalet	[arba'let]

187. Ancient people

primitive (prehistoric)	ibtidai	[ibtida'i]
prehistoric (adj)	tarixdən əvvəlki	[tarih'dæn ævvæl'ki]
ancient (~ civilization)	qədim	[gæ'dim]
Stone Age	Daş dövrü	['daʃ døv'ry]
Bronze Age	Tunc dövrü	['tundʒ døv'ry]
Ice Age	buz dövrü	['buz døv'ry]
tribe	tayfa	[taj'fa]
cannibal	adamyeyən	[adamje'jən]
hunter	ovçu	[ov'ʧu]
to hunt (vi, vt)	ova çıxmaq	[o'va ʧıh'mag]
mammoth	mamont	['mamont]
cave	mağara	[maɣa'ra]
fire	od	[od]
campfire	tonqal	[to'ŋal]
rock painting	qayaüstü rəsmlər	[gajays'ty ræsm'lær]
tool (e.g. stone axe)	iş aləti	['iʃ alæ'ti]
spear	nizə	[ni'zæ]
stone axe	daş baltası	['daʃ balta'sı]
to be at war	müharibə etmək	[myhari'bæ æt'mæk]
to domesticate (vt)	əhliləşdirmək	[æhlilæʃdir'mæk]
idol	büt	[byt]
to worship (vt)	pərəstiş etmək	[pæræs'tiʃ æt'mæk]
superstition	xurafat	[hura'fat]
evolution	təkamül	[tæka'myl]
development	inkişaf	[iŋki'ʃaf]
disappearance	yox olma	['joh ol'ma]
to adapt oneself	uyğunlaşmaq	[ujɣunlaʃ'mag]
archaeology	arxeoloqiya	[arheo'logija]
archaeologist	arxeoloq	[arhe'olog]
archaeological (adj)	arxeoloji	[arheolo'ʒi]
excavation site	qazıntı	[gazın'tı]
excavations	qazıntılar	[gazıntı'lar]
find (object)	tapıntı	[tapın'tı]
fragment	parça	[par'ʧa]

188. Middle Ages

people (population)	xalq	[halg]
peoples	xalqlar	[halg'lar]
tribe	tayfa	[taj'fa]
tribes	tayfalar	[tajfa'lar]
barbarians	barbarlar	[barbar'lar]
Gauls	qallar	[gal'lar]

Goths	qotlar	[got'lar]
Slavs	slavyanlar	[slav'an'lar]
Vikings	vikinqlər	['vikiŋlær]
Romans	romalılar	['romalılar]
Roman (adj)	Roma	['roma]
Byzantines	bizanslılar	[bizanslı'lar]
Byzantium	Bizans	[bi'zans]
Byzantine (adj)	Bizans	[bi'zans]
emperor	imperator	[impe'rator]
leader, chief	rəhbər	[ræh'bær]
powerful (~ king)	qüdrətli	[gydræt'li]
king	kral	[kral]
ruler (sovereign)	hökmdar	[høkm'dar]
knight	rıtsar	['rıtsar]
knightly (adj)	rıtsar	['rıtsar]
feudal lord	mülkədar	[myʎkæ'dar]
feudal (adj)	mülkədar	[myʎkæ'dar]
vassal	vassal	[vas'sal]
duke	hersoq	['hersog]
earl	qraf	[graf]
baron	baron	[ba'ron]
bishop	yepiskop	[e'piskop]
armour	yaraq-əsləhə	[ja'rag æslæ'hæ]
shield	qalxan	[gal'han]
sword	qılınc	[gı'lındʒ]
visor	dəbilqə üzlüyü	[dæbil'gæ yzly'y]
chain armour	dəmir geyim	[dæ'mir ge'jım]
crusade	xaç yürüşü	['hatʃ yry'ʃy]
crusader	əhl-səlib	['æhl sæ'lib]
territory	ərazi	[æra'zi]
to attack (invade)	hücum etmək	[hy'dʒum æt'mæk]
to conquer (vt)	istila etmək	[isti'la æt'mæk]
to occupy (invade)	işğal etmək	[iʃɣ'al æt'mæk]
siege (to be under ~)	mühasirə	[myhasi'ræ]
besieged (adj)	mühasirə olunmuş	[myhasi'ræ olun'muʃ]
to besiege (vt)	mühasirə etmək	[myhasi'ræ æt'mæk]
inquisition	inkvizisiya	[iŋkvi'zisija]
inquisitor	inkvizitor	[iŋkvi'zitor]
torture	işgəncə	[iʃgæn'dʒæ]
cruel (adj)	qəddar	[gæd'dar]
heretic	kafir	[ka'fir]
heresy	küfr	[kyfr]
seafaring	gəmiçilik	[gæmitʃi'lik]
pirate	dəniz qulduru	[dæ'niz guldu'ru]
piracy	dəniz quldurluğu	[dæ'niz guldurluɣ'u]

boarding (attack)	**abordaj**	[abor'daʒ]
loot, booty	**qənimət**	[gæni'mæt]
treasures	**xəzinə**	[hæzi'næ]

discovery	**kəşf etmə**	['kæʃf æt'mæ]
to discover (new land, etc.)	**kəşf etmək**	['kæʃf æt'mæk]
expedition	**ekspedisiya**	[ækspe'disija]

musketeer	**muşketyor**	[muʃket'jor]
cardinal	**kardinal**	[kardi'nal]
heraldry	**heraldika**	[he'raldika]
heraldic (adj)	**heraldik**	[heral'dik]

189. Leader. Chief. Authorities

king	**kral**	[kral]
queen	**kraliçə**	[kra'litʃə]
royal (adj)	**kral**	[kral]
kingdom	**krallıq**	[kral'lıg]

prince	**şahzadə**	[ʃahza'dæ]
princess	**şahzadə xanım**	[ʃahza'dæ ha'nım]

president	**prezident**	[prezi'dent]
vice-president	**vitse-prezident**	['vitse prezi'dent]
senator	**senator**	[se'nator]

monarch	**padşah**	[pad'ʃah]
ruler (sovereign)	**hökmdar**	[høkm'dar]
dictator	**diktator**	[dik'tator]
tyrant	**zülmkar**	[zyʌm'kar]
magnate	**maqnat**	[mag'nat]

director	**direktor**	[di'rektor]
chief	**rəis**	[ræ'is]
manager (director)	**idarə başçısı**	[ida'ræ baʃtʃı'sı]
boss	**boss**	[boss]
owner	**sahib**	[sa'hib]

head (~ of delegation)	**başçı**	[baʃ'tʃı]
authorities	**hakimiyyət**	[hakimi'j:ət]
superiors	**rəhbərlik**	[ræhbær'lik]

governor	**qubernator**	[guber'nator]
consul	**konsul**	['konsul]
diplomat	**diplomat**	[diplo'mat]
mayor	**şəhər icra hakimiyyətinin başçısı**	[ʃæ'hær idʒ'ra hakimij:əti'nin baʃtʃı'sı]
sheriff	**şerif**	[ʃe'rif]

emperor	**imperator**	[impe'rator]
tsar, czar	**çar**	[tʃar]
Pharaoh	**firon**	[fi'ron]
khan	**xan**	[han]

190. Road. Way. Directions

road	yol	[jol]
way (direction)	yol	[jol]
highway	şose	[ʃo'se]
motorway	avtomobil maqistralı	[avtomo'bil magistra'lı]
trunk road	milli yol	[mil'li 'jol]
main road	əsas yol	[æ'sas 'jol]
dirt road	kəndarası yol	[kændara'sı 'jol]
pathway	cığır	[dʒıɣ'ır]
footpath	cığır	[dʒıɣ'ır]
Where?	Harada?	['harada]
Where (to)?	Haraya?	['haraja]
Where … from?	Haradan?	['haradan]
direction (way)	istiqamət	[istiga'mæt]
to point (~ the way)	göstərmək	[gøstær'mæk]
to the left	sola	[so'la]
to the right	sağa	[saɣ'a]
straight ahead (adv)	irəli	[iræ'li]
back (e.g. to turn ~)	geri	[ge'ri]
bend, curve	dönmə yeri	[døn'mæ e'ri]
to turn (~ to the left)	döndərmək	[døndær'mæk]
to make a U-turn	dönmək	[døn'mæk]
to be visible	görünmək	[gøryn'mæk]
to appear (come into view)	görünmək	[gøryn'mæk]
stop, halt (in journey)	dayanma	[dajan'ma]
to rest, to halt (vi)	dincəlmək	[dindʒæl'mæk]
rest (pause)	dincəlmə	[dindʒæl'mæ]
to lose one's way	yolu azmaq	[jo'lu az'mag]
to lead to … (ab. road)	aparmaq	[apar'mag]
to arrive at …	…çıxmaq	[tʃıh'mag]
stretch (of road)	parça	[par'tʃa]
asphalt	asfalt	[as'falt]
kerb	haşiyə	[haʃi'jə]
ditch	arx	[arh]
manhole	lyuk	[lyk]
roadside	yolun qırağı	[jo'lun gıraɣ'ı]
pit, pothole	çuxur	[tʃu'hur]
to go (on foot)	getmək	[get'mæk]
to overtake (vt)	ötüb keçmək	[ø'tyb ketʃ'mæk]
step (footstep)	addım	[ad'dım]
on foot (adv)	piyada	[pija'da]

171

to block (road)	kəsmək	[kæs'mæk]
boom barrier	şlaqbaum	[ʃlag'baum]
dead end	dalan	[da'lan]

191. Breaking the law. Criminals. Part 1

bandit	quldur	[gul'dur]
crime	cinayət	[dʒina'jət]
criminal (person)	cinayətkar	[dʒinajət'kar]

thief	oğru	[oɣ'ru]
to steal (vi, vt)	oğurlamaq	[oɣurla'mag]
stealing, theft	oğurluq	[oɣur'lug]

to kidnap (vt)	qaçırtmaq	[gatʃırt'mag]
kidnapping	qaçırtma	[gatʃırt'ma]
kidnapper	adam oğrusu	[a'dam oɣru'su]

| ransom | fidiyə | [fidi'ja] |
| to demand ransom | fidiyə tələb etmək | [fidi'ja tæ'læb æt'mæk] |

| to rob (vt) | adam soymaq | [a'dam soj'mag] |
| robber | soyğunçu | [sojɣun'tʃu] |

to extort (vt)	zorla pul qoparmaq	['zorla 'pul gopar'mag]
extortionist	zorla pul qoparan	['zorla 'pul gopa'ran]
extortion	zorla pul qoparma	['zorla 'pul gopar'ma]

to murder, to kill	öldürmək	[øldyr'mæk]
murder	qətl	[gætl]
murderer	qatil	[ga'til]

gunshot	atəş	[a'tæʃ]
to fire a shot	güllə atmaq	[gyl'læ at'mag]
to shoot down	güllə ilə vurmaq	[gyl'læ i'læ vur'mag]
to shoot (vi)	atəş açmaq	[a'tæʃ atʃ'mag]
shooting	atəş	[a'tæʃ]

incident (fight, etc.)	hadisə	[hadi'sæ]
fight, brawl	dava-dalaş	[da'va da'laʃ]
victim	qurban	[gur'ban]

to damage (vt)	xarab etmək	[ha'rab æt'mæk]
damage	ziyan	[zi'jan]
dead body	meyit	[me'it]
grave (~ crime)	ağır	[aɣ'ır]

to attack (vt)	hücum etmək	[hy'dʒum æt'mæk]
to beat (dog, person)	vurmaq	[vur'mag]
to beat up	döymək	[døj'mæk]
to take (snatch)	əlindən almaq	[ælin'dæn al'mag]
to stab to death	bıçaqlamaq	[bıtʃagla'mag]
to maim (vt)	şikəst etmək	[ʃi'kæst æt'mæk]
to wound (vt)	yaralamaq	[jarala'mag]

blackmail	şantaj	[ʃan'taʒ]
to blackmail (vt)	şantaj etmək	[ʃan'taʒ æt'mæk]
blackmailer	şantajçı	[ʃantaʒ'tʃı]

protection racket	reket	['reket]
racketeer	reketçi	['reketʃi]
gangster	qanqster	['gaŋster]
mafia	mafiya	['mafija]

pickpocket	cibgir	[dʒib'gir]
burglar	ev yaran	['æv ja'ran]
smuggling	qaçaqçılıq	[gatʃagtʃı'lıg]
smuggler	qaçaqçı	[gatʃag'tʃı]

forgery	saxtalaşdırma	[sahtalaʃdır'ma]
to forge (counterfeit)	saxtalaşdırmaq	[sahtalaʃdır'mag]
fake (forged)	saxta	[sah'ta]

192. Breaking the law. Criminals. Part 2

rape	zorlama	[zorla'ma]
to rape (vt)	zorlamaq	[zorla'mag]
rapist	qadın zorlayan	[ga'dın zorla'jan]
maniac	manyak	[ma'njak]

prostitute (fem.)	fahişə	[fahi'ʃæ]
prostitution	fahişəlik	[fahiʃæ'lik]
pimp	qadın alverçisi	[ga'dın alvertʃi'si]

| drug addict | narkoman | [narko'man] |
| drug dealer | narkotik alverçisi | [narkotik alvertʃisi] |

to blow up (bomb)	partlatmaq	[partlat'mag]
explosion	partlayış	[partla'jıʃ]
to set fire	yandırmaq	[jandır'mag]
incendiary (arsonist)	qəsdən yandıran	['gæsdæn jandı'ran]

terrorism	terrorizm	[terro'rizm]
terrorist	terrorçu	[terror'tʃu]
hostage	girov götürulən adam	[gi'rov gøtyry'læn a'dam]

to swindle (vt)	yalan satmaq	[ja'lan sat'mag]
swindle	yalan	[ja'lan]
swindler	fırıldaqçı	[fırıldag'tʃı]

to bribe (vt)	pulla ələ almaq	['pulla æ'læ al'mag]
bribery	pulla ələ alma	['pulla æ'læ al'ma]
bribe	rüşvət	[ryʃ'væt]

poison	zəhər	[zæ'hær]
to poison (vt)	zəhərləmək	[zæhærlæ'mæk]
to poison oneself	özünü zəhərləmək	[øzy'ny zæhærlæ'mæk]
suicide (act)	intihar	[inti'har]
suicide (person)	intihar edən adam	[inti'har æ'dæn a'dam]

to threaten (vt)	hədələmək	[hædælæ'mæk]
threat	hədə	[hæ'dæ]
to make an attempt	birinin canına qəsd etmək	[biri'nin dʒanı'na 'gæsd æt'mæk]
attempt (attack)	qəsd etmə	['gæsd æt'mæ]

| to steal (a car) | qaçırmaq | [gatʃır'mag] |
| to hijack (a plane) | qaçırmaq | [gatʃır'mag] |

| revenge | intiqam | [inti'gam] |
| to avenge (vt) | intiqam almaq | [inti'gam al'mag] |

to torture (vt)	işgəncə vermək	[iʃgæn'dʒæ ver'mæk]
torture	işgəncə	[iʃgæn'dʒæ]
to torment (vt)	əzab vermək	[æ'zab ver'mæk]

pirate	dəniz qulduru	[dæ'niz guldu'ru]
hooligan	xuliqan	[huli'gan]
armed (adj)	silahlı	[silah'lı]
violence	zorakılıq	[zorakı'lıg]

| spying (n) | casusluq | [dʒasus'lug] |
| to spy (vi) | casusluq etmək | [dʒasus'lug æt'mæk] |

193. Police. Law. Part 1

| justice | ədalət | [æda'læt] |
| court (court room) | məhkəmə | [mæhkæ'mæ] |

judge	hakim	[ha'kim]
jurors	prisyajnı içlasçıları	[pris'jaʒnı idʒlastʃıla'rı]
jury trial	prisyajnılar məhkəməsi	[pris'jaʒnılar mæhkæmæ'si]
to judge (vt)	mühakimə etmək	[myhaki'mæ æt'mæk]

lawyer, barrister	vəkil	[væ'kil]
accused	müqəssir	[mygæs'sir]
dock	müqəssirlər kürsüsü	[mygæssir'lær kyrsy'sy]

| charge | ittiham | [itti'ham] |
| accused | müttəhim | [myttæ'him] |

| sentence | hökm | ['høkm] |
| to sentence (vt) | məhkum etmək | [mæh'kum æt'mæk] |

guilty (culprit)	təqsirkar	[tægsir'kar]
to punish (vt)	cəzalandırmaq	[dʒæzalandır'mag]
punishment	cəza	[dʒæ'za]

fine (penalty)	cərimə	[dʒæri'mæ]
life imprisonment	ömürlük həbs cəzası	[ømyr'lyk 'hæbs dʒæza'sı]
death penalty	ölüm cəzası	[ø'lym dʒæza'sı]
electric chair	elektrik stul	[æelekt'rik 'stul]
gallows	dar ağacı	['dar aɣa'dʒı]
to execute (vt)	edam etmək	[æ'dam æt'mæk]

execution	edam	[æ'dam]
prison, jail	həbsxana	[hæbsha'na]
cell	kamera	['kamera]

escort	mühafizə dəstəsi	[myhafi'zæ dæstæ'si]
prison officer	gözətçi	[gøzæ'tʃi]
prisoner	dustaq	[dus'tag]

| handcuffs | əl qandalları | ['æl gandalla'rı] |
| to handcuff (vt) | əl qandalları vurmaq | ['æl gandalla'rı vur'mag] |

prison break	qaçış	[ga'tʃıʃ]
to break out (vi)	qaçmaq	[gatʃ'mag]
to disappear (vi)	yox olmaq	['joh ol'mag]
to release (from prison)	azad etmək	[a'zad æt'mæk]
amnesty	əhf	[æhf]

police	polis	[po'lis]
policeman	polis	[po'lis]
police station	polis idarəsi	[po'lis idaræ'si]
truncheon	rezin dəyənək	[re'zin dæjə'næk]
loudspeaker	rupor	['rupor]

patrol car	patrul maşını	[pat'rul maʃı'nı]
siren	sirena	[si'rena]
to turn on the siren	sirenanı qoşmaq	[si'renanı goʃ'mag]
siren call	sirena səsi	[si'rena sæ'si]

crime scene	hadisə yeri	[hadi'sæ e'ri]
witness	şahid	[ʃa'hid]
freedom	azadlıq	[azad'lıg]
accomplice	cinayət ortağı	[dʒina'jət ortaɣ'ı]
to flee (vi)	gözdən itmək	[gøz'dæn it'mæk]
trace (to leave a ~)	iz	[iz]

194. Police. Law. Part 2

search (for a criminal)	axtarış	[ahta'rıʃ]
to look for ...	axtarmaq	[ahtar'mag]
suspicion	şübhə	[ʃyb'hæ]
suspicious (suspect)	şübhəli	[ʃybhæ'li]
to stop (cause to halt)	dayandırmaq	[dajandır'mag]
to detain (keep in custody)	saxlamaq	[sahla'mag]

case (lawsuit)	iş	[iʃ]
investigation	istintaq	[istin'tag]
detective	detektiv	[detek'tiv]
investigator	müstəntiq	[mystæn'tig]
version	versiya	['versija]

motive	əsas	[æ'sas]
interrogation	dindirilmə	[dindiril'mæ]
to interrogate (vt)	dindirmək	[dindir'mæk]
to question (vt)	sorğulamaq	[sorɣula'mag]

checking (police ~)	yoxlama	[johla'ma]
round-up	basqın	[bas'gın]
search (~ warrant)	axtarış	[ahta'rıʃ]
chase (pursuit)	təqib etmə	[tæ'gib æt'mæ]
to pursue, to chase	təqib etmək	[tæ'gib æt'mæk]
to track (a criminal)	izləmək	[izlæ'mæk]

arrest	həbs	[hæbs]
to arrest (sb)	həbs etmək	['hæbs æt'mæk]
to catch (thief, etc.)	tutmaq	[tut'mag]
capture	tutma	[tut'ma]

document	sənəd	[sæ'næd]
proof (evidence)	sübut	[sy'but]
to prove (vt)	sübut etmək	[sy'but æt'mæk]
footprint	iz	[iz]
fingerprints	barmaq izləri	[bar'mag izlæ'ri]
piece of evidence	dəlil	[dæ'lil]

alibi	alibi	['alibi]
innocent (not guilty)	günahsız	[gynah'sız]
injustice (unjust act)	ədalətsizlik	[ædalætsiz'lik]
unjust, unfair (adj)	ədalətsiz	[ædalæ'tsiz]

crime (adj)	kriminal	[krimi'nal]
to confiscate (vt)	müsadirə etmək	[mysadi'ræ æt'mæk]
drug (illegal substance)	narkotik maddə	[narko'tik mad'dæ]
weapon, gun	silah	[si'lah]
to disarm (vt)	tərksilah etmək	[tærksi'lah æt'mæk]
to order (command)	əmr etmək	['æmr æt'mæk]
to disappear (vi)	yox olmaq	['joh ol'mag]

law	qanun	[ga'nun]
legal (adj)	qanuni	[ganu'ni]
illegal (adj)	qanunsuz	[ganun'suz]

responsibility	məsuliyyət	[mæsuli'j:ət]
responsible (adj)	məsul	[mæ'sul]

NATURE

The Earth. Part 1

195. Outer space

cosmos	kosmos	['kosmos]
space (as adj)	kosmik	[kos'mik]
outer space	kosmik fəza	[kos'mik fæ'za]
world	dünya	[dyn'ja]
universe	kainat	[kai'nat]
galaxy	qalaktika	[ga'laktika]
star	ulduz	[ul'duz]
constellation	bürc	[byrʤ]
planet	planet	[pla'net]
satellite	peyk	[pejk]
meteorite	meteorit	[meteo'rit]
comet	kometa	[ko'meta]
asteroid	asteroid	[aste'roid]
orbit	orbita	[or'bita]
to rotate (vi)	fırlanmaq	[fırlan'maq]
atmosphere	atmosfer	[atmos'fer]
the Sun	Günəş	[gy'næʃ]
solar system	Günəş sistemi	[gy'næʃ siste'mi]
solar eclipse	günəşin tutulması	[gynæ'ʃin tutulma'sı]
the Earth	Yer	[er]
the Moon	Ay	[aj]
Mars	Mars	[mars]
Venus	Venera	[ve'nera]
Jupiter	Yupiter	[y'piter]
Saturn	Saturn	[sa'turn]
Mercury	Merkuri	[mer'kurij]
Uranus	Uran	[u'ran]
Neptune	Neptun	[nep'tun]
Pluto	Pluton	[plu'ton]
Milky Way	Ağ Yol	['aɣ 'jol]
Great Bear	Böyük ayı bürcü	[bø'yk a'jı byr'ʤy]
North Star	Qütb ulduzu	['gytb uldu'zu]
Martian	marslı	[mars'lı]
extraterrestrial	başqa planetdən gələn	[baʃ'ga planet'dæn gæ'læn]

| alien | gəlmə | [gæl'mæ] |
| flying saucer | uçan boşqab | [u'tʃan boʃgab] |

spaceship	kosmik gəmi	[kos'mik gæ'mi]
space station	orbital stansiya	[orbi'tal 'stansija]
blast-off	start	[start]

engine	mühərrik	[myhær'rik]
nozzle	ucluq	[udʒ'lug]
fuel	yanacaq	[jana'dʒag]

cockpit, flight deck	kabina	[ka'bina]
aerial	antenna	[an'teŋa]
porthole	illüminator	[illymi'nator]
solar battery	günəş batareyası	[gy'næʃ bata'rejası]
spacesuit	skafandr	[ska'fandr]

| weightlessness | çəkisizlik | [tʃəkisiz'lik] |
| oxygen | oksigen | [oksi'gen] |

| docking (in space) | uc-uca calama | ['udʒ u'dʒa dʒala'ma] |
| to dock (vi, vt) | uc-uca calamaq | ['udʒ u'dʒa dʒala'mag] |

observatory	observatoriya	[observa'torija]
telescope	teleskop	[teles'kop]
to observe (vt)	müşaidə etmək	[myʃai'dæ æt'mæk]
to explore (vt)	araşdırmaq	[araʃdɪr'mag]

196. The Earth

the Earth	Yer	[er]
globe (the Earth)	yer kürəsi	['er kyræ'si]
planet	planet	[pla'net]

atmosphere	atmosfer	[atmos'fer]
geography	coğrafiya	[dʒoɣ'rafija]
nature	təbiət	[tæbi'æt]

globe (table ~)	qlobus	['globus]
map	xəritə	[hæri'tæ]
atlas	atlas	['atlas]

| Europe | Avropa | [av'ropa] |
| Asia | Asiya | ['asija] |

| Africa | Afrika | ['afrika] |
| Australia | Avstraliya | [avst'ralija] |

America	Amerika	[a'merika]
North America	Şimali Amerika	[ʃima'li a'merika]
South America	Cənubi Amerika	[dʒænu'bi a'merika]

| Antarctica | Antarktida | [antark'tida] |
| the Arctic | Arktika | ['arktika] |

197. Cardinal directions

north	şimal	[ʃi'mal]
to the north	şimala	[ʃima'la]
in the north	şimalda	[ʃimal'da]
northern (adj)	şimali	[ʃima'li]

south	cənub	[dʒæ'nub]
to the south	cənuba	[dʒænu'ba]
in the south	cənubda	[dʒænub'da]
southern (adj)	cənubi	[dʒænu'bi]

west	qərb	[gærb]
to the west	qərbə	[gær'bæ]
in the west	qərbdə	[gærb'dæ]
western (adj)	qərb	[gærb]

east	şərq	[ʃærg]
to the east	şərqə	[ʃær'gæ]
in the east	şərqdə	[ʃærg'dæ]
eastern (adj)	şərq	[ʃærg]

198. Sea. Ocean

sea	dəniz	[dæ'niz]
ocean	okean	[oke'an]
gulf (bay)	körfəz	[kør'fæz]
straits	boğaz	[bo'gaz]

dry land	quru	[gu'ru]
continent (mainland)	materik	[mate'rik]
island	ada	[a'da]
peninsula	yarımada	[jarıma'da]
archipelago	arxipelaq	[arhipe'lag]

bay	buxta	['buhta]
harbour	liman	[li'man]
lagoon	laquna	[la'guna]
cape	burun	[bu'run]

atoll	mərcan adası	[mær'dʒan ada'sı]
reef	rif	[rif]
coral	mərcan	[mær'dʒan]
coral reef	mərcan rifi	[mær'dʒan ri'fi]

deep (adj)	dərin	[dæ'rin]
depth (deep water)	dərinlik	[dærin'lik]
abyss	dərinlik	[dærin'lik]
trench (e.g. Mariana ~)	çuxur	[tʃu'hur]

current, stream	axın	[a'hın]
to surround (bathe)	əhatə etmək	[æha'tæ æt'mæk]
shore	sahil	[sa'hil]

coast	sahilboyu	[sahilbo'y]
high tide	yüksəlmə	[yksæl'mæ]
low tide	çəkilmə	[tʃəkil'mæ]
sandbank	dayaz yer	[da'jaz 'er]
bottom	dib	[dib]

wave	dalğa	[dalɣ'a]
crest (~ of a wave)	ləpə beli	[læ'pæ be'li]
froth (foam)	köpük	[kø'pyk]

hurricane	qasırğa	[gasırɣ'a]
tsunami	tsunami	[ʦu'nami]
calm (dead ~)	tam sakitlik	['tam sakit'lik]
quiet, calm (adj)	sakit	[sa'kit]

pole	polyus	['polys]
polar (adj)	qütbi	[gyt'bi]

latitude	en dairəsi	['æn dairæ'si]
longitude	uzunluq dairəsi	[uzun'lug dairæ'si]
parallel	paralel	[para'lel]
equator	ekvator	[æk'vator]

sky	səma	[sæ'ma]
horizon	üfüq	[y'fyg]
air	hava	[ha'va]

lighthouse	mayak	[ma'jak]
to dive (vi)	dalmaq	[dal'mag]
to sink (ab. boat)	batmaq	[bat'mag]
treasures	xəzinə	[hæzi'næ]

199. Seas & Oceans names

Atlantic Ocean	Atlantik okean	[atlan'tik oke'an]
Indian Ocean	Hind okeanı	['hind okea'nı]
Pacific Ocean	Sakit okean	[sa'kit oke'an]
Arctic Ocean	Şimal buzlu okeanı	[ʃi'mal buz'lu oke'an]

Black Sea	Qara dəniz	[ga'ra dæ'niz]
Red Sea	Qırmızı dəniz	[gırmı'zı dæ'niz]
Yellow Sea	Sarı dəniz	[sa'rı dæ'niz]
White Sea	Ağ dəniz	['aɣ dæ'niz]

Caspian Sea	Xəzər dənizi	[hæ'zær dæni'zi]
Dead Sea	Ölü dənizi	[ø'ly dæni'zi]
Mediterranean Sea	Aralıq dənizi	[ara'lıg dæni'zi]

Aegean Sea	Egey dənizi	[æ'gej dæni'zi]
Adriatic Sea	Adriatik dənizi	[adria'tik dæni'zi]

Arabian Sea	Ərəb dənizi	[æ'ræb dæni'zi]
Sea of Japan	Yapon dənizi	[ja'pon dæni'zi]
Bering Sea	Berinq dənizi	['beriŋ dæni'zi]

South China Sea	Cənubi Çin dənizi	[ʤænu'bi 'ʧin dæni'zi]
Coral Sea	Mərcan dənizi	[mær'ʤan dæni'zi]
Tasman Sea	Tasman dənizi	[tas'man dæni'zi]
Caribbean Sea	Karib dənizi	[ka'rib dæni'zi]

| Barents Sea | Barens dənizi | ['barens dæni'zi] |
| Kara Sea | Kars dənizi | ['kars dæni'zi] |

North Sea	Şimal dənizi	[ʃi'mal dæni'zi]
Baltic Sea	Baltik dənizi	[bal'tik dæni'zi]
Norwegian Sea	Norveç dənizi	[nor'veʧ dæni'zi]

200. Mountains

mountain	dağ	[daɣ]
mountain range	dağ silsiləsi	['daɣ silsilæ'si]
mountain ridge	sıra dağlar	[sı'ra daɣ'lar]

summit, top	baş	[baʃ]
peak	zirvə	[zir'væ]
foot (of mountain)	ətək	[æ'tæk]
slope (mountainside)	yamac	[ja'maʤ]

volcano	yanardağ	[janar'daɣ]
active volcano	feal yanardağ	[fæ'al janar'daɣ]
dormant volcano	sönmüş yanardağ	[søn'myʃ janar'daɣ]

eruption	püskürmə	[pyskyr'mæ]
crater	yanardağ ağzı	[janar'daɣ aɣ'zı]
magma	maqma	['magma]
lava	lava	['lava]
molten (~ lava)	qızmar	[gız'mar]

canyon	kanyon	[ka'ɲion]
gorge	dərə	[dæ'ræ]
crevice	dar dərə	['dar dæ'ræ]
pass, col	dağ keçidi	['daɣ ketʃi'di]
plateau	plato	['plato]
cliff	qaya	[ga'ja]
hill	təpə	[tæ'pæ]

glacier	buzlaq	[buz'lag]
waterfall	şəlalə	[ʃæla'læ]
geyser	qeyzer	['gejzer]
lake	göl	['gøʌ]

plain	düzən	[dy'zæn]
landscape	mənzərə	[mænzæ'ræ]
echo	əks-səda	['æks sæ'da]

alpinist	alpinist	[alpi'nist]
rock climber	qayalara dırmaşan idmançı	[gajala'ra dırma'ʃan idman'ʧı]
to conquer (in climbing)	fəth etmək	['fæth æt'mæk]
climb (an easy ~)	dırmaşma	[dırmaʃ'ma]

181

201. Mountains names

Alps	Alp dağları	['alp dayla'rı]
Mont Blanc	Monblan	[monb'lan]
Pyrenees	Pireney	[pire'nej]
Carpathians	Karpat	[kar'pat]
Ural Mountains	Ural dağları	[u'ral dayla'rı]
Caucasus	Qafqaz	[gaf'gaz]
Elbrus	Elbrus	[ælb'rus]
Altai	Altay	[al'taj]
Tien Shan	Tyan-Şan	['tjan 'ʃan]
Pamir Mountains	Pamir	[pa'mir]
Himalayas	Himalay	[gima'laj]
Everest	Everest	[æve'rest]
Andes	And dağları	['and dayla'rı]
Kilimanjaro	Kilimancaro	[kiliman'dʒaro]

202. Rivers

river	çay	[tʃaj]
spring (natural source)	çeşmə	[tʃeʃ'mæ]
riverbed	çay yatağı	['tʃaj jatay'ı]
basin	hovuz	[ho'vuz]
to flow into ...	tökülmək	[tøkyl'mæk]
tributary	axın	[a'hın]
bank (of river)	sahil	[sa'hil]
current, stream	axın	[a'hın]
downstream (adv)	axınla aşağıya doğru	[a'hınla aʃayı'ja doy'ru]
upstream (adv)	axınla yuxarıya doğru	[a'hınla yharı'ja doy'ru]
inundation	daşqın	[daʃ'gın]
flooding	sel	[sel]
to overflow (vi)	daşmaq	[daʃ'mag]
to flood (vt)	su basmaq	['su bas'mag]
shallows (shoal)	say	[saj]
rapids	kandar	[kan'dar]
dam	bənd	[bænd]
canal	kanal	[ka'nal]
reservoir (artificial lake)	su anbarı	['su anba'rı]
sluice, lock	şlyuz	[ʃlyz]
water body (pond, etc.)	nohur	[no'hur]
swamp, bog	bataqlıq	[batag'lıg]
marsh	bataq	[ba'tag]
whirlpool	qıjov	[gı'ʒov]
stream (brook)	kiçik çay	[ki'tʃik 'tʃaj]

drinking (ab. water)	içməli	[itʃmæ'li]
fresh (~ water)	şirin	[ʃi'rin]
ice	buz	[buz]
to ice over	donmaq	[don'mag]

203. Rivers names

Seine	Sena	['sena]
Loire	Luara	[lu'ara]
Thames	Temza	['temza]
Rhine	Reyn	[rejn]
Danube	Dunay	[du'naj]
Volga	Volqa	['volga]
Don	Don	[don]
Lena	Lena	['lena]
Yellow River	Xuanxe	[huan'hæ]
Yangtze	Yanqdzı	[jaŋ'dzı]
Mekong	Mekonq	[me'koŋ]
Ganges	Qanq	[gaŋ]
Nile	Nil	[nil]
Congo	Konqo	['koŋo]
Okavango	Okavanqo	[oka'vaŋo]
Zambezi	Zambezi	[zam'bezi]
Limpopo	Limpopo	[limpo'po]
Mississippi River	Missisipi	[mississipi]

204. Forest

forest	meşə	[me'ʃæ]
forest (as adj)	meşə	[me'ʃæ]
thick forest	sıx meşəlik	['sıh meʃæ'lik]
grove	ağaclıq	[aɣadʒ'lıg]
clearing	tala	[ta'la]
thicket	cəngəllik	[dʒæŋæl'lik]
scrubland	kolluq	[kol'lug]
footpath	cığır	[dʒıɣ'ır]
gully	yarğan	[jarɣ'an]
tree	ağac	[aɣ'adʒ]
leaf	yarpaq	[jar'pag]
leaves	yarpaqlar	[jarpag'lar]
falling leaves	yarpağın tökülməsi	[jarpaɣ'ın tøkylmæ'si]
to fall (ab. leaves)	tökülmək	[tøkyl'mæk]

top (of the tree)	baş	[baʃ]
branch	budaq	[bu'dag]
bough	budaq	[bu'dag]
bud (on shrub, tree)	tumurcuq	[tumur'dʒug]
needle (of pine tree)	iynə	[ij'næ]
fir cone	qoza	[go'za]

hollow (in a tree)	oyuq	[o'yg]
nest	yuva	[y'va]
burrow (animal hole)	yuva	[y'va]

trunk	gövdə	[gøv'dæ]
root	kök	['køk]
bark	qabıq	[ga'bıg]
moss	mamır	[ma'mır]

to uproot (vt)	kötük çıxarmaq	[kø'tyk tʃıhar'mag]
to chop down	kəsmək	[kæs'mæk]
to deforest (vt)	qırıb qurtarmaq	[gı'rıb gurtar'mag]
tree stump	kötük	[kø'tyk]

campfire	tonqal	[to'ŋal]
forest fire	yanğın	[jaŋɣ'ın]
to extinguish (vt)	söndürmək	[søndyr'mæk]

forest ranger	meşəbəyi	[meʃæbæ'jı]
protection	qoruma	[goru'ma]
to protect (~ nature)	mühafizə etmək	[myhafi'zæ æt'mæk]
poacher	brakonyer	[brako'njer]
trap (e.g. bear ~)	tələ	[tæ'læ]

to gather, to pick (vt)	yığmaq	[jıɣ'mag]
to lose one's way	yolu azmaq	[jo'lu az'mag]

205. Natural resources

natural resources	təbii ehtiyatlar	[tæbi'i æhtijat'lar]
minerals	yeraltı sərvətlər	[eral'tı særvæt'lær]
deposits	yataqlar	[jatag'lar]
field (e.g. oilfield)	yataq	[ja'tag]

to mine (extract)	hasil etmək	[ha'sil æt'mæk]
mining (extraction)	hasilat	[hasi'lat]
ore	filiz	[fi'liz]
mine (e.g. for coal)	mədən	[mæ'dæn]
mine shaft, pit	quyu	[gu'y]
miner	şaxtaçı	['ʃahtatʃı]

gas	qaz	[gaz]
gas pipeline	qaz borusu	['gaz boru'su]

oil (petroleum)	neft	[neft]
oil pipeline	neft borusu	['neft boru'su]
oil rig	neft qülləsi	['neft gyllæ'si]

derrick	**neft buruğu**	['neft buruɣ'u]
tanker	**tanker**	['taŋker]
sand	**qum**	[gum]
limestone	**əhəngdaşı**	[æhæŋda'ʃɪ]
gravel	**çınqıl**	[ʧɪ'ŋɪl]
peat	**torf**	[torf]
clay	**gil**	[gil]
coal	**kömür**	[kø'myr]
iron	**dəmir**	[dæ'mir]
gold	**qızıl**	[gɪ'zɪl]
silver	**gümüş**	[gy'myʃ]
nickel	**nikel**	['nikel]
copper	**mis**	[mis]
zinc	**sink**	[siŋk]
manganese	**manqan**	[ma'ŋan]
mercury	**civə**	[ʤi'væ]
lead	**qurğuşun**	[gurɣu'ʃun]
mineral	**mineral**	[mine'ral]
crystal	**kristal**	[kris'tal]
marble	**mərmər**	[mær'mær]
uranium	**uran**	[u'ran]

The Earth. Part 2

206. Weather

weather	hava	[ha'va]
weather forecast	hava proqnozu	[ha'va progno'zu]
temperature	temperatur	[tempera'tur]
thermometer	istilik ölçən	[isti'lik øl'ʧən]
barometer	barometr	[ba'rometr]
humidity	rütubət	[rytu'bæt]
heat (of summer)	çox isti hava	['ʧoh is'ti ha'va]
hot (torrid)	çox isti	['ʧoh is'ti]
it's hot	çox istidir	['ʧoh is'tidir]
it's warm	istidir	[is'tidir]
warm (moderately hot)	isti	[is'ti]
it's cold	soyuqdur	[so'ygdur]
cold (adj)	soyuq	[so'yg]
sun	günəş	[gy'næʃ]
to shine (vi)	içıq saçmaq	[i'ʃıg saʧ'mag]
sunny (day)	günəşli	[gynæʃ'li]
to come up (vi)	çıxmaq	[ʧıh'mag]
to set (vi)	batmaq	[bat'mag]
cloud	bulud	[bu'lud]
cloudy (adj)	buludlu	[bulud'lu]
rain cloud	qara bulud	[ga'ra bu'lud]
somber (gloomy)	tutqun	[tut'gun]
rain	yağış	[jaɣ'ıʃ]
it's raining	yağır	[jaɣ'ır]
rainy (day)	yağışlı	[jaɣıʃ'lı]
to drizzle (vi)	çiskinləmək	[ʧiskinlæ'mæk]
pouring rain	şiddətli yağış	[ʃiddæt'li jaɣ'ıʃ]
downpour	sel	[sel]
heavy (e.g. ~ rain)	şiddətli	[ʃiddæt'li]
puddle	su gölməçəsi	['su gølmæʧə'si]
to get wet (in rain)	islanmaq	[islan'mag]
fog (mist)	duman	[du'man]
foggy	dumanlı	[duman'lı]
snow	qar	[gar]
it's snowing	qar yağır	['gar jaɣ'ır]

207. Severe weather. Natural disasters

thunderstorm	tufan	[tu'fan]
lightning (~ strike)	şimşək	[ʃim'ʃæk]
to flash (vi)	çaxmaq	[ʧah'mag]
thunder	göy gurultusu	['gøj gyrultu'su]
to thunder (vi)	guruldamaq	[gyrulda'mag]
it's thundering	göy guruldayır	['gøj gyrulda'jır]
hail	dolu	[do'lu]
it's hailing	dolu yağır	[do'lu jaɣ'ır]
to flood (vt)	su basmaq	['su bas'mag]
flood, inundation	daşqın	[daʃ'gın]
earthquake	zəlzələ	[zælzæ'læ]
tremor, quake	təkan	[tæ'kan]
epicentre	mərkəz	[mær'kæz]
eruption	püskürmə	[pyskyr'mæ]
lava	lava	['lava]
twister	burağan	[buraɣ'an]
tornado	tornado	[tor'nado]
typhoon	şiddətli fırtına	[ʃiddæt'li fırtı'na]
hurricane	qasırğa	[gasırɣ'a]
storm	fırtına	[fırtı'na]
tsunami	tsunami	[ʦu'nami]
cyclone	siklon	[sik'lon]
bad weather	pis hava	['pis ha'va]
fire (accident)	yanğın	[janɣ'ın]
disaster	fəlakət	[fæla'kæt]
meteorite	meteorit	[meteo'rit]
avalanche	qar uçqunu	['gar uʧgu'nu]
snowslide	qar uçqunu	['gar uʧgu'nu]
blizzard	çovğun	[ʧovɣ'un]
snowstorm	boran	[bo'ran]

208. Noises. Sounds

quiet, silence	səssizlik	[sæssiz'lik]
sound	səs	[sæs]
noise	gurultu	[gyrul'tu]
to make noise	gurultu salmaq	[gyrul'tu sal'mag]
noisy (adj)	gurultulu	[gyrultu'lu]
loudly (to speak, etc.)	ucadan	[uʤa'dan]
loud (voice, etc.)	gurultulu	[gyrultu'lu]
constant (continuous)	daimi	[dai'mi]

shout (n)	çığırtı	[tʃɪɣɪr'tɪ]
to shout (vi)	çığırmaq	[tʃɪɣɪr'mag]
whisper	pıçıltı	[pɪtʃɪl'tɪ]
to whisper (vi, vt)	pıçıldamaq	[pɪtʃɪlda'mag]

| barking (of dog) | hürmə | [hyr'mæ] |
| to bark (vi) | hürmək | [hyr'mæk] |

groan (of pain)	inilti	[inil'ti]
to groan (vi)	inildəmək	[inildæ'mæk]
cough	öskürək	[øsky'ræk]
to cough (vi)	öskürmək	[øskyr'mæk]

whistle	fışqırıq	[fɪʃgɪ'rɪg]
to whistle (vi)	fışqırıq çalmaq	[fɪʃgɪ'rɪg tʃal'mag]
knock (at the door)	taqqıltı	[taggɪl'tɪ]
to knock (at the door)	taqqıldatmaq	[taggɪldat'mag]

| to crack (vi) | şaqqıldamak | [ʃaggɪlda'mag] |
| crack (plank, etc.) | şaqqıltı | [ʃaggɪl'tɪ] |

siren	sirena	[si'rena]
whistle (factory's ~)	fit	[fit]
to whistle (ship, train)	fit vermək	['fit ver'mæk]
honk (signal)	siqnal	[sig'nal]
to honk (vi)	siqnal vermək	[sig'nal ver'mæk]

209. Winter

winter (n)	qış	[gɪʃ]
winter (as adj)	qış	[gɪʃ]
in winter	qışda	[gɪʃ'da]

snow	qar	[gar]
it's snowing	qar yağır	['gar jaɣ'ır]
snowfall	qar yağması	['gar jaɣma'sı]
snowdrift	qar təpəsi	['gar tæpæ'si]

snowflake	qar dənəciyi	['gar dænædʒi'jı]
snowball	qartopu	[garto'pu]
snowman	qar heykəl	['gar hej'kæl]
icicle	sallaq buz	[sal'lag 'buz]

December	dekabr	[de'kabr]
January	yanvar	[jan'var]
February	fevral	[fev'ral]

| heavy frost | şaxta | [ʃah'ta] |
| frosty (weather, air) | şaxtalı | [ʃahta'lı] |

below zero (adv)	sıfırdan aşağı	['sıfırdan aʃaɣ'ı]
first frost	səhər şaxtası	[sæ'hær ʃahta'sı]
hoarfrost	qırov	[gı'rov]
cold (cold weather)	soyuq	[so'yg]

it's cold	soyuqdur	[so'ygdur]
fur coat	kürk	[kyrk]
mittens	təkbarmaq əlcək	[tækbar'mag æl'dʒæk]

to fall ill	xəstələnmək	[hæstælæn'mæk]
cold (illness)	soyuqdəymə	[soygdæj'mæ]
to catch a cold	özünü soyuğa vermək	[øzy'ny soyɣ'a ver'mæk]

ice	buz	[buz]
black ice	yerin buz bağlaması	[e'rin 'buz baɣlama'sı]
to ice over	donmaq	[don'mag]
ice floe	buz kütləsi	['buz kytlæ'si]

skis	xizək	[hi'zæk]
skier	xizəkçi	[hizæk'tʃi]
to ski (vi)	xizək sürmək	[hi'zæk syr'mæk]
to skate (vi)	konki sürmək	[ko'ŋki syr'mæk]

Fauna

210. Mammals. Predators

predator	yırtıcı	[jɪrtɪ'dʒɪ]
tiger	pələng	[pæ'læŋ]
lion	şir	[ʃir]
wolf	canavar	[dʒana'var]
fox	tülkü	[tyl'ky]

jaguar	yaquar	[jagu'ar]
leopard	leopard	[leo'pard]
cheetah	gepard	[ge'pard]

black panther	panter	[pan'ter]
puma	puma	['puma]
snow leopard	qar bəbiri	['gar bæbi'ri]
lynx	vaşaq	[va'ʃag]

coyote	koyot	[ko'jot]
jackal	çaqqal	[tʃag'gal]
hyena	kaftar	[kʲaf'tar]

211. Wild animals

animal	heyvan	[hej'van]
beast (animal)	vəhşi heyvan	[væh'ʃi hæj'van]

squirrel	sincab	[sin'dʒab]
hedgehog	kirpi	[kir'pi]
hare	dovşan	[dov'ʃan]
rabbit	ev dovşanı	['æv dovʃa'nı]

badger	porsuq	[por'sug]
raccoon	yenot	[e'not]
hamster	dağsiçanı	['daɣsitʃanı]
marmot	marmot	[mar'mot]

mole	köstəbək	[køstæ'bæk]
mouse	siçan	[si'tʃan]
rat	siçovul	[sitʃo'vul]
bat	yarasa	[jara'sa]

ermine	sincab	[sin'dʒab]
sable	samur	[sa'mur]
marten	dələ	[dæ'læ]
weasel	gəlincik	[gelin'dʒik]
mink	su samuru	['su samu'ru]

| beaver | qunduz | [gun'duz] |
| otter | susamuru | [susamu'ru] |

horse	at	[at]
moose	sığın	[sɪɣ'ın]
deer	maral	[ma'ral]
camel	dəvə	[dæ'væ]

bison	bizon	[bi'zon]
aurochs	zubr	[zubr]
buffalo	camış	[dʒa'mıʃ]

zebra	zebra	['zebra]
antelope	antilop	[anti'lop]
roe deer	cüyür	[dʒy'yr]
fallow deer	xallı maral	[hal'lı ma'ral]
chamois	dağ keçisi	['daɣ ketʃi'si]
wild boar	qaban	[ga'ban]

whale	balina	[ba'lina]
seal	suiti	[sui'ti]
walrus	morj	[morʒ]
fur seal	dəniz pişiyi	[dæ'niz piʃi'jı]
dolphin	delfin	[del'fin]

bear	ayı	[a'jı]
polar bear	ağ ayı	['aɣ a'jı]
panda	panda	['panda]

monkey	meymun	[mej'mun]
chimpanzee	şimpanze	[ʃimpan'ze]
orangutan	oranqutan	[oraŋu'tan]
gorilla	qorilla	[go'rilla]
macaque	makaka	[ma'kaka]
gibbon	gibbon	[gib'bon]

elephant	fil	[fil]
rhinoceros	kərgədən	[kærgæ'dan]
giraffe	zürafə	[zyra'fæ]
hippopotamus	begemot	[bege'mot]

| kangaroo | kenquru | [keŋu'ru] |
| koala (bear) | koala | [ko'ala] |

mongoose	manqust	[ma'ŋust]
chinchilla	şinşilla	[ʃin'ʃilla]
skunk	skuns	[skuns]
porcupine	oxlu kirpi	[oh'lu kir'pi]

212. Domestic animals

cat	pişik	[pi'ʃik]
tomcat	pişik	[pi'ʃik]
dog	it	[it]

horse	at	[at]
stallion	ayğır	[ajɣ'ır]
mare	madyan	[mad'jan]

cow	inək	[i'næk]
bull	buğa	[buɣ'a]
ox	öküz	[ø'kyz]

sheep	qoyun	[go'yn]
ram	qoyun	[go'yn]
goat	keçi	[ke'tʃi]
billy goat, he-goat	erkək keçi	[ærkæk ke'tʃi]

| donkey | eşşək | [æ'ʃæk] |
| mule | qatır | [ga'tır] |

pig	donuz	[do'nuz]
piglet	çoşka	[tʃoʃ'ka]
rabbit	ev dovşanı	['æv dovʃa'nı]

| hen (chicken) | toyuq | [to'yg] |
| cock | xoruz | [ho'ruz] |

duck	ördək	[ør'dæk]
drake	yaşılbaş	[jaʃıl'baʃ]
goose	qaz	[gaz]

| stag turkey | hind xoruzu | ['hind horu'zu] |
| turkey (hen) | hind toyuğu | ['hind toyɣ'u] |

domestic animals	ev heyvanları	['æv hejvanla'rı]
tame (e.g. ~ hamster)	əhliləşdirilmiş	[æhlilæʃdiril'miʃ]
to tame (vt)	əhliləşdirmək	[æhlilæʃdir'mæk]
to breed (vt)	yetişdirmək	[etiʃdir'mæk]

farm	ferma	['ferma]
poultry	ev quşları	['æv guʃla'rı]
cattle	mal-qara	['mal ga'ra]
herd (cattle)	sürü	[sy'ry]

stable	tövlə	[tøv'læ]
pigsty	donuz damı	[do'nuz da'mı]
cowshed	inək damı	[i'næk da'mı]
rabbit hutch	ev dovşanı saxlanılan yer	['æv dovʃa'nı sahlanı'lan 'er]
hen house	toyuq damı	[to'yg da'mı]

213. Dogs. Dog breeds

dog	it	[it]
sheepdog	çoban iti	[tʃo'ban i'ti]
poodle	pudel	['pudel]
dachshund	taksa	['taksa]
bulldog	buldoq	[bul'dog]
boxer	boksyor	[boks'jor]

mastiff	mastif	[mas'tif]
rottweiler	rotveyler	[rot'vejler]
Doberman	doberman	[dober'man]

basset	basset	['basset]
bobtail	bobteyl	[bob'tejl]
Dalmatian	dalmat iti	[dal'mat i'ti]
cocker spaniel	koker-spaniel	['koker spani'el]

| Newfoundland | nyufaundlend | [ɲjy'faundlend] |
| Saint Bernard | senbernar | [senber'nar] |

husky	xaski	['haski]
Chow Chow	çau-çau	['ʧau 'ʧau]
spitz	şpis	[ʃpiʦ]
pug	mops	[mops]

214. Sounds made by animals

barking (n)	hürmə	[hyr'mæ]
to bark (vi)	hürmək	[hyr'mæk]
to miaow (vi)	miyovlamaq	[mijovla'mag]
to purr (vi)	mırıldamaq	[mırılda'mag]

to moo (vi)	movuldamaq	[movulda'mag]
to bellow (bull)	böyürmək	[bøyr'mæk]
to growl (vi)	nərildəmək	[nærildæ'mæk]

howl (n)	ulama	[ula'ma]
to howl (vi)	ulamaq	[ula'mag]
to whine (vi)	zingildəmək	[ziŋildæ'mæk]

to bleat (sheep)	mələmək	[mælæ'mæk]
to oink, to grunt (pig)	xortuldamaq	[hortulda'mag]
to squeal (vi)	ciyildəmək	[ʤijıldæ'mæk]

to croak (vi)	vaqqıltı	[vaggıl'tı]
to buzz (insect)	vızıldamaq	[vızılda'mag]
to stridulate (vi)	cırıldamaq	[ʤırılda'mag]

215. Young animals

cub	bala	[ba'la]
kitten	pişik balası	[pi'ʃik bala'sı]
baby mouse	siçan balası	[si'ʧan bala'sı]
pup, puppy	küçük	[ky'ʧuk]

leveret	dovşan balası	[dov'ʃan bala'sı]
baby rabbit	ev dovşanı balası	['æv dovʃa'nı bala'sı]
wolf cub	canavar balası	[ʤana'var bala'sı]
fox cub	tülkü balası	[tyl'ky bala'sı]
bear cub	ayı balası	[a'jı bala'sı]

lion cub	şir balası	['ʃir bala'sı]
tiger cub	pələng balası	[pæ'læŋ bala'sı]
elephant calf	fil balası	['fil bala'sı]

piglet	çoşka	[ʧoʃ'ka]
calf (young cow, bull)	inək balası	[i'næk bala'sı]
kid (young goat)	keçi balası	[ke'ʧi bala'sı]
lamb	quzu	[gu'zu]
fawn (deer)	maral balası	[ma'ral bala'sı]
young camel	dəvə balası	[dæ'væ bala'sı]

| baby snake | ilan balası | [i'lan bala'sı] |
| baby frog | qurbağa balası | [gurbaɣ'a bala'sı] |

nestling	quş balası	['guʃ bala'sı]
chick (of chicken)	cücə	[ʤy'ʤæ]
duckling	ördək balası	[ør'dæk bala'sı]

216. Birds

bird	quş	[guʃ]
pigeon	göyərçin	[gøjər'ʧin]
sparrow	sərçə	[sær'ʧə]
tit	arıquşu	[arıgu'ʃu]
magpie	sağsağan	[saɣsaɣ'an]

raven	qarğa	[garɣ'a]
crow	qarğa	[garɣ'a]
jackdaw	dolaşa	[dola'ʃa]
rook	zağca	[zaɣ'ʤa]

duck	ördək	[ør'dæk]
goose	qaz	[gaz]
pheasant	qırqovul	[gırgo'vul]

eagle	qartal	[gar'tal]
hawk	qırğı	[gırɣ'ı]
falcon	şahin	[ʃa'hin]
vulture	qrif	[grif]
condor	kondor	[kon'dor]

swan	sona	[so'na]
crane	durna	[dur'na]
stork	leylək	[lej'læk]

parrot	tutuquşu	[tutugu'ʃu]
hummingbird	kolibri	[ko'libri]
peacock	tovuz	[to'vuz]

ostrich	straus	['straus]
heron	vağ	[vaɣ]
flamingo	qızılqaz	[gızıl'gaz]
pelican	qutan	[gu'tan]
nightingale	bülbül	[byʎ'byʎ]

swallow	qaranquş	[gara'ŋuʃ]
thrush	qaratoyuq	[garato'yg]
song thrush	ötən qaratoyuq	[ø'tæn garato'yg]
blackbird	qara qaratoyuq	[ga'ra garato'yg]

swift	uzunqanad	[u'zuŋa'nad]
lark	torağay	[toraɣ'aj]
quail	bidirçin	[biʌdir'ʧin]

woodpecker	ağacdələn	[aɣadʒdæ'læn]
cuckoo	ququ quşu	[gu'gu gu'ʃu]
owl	bayquş	[baj'guʃ]
eagle owl	yapalaq	[japa'lag]
wood grouse	Sibir xoruzu	[si'bir horu'zu]
black grouse	tetra quşu	['tetra gu'ʃu]
partridge	kəklik	[kæk'lik]

starling	sığırçın	[sɪɣɪr'ʧɪn]
canary	sarıbülbül	[sarıbyʌ'byʌ]
hazel grouse	qarabağır	[garabaɣ'ır]
chaffinch	alacəhrə	[alaʧəh'ræ]
bullfinch	qar quşu	['gar gu'ʃu]

seagull	qağayı	[gaga'jı]
albatross	albatros	[albat'ros]
penguin	pinqvin	[piŋ'vin]

217. Birds. Singing and sounds

to sing (vi)	oxumaq	[ohu'mag]
to call (animal, bird)	çığırmaq	[ʧıɣır'mag]
to crow (cock)	banlamaq	[banla'mag]
cock-a-doodle-doo	ququluqu	[guggulu'gu]

to cluck (hen)	qaqqıldamaq	[gaggılda'mag]
to caw (vi)	qarıldamaq	[garılda'mag]
to quack (duck)	vaqqıldamaq	[vaggılda'mag]
to cheep (vi)	ciyildəmək	[dʒijıldæ'mæk]
to chirp, to twitter	cəh-cəh vurmaq	['dʒæh 'dʒæh vur'mag]

218. Fish. Marine animals

bream	çapaq	[ʧa'pag]
carp	karp	[karp]
perch	xanı balığı	[ha'nı balıɣ'ı]
catfish	naqqa	[nag'ga]
pike	durnabalığı	[durnabalıɣ'ı]

salmon	qızılbalıq	[gızılba'lıg]
sturgeon	nərə balığı	[næ'ræ balıɣ'ı]
herring	siyənək	[sijə'næk]
Atlantic salmon	somğa	[somɣ'a]

| mackerel | skumbriya | ['skumbrija] |
| flatfish | qalxan balığı | [gal'han balıɣ'ı] |

zander, pike perch	suf balığı	['suf balıɣ'ı]
cod	treska	[tres'ka]
tuna	tunes	[tu'nes]
trout	alabalıq	[alaba'lıg]

eel	angvil balığı	[aŋ'vil balıɣ'ı]
electric ray	elektrikli skat	[ælektrik'li 'skat]
moray eel	müren balığı	[my'ren balıɣ'ı]
piranha	piranya balığı	[pi'ranja balıɣ'ı]

shark	köpək balığı	[kø'pæk balıɣ'ı]
dolphin	delfin	[del'fin]
whale	balina	[ba'lina]

crab	qısaquyruq	[gısaguj'rug]
jellyfish	meduza	[me'duza]
octopus	səkkizayaqlı ilbiz	[sækkizajag'lı il'biz]

starfish	dəniz ulduzu	[dæ'niz uldu'zu]
sea urchin	dəniz kirpisi	[dæ'niz kirpi'si]
seahorse	dəniz atı	[dæ'niz a'tı]

oyster	istridyə	[istrid'jə]
prawn	krevet	[kre'vet]
lobster	omar	[o'mar]
spiny lobster	lanqust	[la'ŋust]

219. Amphibians. Reptiles

| snake | ilan | [i'lan] |
| venomous (snake) | zəhərli | [zæhær'li] |

viper	gürzə	[gyr'zæ]
cobra	kobra	['kobra]
python	piton	[pi'ton]
boa	boa	[bo'a]
grass snake	koramal	[kora'mal]
rattle snake	zınqırovlu ilan	[zıŋırov'lu i'lan]
anaconda	anakonda	[ana'konda]

lizard	kərtənkələ	[kærtæŋkæ'læ]
iguana	iquana	[igu'ana]
monitor lizard	çöl kərtənkələsi	['tʃol kærtæŋkælæ'si]
salamander	salamandr	[sala'mandr]
chameleon	buğələmun	[buɣælæ'mun]
scorpion	əqrəb	[æg'ræb]

turtle	tısbağa	[tısbaɣ'a]
frog	qurbağa	[gurbaɣ'a]
toad	quru qurbağası	[gu'ru gurbaɣa'sı]
crocodile	timsah	[tim'sah]

220. Insects

insect	həşarat	[hæʃaˈrat]
butterfly	kəpənək	[kæpæˈnæk]
ant	qarışqa	[garɪʃˈga]
fly	milçək	[milˈtʃək]
mosquito	ağcaqanad	[aɣdʒagaˈnad]
beetle	böcək	[bøˈdʒæk]

wasp	arı	[aˈrɪ]
bee	bal arısı	[ˈbal arɪˈsɪ]
bumblebee	eşşək arısı	[æˈʃæk arɪˈsɪ]
gadfly	mozalan	[mozaˈlan]

| spider | hörümçək | [hørymˈtʃək] |
| spider's web | hörümçək toru | [hørymˈtʃək toru] |

dragonfly	cırcırama	[dʒɪrdʒɪraˈma]
grasshopper	şala cırcıraması	[ʃaˈla dʒɪrdʒɪramaˈsɪ]
moth (night butterfly)	pərvanə	[pærvaˈnæ]

cockroach	tarakan	[taraˈkan]
tick	gənə	[gæˈnæ]
flea	birə	[biˈræ]
midge	mığmığa	[mɪɣmɪɣˈa]

locust	çəyirtkə	[tʃəjɪrtˈkæ]
snail	ilbiz	[ilˈbiz]
cricket	sisəy	[siˈsæj]
firefly	işıldaquş	[iʃɪldaˈguʃ]
ladybird	xanımböcəyi	[hanɪmbødʒæˈjɪ]
cockchafer	may böcəyi	[ˈmaj bødʒæˈjɪ]

leech	zəli	[zæˈli]
caterpillar	kəpənək qurdu	[kæpæˈnæk gurˈdu]
earthworm	qurd	[gurd]
larva	sürfə	[syrˈfæ]

221. Animals. Body parts

beak	dimdik	[dimˈdik]
wings	qanadlar	[ganadˈlar]
foot (of bird)	pəncə	[pænˈdʒæ]
feathering	tük	[tyk]
feather	lələk	[læˈlæk]
crest	kəkil	[kæˈkil]

gill	qəlsəmə	[gælsæˈmæ]
spawn	kürü	[kyˈry]
larva	sürfə	[syrˈfæ]
fin	üzgəc	[yzˈgædʒ]
scales (of fish, reptile)	pul	[pul]
fang (of wolf, etc.)	köpək dişi	[køˈpæk diˈʃi]

paw (e.g. cat's ~)	pəncə	[pæn'dʒæ]
muzzle (snout)	üz	[yz]
mouth (of cat, dog)	ağız	[aɣ'ız]
tail	quyruq	[guj'rug]
whiskers	bığ	[bıɣ]

hoof	dırnaq	[dır'nag]
horn	buynuz	[buj'nuz]

carapace	qın	[gın]
shell (of mollusc)	balıqqulağı	[balıggulaɣ'ı]
eggshell	qabıq	[ga'bıg]

hair (e.g. dog's ~)	yun	[yn]
pelt	dəri	[dæ'ri]

222. Actions of animals

to fly (vi)	üçmaq	[utʃ'mag]
to make circles	dövrə vurmaq	[døv'ræ vur'mag]
to fly away	uçub qetmək	[u'tʃub get'mæk]
to flap (~ the wings)	qanad çalmaq	[ga'nad tʃal'mag]

to peck (vi)	dimdikləmək	[dimdiklæ'mæk]
to sit on (vt)	kürt yatmaq	['kyrt jat'mag]
to hatch out (vi)	yumurtadan çıxmaq	[ymurta'dan tʃıh'mag]
to build the nest	yuva tikmək	[y'va tik'mæk]

to slither, to crawl	sürünmək	[syryn'mæk]
to sting, to bite (insect)	vurmaq	[vur'mag]
to bite (ab. animal)	qapmaq	[gap'mag]

to sniff (vt)	iyləmək	[ijlæ'mæk]
to bark (vi)	hürmək	[hyr'mæk]
to hiss (snake)	fışıldamaq	[fıʃılda'mag]
to scare (vt)	qorxutmaq	[gorhut'mag]
to attack (vt)	hücum etmək	[hy'dʒum æt'mæk]

to gnaw (bone, etc.)	gəmirmək	[gæmir'mæk]
to scratch (with claws)	cızmaq	[dʒız'mag]
to hide (vi)	gizlənmək	[gizlæn'mæk]

to play (kittens, etc.)	oynamaq	[ojna'mag]
to hunt (vi, vt)	ova çıxmaq	[o'va tʃıh'mag]
to hibernate (vi)	yatmaq	[jat'mag]
to become extinct	qırılıb qurtarmaq	[gırı'lıb gurtar'mag]

223. Animals. Habitats

habitat	yaşayış mühiti	[jaʃa'jıʃ myhi'ti]
migration	köç	['køtʃ]
mountain	dağ	[daɣ]

| reef | rif | [rif] |
| cliff | qaya | [ga'ja] |

forest	meşə	[me'ʃæ]
jungle	cəngəllik	[dʒæŋæl'lik]
savanna	savanna	[sa'vaŋa]
tundra	tundra	['tundra]

steppe	çöl	['tʃol]
desert	səhra	[sæh'ra]
oasis	oazis	[o'azis]

sea	dəniz	[dæ'niz]
lake	göl	['gøʎ]
ocean	okean	[oke'an]

swamp	bataqlıq	[batag'lıg]
freshwater (adj)	şirin sulu	[ʃi'rin su'lu]
pond	gölcük	[gøʎ'dʒyk]
river	çay	[tʃaj]

den	ayı yuvası	[a'jı yva'sı]
nest	yuva	[y'va]
hollow (in a tree)	oyuq	[o'yg]
burrow (animal hole)	yuva	[y'va]
anthill	qarışqa yuvası	[garıʃ'ga yva'sı]

224. Animal care

| zoo | heyvanat parkı | [hæjva'nat par'kı] |
| nature reserve | qoruq yeri | [go'rug e'ri] |

breeder, breed club	heyvan yetişdirmə müəssisəsi	[hej'van etiʃdir'mæ myæssisæ'si]
open-air cage	volyer	[vol'jer]
cage	qəfəs	[gæ'fæs]
kennel	it damı	['it da'mı]

dovecot	göyərçin damı	[gøjər'tʃin da'mı]
aquarium	akvarium	[ak'varium]
dolphinarium	delfinarium	[delfi'narium]

to breed (animals)	yetişdirmək	[etiʃdir'mæk]
brood, litter	nəsil	[næ'sil]
to tame (vt)	əhliləşdirmək	[æhlilæʃdir'mæk]
feed (for animal)	yem	[em]
to feed (vt)	yedirmək	[edir'mæk]
to train (animals)	heyvanı təlim etmək	[hejva'nı tæ'lim æt'mæk]

pet shop	heyvan mağazası	[hej'van maɣ'azası]
muzzle (for dog)	buruntaq	[burun'tag]
collar	xalta	[hal'ta]
name (of animal)	ad	[ad]
pedigree (of dog)	şəcərə tarixi	[sædʒæ'ræ tari'hi]

225. Animals. Miscellaneous

pack (wolves)	sürü	[sy'ry]
flock (birds)	qatar	[ga'tar]
shoal (fish)	dəstə	[dæs'tæ]
herd of horses	ilxı	[il'hı]

male (n)	erkək	[ær'kæk]
female	dişi	[di'ʃi]

hungry (adj)	ac	[adʒ]
wild (adj)	vəhşi	[væh'ʃi]
dangerous (adj)	təhlükəli	[tæhlykæ'li]

226. Horses

horse	at	[at]
breed (race)	cins	[dʒins]

foal (of horse)	dayça	[daj'tʃa]
mare	madyan	[mad'jan]

mustang	mustanq	[mus'taŋ]
pony (small horse)	poni	['poni]
draught horse	ağır yük atı	[aɣ'ır 'yk a'tı]

mane	yal	[jal]
tail	quyruq	[guj'rug]

hoof	dırnaq	[dır'nag]
horseshoe	nal	[nal]
to shoe (vt)	nal vurmaq	['nal vur'mag]
blacksmith	nalbənd	[nal'bænd]

saddle	yəhər	[jə'hær]
stirrup	üzəngi	[yzæ'ŋi]
bridle	yüyən	[y'jən]
reins	cilov	[dʒi'lov]
whip (for riding)	qamçı	[gam'tʃı]

rider	at sürən	['at sy'ræn]
to break in (horse)	yerişə öyrətmək	[eri'ʃæ øjræt'mæk]
to saddle (vt)	yəhərləmək	[jəhærlæ'mæk]
to mount a horse	yəhər qoyub minmək	[jə'hær go'yb min'mæk]

gallop	dördayaq yeriş	[dørda'jag e'riʃ]
to gallop (vi)	dördayaq getmək	[dørda'jag get'mæk]
trot (n)	löhrəm yeriş	[løh'ræm e'riʃ]
at a trot (adv)	löhrəm yerişlə	[løh'ræm e'riʃlæ]

racehorse	cıdır atı	[dʒı'dır a'tı]
races	cıdır	[dʒı'dır]
stable	tövlə	[tøv'læ]

to feed (vt)	**yedirmək**	[edir'mæk]
hay	**quru ot**	[gu'ru 'ot]
to water (animals)	**suvarmaq**	[suvar'mag]
to wash (horse)	**təmizləmək**	[tæmizlæ'mæk]
to hobble (vt)	**buxovlamaq**	[buhovla'mag]
to graze (vi)	**otlamaq**	[otla'mag]
to neigh (vi)	**kişnəmək**	[kiʃnæ'mæk]
to jib, to kick out	**təpmək**	[tæp'mæk]

Flora

227. Trees

tree	ağac	[aɣˈadʒ]
deciduous (adj)	yarpaqlı	[jarpagˈlı]
coniferous (adj)	iynəli	[ijnæˈli]
evergreen (adj)	həmişəyaşıl	[hæmiʃæjaˈʃıl]
apple tree	alma	[alˈma]
pear tree	armud	[arˈmud]
sweet cherry tree	gilas	[giˈlas]
sour cherry tree	albalı	[albaˈlı]
plum tree	gavalı	[gavaˈlı]
birch	tozağacı	[tozaɣaˈdʒı]
oak	palıd	[paˈlıd]
linden tree	cökə	[dʒøˈkæ]
aspen	ağcaqovaq	[aɣdʒagoˈvag]
maple	ağcaqayın	[aɣdʒagaˈjın]
spruce	küknar	[kykˈnar]
pine	şam	[ʃam]
larch	qara şam ağacı	[gaˈra ʃam aɣaˈdʒı]
fir	ağ şam ağacı	[aɣ ʃam aɣadʒı]
cedar	sidr	[sidr]
poplar	qovaq	[goˈvag]
rowan	quşarmudu	[guʃarmuˈdu]
willow	söyüd	[søˈyd]
alder	qızılağac	[gızılaɣadʒ]
beech	fıstıq	[fısˈtıg]
elm	qarağac	[garaɣˈadʒ]
ash (tree)	göyrüş	[gøjˈryʃ]
chestnut	şabalıd	[ʃabaˈlıd]
magnolia	maqnoliya	[magˈnolija]
palm tree	palma	[ˈpalma]
cypress	sərv	[særv]
mangrove	manqra ağacı	[ˈmanqra aɣaˈdʒı]
baobab	baobab	[baoˈbab]
eucalyptus	evkalipt	[ævkaˈlipt]
sequoia	sekvoya	[sekˈvoja]

228. Shrubs

bush	kol	[ˈkøl]
shrub	kolluq	[kolˈlug]

grapevine	üzüm	[y'zym]
vineyard	üzüm bağı	[y'zym baɣ'ı]

raspberry bush	moruq	[mo'rug]
redcurrant bush	qırmızı qarağat	[gırmı'zı garaɣ'at]
gooseberry bush	krıjovnik	[krı'ʒovnik]

acacia	akasiya	[a'kasija]
barberry	zərinc	[zæ'rindʒ]
jasmine	jasmin	[ʒas'min]

juniper	ardıc kolu	[ar'dıdʒ ko'lu]
rosebush	qızılgül kolu	[gızıl'gyʎ ko'lu]
dog rose	itburnu	[itbur'nu]

229. Mushrooms

mushroom	göbələk	[gøbæ'læk]
edible mushroom	yeməli göbələk	[emæ'li gøbæ'læk]
toadstool	zəhərli göbələk	[zæhær'li gøbæ'læk]
cap (of mushroom)	papaq	[pa'pag]
stipe (of mushroom)	gövdə	[gøv'dæ]

cep, penny bun	ağ göbələk	['aɣ gøbæ'læk]
orange-cap boletus	qırmızıbaş göbələk	[gırmızı'baʃ gøbæ'læk]
birch bolete	qara göbələk	[ga'ra gøbæ'læk]
chanterelle	sarı göbələk	[sa'rı gøbæ'læk]
russula	zol-zol papaqlı göbələk	['zol 'zol papag'lı gøbæ'læk]

morel	quzugöbələyi	[guzugøbælæ'jı]
fly agaric	milşəkqıran	[milʃəkgı'ran]
death cap	zəhərli göbələk	[zæhær'li gøbæ'læk]

230. Fruits. Berries

apple	alma	[al'ma]
pear	armud	[ar'mud]
plum	gavalı	[gava'lı]

strawberry	bağ çiyələyi	['baɣ tʃijəlæ'jı]
sour cherry	albalı	[alba'lı]
sweet cherry	gilas	[gi'las]
grape	üzüm	[y'zym]

raspberry	moruq	[mo'rug]
blackcurrant	qara qarağat	[ga'ra garaɣ'at]
redcurrant	qırmızı qarağat	[gırmı'zı garaɣ'at]
gooseberry	krıjovnik	[krı'ʒovnik]
cranberry	quşüzümü	[guʃyzy'my]

orange	portağal	[portaɣ'al]
tangerine	mandarin	[manda'rin]

pineapple	ananas	[ana'nas]
banana	banan	[ba'nan]
date	xurma	[hur'ma]

lemon	limon	[li'mon]
apricot	ərik	[æ'rik]
peach	şaftalı	[ʃafta'lı]
kiwi	kivi	['kivi]
grapefruit	qreypfrut	['grejpfrut]

berry	giləmeyvə	[gilæmej'væ]
berries	giləmeyvələr	[gilæmejvæ'lær]
cowberry	mərsin	[mær'sin]
wild strawberry	çiyələk	[ʧije'læk]
bilberry	qaragilə	[garagi'læ]

231. Flowers. Plants

| flower | gül | [gyʎ] |
| bouquet (of flowers) | gül dəstəsi | ['gyʎ dæstæ'si] |

rose (flower)	qızılgül	[gızıl'gyʎ]
tulip	lalə	[la'læ]
carnation	qərənfil	[gæræn'fil]
gladiolus	qladiolus	[gladi'olus]

cornflower	peyğəmbərçiçəyi	[pejɣæmbærʧiʧə'jı]
bluebell	zəngçiçəyi	[zæŋʧiʧə'jı]
dandelion	zəncirotu	[zændʒiro'tu]
camomile	çobanyastığı	[ʧobanjastıɣ'ı]

aloe	əzvay	[æz'vaj]
cactus	kaktus	['kaktus]
rubber plant, ficus	fikus	['fikus]

lily	zanbaq	[zan'bag]
geranium	ətirşah	[ætir'ʃah]
hyacinth	giasint	[gia'sint]

mimosa	küsdüm ağacı	[kys'dym aɣa'dʒı]
narcissus	nərgizgülü	[nærgizgy'ly]
nasturtium	ərikgülü	[ærikgy'ly]

orchid	səhləb çiçəyi	[sæh'læb ʧiʧə'jı]
peony	pion	[pi'on]
violet	bənövşə	[bænøv'ʃæ]

pansy	alabəzək bənövşə	[alabæ'zæk bænøv'ʃæ]
forget-me-not	yaddaş çiçəyi	[jad'daʃ ʧiʧə'jı]
daisy	qızçiçəyi	[gızʧiʧə'jı]

poppy	lalə	[la'læ]
hemp	çətənə	[ʧətæ'næ]
mint	nanə	[na'næ]

| lily of the valley | inciçiçəyi | [inʤitʃitʃə'jı] |
| snowdrop | novruzgülü | [novruzgy'ly] |

nettle	gicitkən	[gitʃit'kæn]
sorrel	quzuqulağı	[guzugulaɣ'ı]
water lily	ağ suzanbağı	['aɣ suzanbaɣ'ı]
fern	ayıdöşəyi	[ajıdøʃæ'jı]
lichen	şibyə	[ʃib'jə]

tropical glasshouse	oranjereya	[oranʒe'reja]
grass lawn	qazon	[ga'zon]
flowerbed	çiçək ləki	[tʃi'tʃək læ'ki]

plant	bitki	[bit'ki]
grass	ot	[ot]
blade of grass	ot saplağı	['ot saplaɣ'ı]

leaf	yarpaq	[jar'pag]
petal	ləçək	[læ'tʃək]
stem	saplaq	[sap'lag]
tuber	kök yumrusu	['køk ymru'su]

| young plant (shoot) | cücərti | [ʤyʤær'ti] |
| thorn | tikan | [ti'kan] |

to blossom (vi)	çiçək açmaq	[tʃi'tʃək atʃ'mag]
to fade, to wither	solmaq	[sol'mag]
smell (odour)	ətir	[æ'tir]
to cut (flowers)	kəsmək	[kæs'mæk]
to pick (a flower)	dərmək	[dær'mæk]

232. Cereals, grains

grain	dən	[dæn]
cereals (plants)	dənli bitkilər	[dæn'li bitki'lær]
ear (of barley, etc.)	sümbül	[sym'byʎ]

wheat	taxıl	[ta'hıl]
rye	covdar	[ʤov'dar]
oats	yulaf	[y'laf]

| millet | darı | [da'rı] |
| barley | arpa | [ar'pa] |

maize	qarğıdalı	[garɣıda'lı]
rice	düyü	[dy'y]
buckwheat	qarabaşaq	[garaba'ʃag]

| pea | noxud | [no'hud] |
| kidney bean | lobya | [lob'ja] |

soya	soya	['soja]
lentil	mərcimək	[mærʤi'mæk]
beans (broad ~)	paxla	[pah'la]

233. Vegetables. Greens

vegetables	tərəvəz	[tæræ'væz]
greens	göyərti	[gøjər'ti]
tomato	pomidor	[pomi'dor]
cucumber	xiyar	[hi'jar]
carrot	kök	['køk]
potato	kartof	[kar'tof]
onion	soğan	[soɣ'an]
garlic	sarımsaq	[sarım'sag]
cabbage	kələm	[kæ'læm]
cauliflower	gül kələm	['gyʎ kæ'læm]
Brussels sprouts	Brüssel kələmi	['bryssel kælæ'mi]
beetroot	çuğundur	[ʧuɣun'dur]
aubergine	badımcan	[badım'ʤan]
marrow	yunan qabağı	[ɣ'nan gabaɣ'ı]
pumpkin	balqabaq	[balga'bag]
turnip	şalğam	[ʃalɣ'am]
parsley	petruşka	[petruʃ'ka]
dill	şüyüt	[ʃy'yt]
lettuce	salat	[sa'lat]
celery	kərəviz	[kæræ'viz]
asparagus	qulançar	[gulan'ʧar]
spinach	ispanaq	[ispa'nag]
pea	noxud	[no'hud]
beans	paxla	[pah'la]
maize	qarğıdalı	[garɣıda'lı]
kidney bean	lobya	[lob'ja]
bell pepper	biber	[bi'bær]
radish	turp	[turp]
artichoke	ənginar	[æɲi'nar]

REGIONAL GEOGRAPHY

Countries. Nationalities

234. Western Europe

Europe	Avropa	[av'ropa]
European Union	Avropa Birliyi	[av'ropa birli'jı]
European (n)	avropalı	[av'ropalı]
European (adj)	Avropa	[av'ropa]

Austria	Avstriya	['avstrija]
Austrian (masc.)	avstriyalı	['avstrijalı]
Austrian (fem.)	avstriyalı qadın	['avstrijalı ga'dın]
Austrian (adj)	Avstriya	['avstrija]

Great Britain	Böyük Britaniya	[bø'yk bri'tanija]
England	İngiltərə	[i'ŋiltæræ]
British (masc.)	ingilis	[iŋi'lis]
British (fem.)	ingilis qadın	[iŋi'lis ga'dın]
English, British (adj)	ingilis	[iŋi'lis]

Belgium	Belçika	['beltʃika]
Belgian (masc.)	belçikalı	['beltʃikalı]
Belgian (fem.)	belçikalı qadın	['beltʃikalı ga'dın]
Belgian (adj)	Belçika	['beltʃika]

Germany	Almaniya	[al'manija]
German (masc.)	alman	[al'man]
German (fem.)	alman qadını	[al'man gadı'nı]
German (adj)	alman	[al'man]

Netherlands	Niderland	[nider'land]
Holland	Hollandiya	[hol'landija]
Dutchman	hollandiyalı	[hol'landijalı]
Dutchwoman	hollandiyalı qadın	[hol'landijalı ga'dın]
Dutch (adj)	Hollandiya	[hol'landija]

Greece	Yunanıstan	[ynanıs'tan]
Greek (masc.)	yunan	[y'nan]
Greek (fem.)	yunan qadını	[y'nan gadı'nı]
Greek (adj)	yunan	[y'nan]

Denmark	Danimarka	[dani'marka]
Dane (masc.)	danimarkalı	[dani'markalı]
Dane (fem.)	danimarkalı qadın	[dani'markalı ga'dın]
Danish (adj)	Danimarka	[dani'marka]
Ireland	İrlandiya	[ir'landija]
Irishman	irlandiyalı	[ir'landijalı]

| Irishwoman | irlandiyalı qadın | [ir'landijalı ga'dın] |
| Irish (adj) | İrlandiya | [ir'landija] |

Iceland	İslandiya	[is'landija]
Icelander (masc.)	islandiyalı	[is'landijalı]
Icelander (fem.)	islandiyalı qadın	[is'landijalı ga'dın]
Icelandic (adj)	İslandiya	[is'landija]

Spain	İspaniya	[is'panija]
Spaniard (masc.)	ispaniyalı	[is'panijalı]
Spaniard (fem.)	ispan qadını	[is'pan gadı'nı]
Spanish (adj)	ispan	[is'pan]

Italy	İtaliya	[i'talija]
Italian (masc.)	italyan	[ita'ʎjan]
Italian (fem.)	italyan qadın	[ita'ʎjan ga'dın]
Italian (adj)	italyan	[ita'ʎjan]

Cyprus	Kıbrıs	['kıbrıs]
Cypriot (masc.)	kıbrıslı	['kıbrıslı]
Cypriot (fem.)	kıbrıslı qadın	['kıbrıslı ga'dın]
Cypriot (adj)	kıbrıs	['kıbrıs]

Malta	Malta	['malta]
Maltese (masc.)	maltalı	['maltalı]
Maltese (fem.)	maltalı qadın	['maltalı ga'dın]
Maltese (adj)	Malta	['malta]

Norway	Norveç	[nor'vetʃ]
Norwegian (masc.)	norveçli	[norvetʃ'li]
Norwegian (fem.)	norveçli qadın	[norvetʃ'li ga'dın]
Norwegian (adj)	Norveç	[nor'vetʃ]

Portugal	Portuqaliya	[portu'galija]
Portuguese (masc.)	portuqaliyalı	[portu'galijalı]
Portuguese (fem.)	portuqaliyalı qadın	[portu'galijalı ga'dın]
Portuguese (adj)	Portuqal	[portu'gal]

Finland	Finlyandiya	[fin'ʎandija]
Finn (masc.)	fin	[fin]
Finn (fem.)	fin qadın	['fin ga'dın]
Finnish (adj)	fin	[fin]

France	Fransa	['fransa]
Frenchman	fransız	[fran'sız]
Frenchwoman	fransız qadın	[fran'sız ga'dın]
French (adj)	fransız	[fran'sız]

Sweden	İsveç	[is'vetʃ]
Swede (masc.)	isveçli	[isvetʃ'li]
Swede (fem.)	isveçli qadın	[isvetʃ'li ga'dın]
Swedish (adj)	İsveç	[is'vetʃ]

Switzerland	İsveçrə	[is'vetʃræ]
Swiss (masc.)	isveçrəli	[is'vetʃræli]
Swiss (fem.)	isveçrəli qadın	[is'vetʃræli ga'dın]

Swiss (adj)	İsveçrə	[isˈvetʃræ]
Scotland	Şotlandiya	[ʃotˈlandija]
Scottish (masc.)	şotlandiyalı	[ʃotˈlandijalı]
Scottish (fem.)	şotlandiyalı qadın	[ʃotˈlandijalı gaˈdın]
Scottish (adj)	Şotlandiya	[ʃotˈlandija]

Vatican	Vatikan	[vatiˈkan]
Liechtenstein	Lixtenşteyn	[lihtenʃˈtejn]
Luxembourg	Lüksemburq	[lyksemˈburg]
Monaco	Monako	[moˈnako]

235. Central and Eastern Europe

Albania	Albaniya	[alˈbanija]
Albanian (masc.)	albaniyalı	[alˈban]
Albanian (fem.)	alban qadını	[alˈban gadıˈnı]
Albanian (adj)	alban	[alˈban]

Bulgaria	Bolqarıstan	[bolgarısˈtan]
Bulgarian (masc.)	bolqar	[bolˈgar]
Bulgarian (fem.)	bolqar qadını	[bolˈgar gadıˈnı]
Bulgarian (adj)	bolqar	[bolˈgar]

Hungary	Macarıstan	[madʒarısˈtan]
Hungarian (masc.)	macar	[maˈdʒar]
Hungarian (fem.)	macar qadını	[maˈdʒar gadıˈnı]
Hungarian (adj)	macar	[maˈdʒar]

Latvia	Latviya	[ˈlatvija]
Latvian (masc.)	latviyalı	[ˈlatvijalı]
Latvian (fem.)	latviyalı qadın	[ˈlatvijalı gaˈdın]
Latvian (adj)	Latviya	[ˈlatvija]

Lithuania	Litva	[litˈva]
Lithuanian (masc.)	litvalı	[litvaˈlı]
Lithuanian (fem.)	litvalı qadın	[litvaˈlı gaˈdın]
Lithuanian (adj)	Litva	[litˈva]

Poland	Polşa	[ˈpolʃa]
Pole (masc.)	polyak	[polˈjak]
Pole (fem.)	polyak qadın	[polˈjak gaˈdın]
Polish (adj)	polyak	[polˈjak]

Romania	Rumıniya	[ruˈmınija]
Romanian (masc.)	rumın	[ruˈmın]
Romanian (fem.)	rumın qadını	[ruˈmın gadıˈnı]
Romanian (adj)	rumın	[ruˈmın]

Serbia	Serbiya	[ˈserbija]
Serbian (masc.)	serb	[serb]
Serbian (fem.)	serb qadın	[ˈserb gaˈdın]
Serbian (adj)	serb	[serb]
Slovakia	Slovakiya	[sloˈvakija]
Slovak (masc.)	slovak	[sloˈvak]

| Slovak (fem.) | slovak qadın | [slo'vak ga'dın] |
| Slovak (adj) | slovak | [slo'vak] |

Croatia	Xorvatiya	[hor'vatija]
Croatian (masc.)	xorvat	[hor'vat]
Croatian (fem.)	xorvat qadın	[hor'vat ga'dın]
Croatian (adj)	xorvat	[hor'vat]

Czech Republic	Çexiya	['tʃehija]
Czech (masc.)	çex	[tʃeh]
Czech (fem.)	çex qadın	['tʃeh ga'dın]
Czech (adj)	çex	[tʃeh]

Estonia	Estoniya	[æs'tonija]
Estonian (masc.)	eston	[æs'ton]
Estonian (fem.)	eston qadın	[æs'ton ga'dın]
Estonian (adj)	eston	[æs'ton]

Bosnia-Herzegovina	Bosniya və Hersoqovina	['bosnija 'væ hersogo'vina]
Macedonia	Makedoniya	[make'donija]
Slovenia	Sloveniya	[slo'venija]
Montenegro	Qaradağ	[ga'radaɣ]

236. Former USSR countries

Azerbaijan	Azərbaycan	[azærbaj'dʒan]
Azerbaijani (masc.)	azərbaycanlı	[azærbajdʒan'lı]
Azerbaijani (fem.)	azərbaycanlı qadın	[azærbajdʒan'lı ga'dın]
Azerbaijani (adj)	Azərbaycan	[azærbaj'dʒan]

Armenia	Ermənistan	[ærmænis'tan]
Armenian (masc.)	erməni	[ærmæ'ni]
Armenian (fem.)	erməni qadını	[ærmæ'ni gadı'nı]
Armenian (adj)	erməni	[ærmæ'ni]

Belarus	Belarus	[bela'rus]
Belarusian (masc.)	belarus	[bela'rus]
Belarusian (fem.)	belarus qadını	[bela'rus gadı'nı]
Belarusian (adj)	belarus	[bela'rus]

Georgia	Gürcüstan	[gyrdʒys'tan]
Georgian (masc.)	gürcü	[gyr'dʒy]
Georgian (fem.)	gürcü qadını	[gyr'dʒy gadı'nı]
Georgian (adj)	gürcü	[gyr'dʒy]

Kazakhstan	Qazaxstan	[gazahs'tan]
Kazakh (masc.)	qazax	[ga'zah]
Kazakh (fem.)	qazax qadın	[ga'zah ga'dın]
Kazakh (adj)	qazax	[ga'zah]

Kirghizia	Qırğızıstan	[gırɣızıs'tan]
Kirghiz (masc.)	qırğız	[gırɣ'ız]
Kirghiz (fem.)	qırğız qadını	[gırɣ'ız gadı'nı]
Kirghiz (adj)	qırğız	[gırɣ'ız]

Moldavia	Moldova	[mol'dova]
Moldavian (masc.)	moldovalı	[mol'dovalı]
Moldavian (fem.)	moldovalı qadın	[mol'dovalı ga'dın]
Moldavian (adj)	Moldova	[mol'dova]

Russia	Rusiya	['rusija]
Russian (masc.)	rus	[rus]
Russian (fem.)	rus qadını	['rus gadı'nı]
Russian (adj)	rus	[rus]

Tajikistan	Tacikistan	[tadʒikis'tan]
Tajik (masc.)	tacik	[ta'dʒik]
Tajik (fem.)	tacik qadın	[ta'dʒik ga'dın]
Tajik (adj)	tacik	[ta'dʒik]

Turkmenistan	Türkmənistan	[tyrkmænis'tan]
Turkmen (masc.)	türkmən	[tyrk'mæn]
Turkmen (fem.)	türkmən qadın	[tyrk'mæn ga'dın]
Turkmenian (adj)	türkmən	[tyrk'mæn]

Uzbekistan	Özbəkistan	[øzbækis'tan]
Uzbek (masc.)	özbək	[øz'bæk]
Uzbek (fem.)	özbək qadın	[øz'bæk ga'dın]
Uzbek (adj)	özbək	[øz'bæk]

Ukraine	Ukrayna	[uk'rajna]
Ukrainian (masc.)	ukraynalı	[uk'rajnalı]
Ukrainian (fem.)	ukraynalı qadın	[uk'rajnalı ga'dın]
Ukrainian (adj)	Ukrayna	[uk'rajna]

237. Asia

Asia	Asiya	['asija]
Asian (adj)	Asiya	['asija]

Vietnam	Vyetnam	[vjet'nam]
Vietnamese (masc.)	vyetnamlı	[vjetnam'lı]
Vietnamese (fem.)	vyetnamlı qadın	[vjetnam'lı ga'dın]
Vietnamese (adj)	Vyetnam	[vjet'nam]

India	Hindistan	[hindis'tan]
Indian (masc.)	hind	[hind]
Indian (fem.)	hind qadını	['hind gadı'nı]
Indian (adj)	hind	[hind]

Israel	İsrail	[isra'il]
Israeli (masc.)	israilli	[israil'li]
Israeli (fem.)	israilli qadın	[israil'li ga'dın]
Israeli (adj)	İsrail	[isra'il]

Jew (n)	yahudi	[jahu'di]
Jewess (n)	yahudi qadın	[jahu'di ga'dın]
Jewish (adj)	yahudi	[jahu'di]
China	Çin	[tʃin]

211

Chinese (masc.)	çinli	[tʃin'li]
Chinese (fem.)	çinli qadın	[tʃin'li ga'dın]
Chinese (adj)	Çin	[tʃin]

Korean (masc.)	koreyalı	[ko'rejalı]
Korean (fem.)	koreyalı qadın	[ko'rejalı ga'dın]
Korean (adj)	Koreya	[ko'reja]

Lebanon	Livan	[li'van]
Lebanese (masc.)	livanlı	[livan'lı]
Lebanese (fem.)	livanlı qadın	[livan'lı ga'dın]
Lebanese (adj)	Livan	[li'van]

Mongolia	Monqolustan	[moŋolus'tan]
Mongolian (masc.)	monqol	[mo'ŋol]
Mongolian (fem.)	monqol qadın	[mo'ŋol ga'dın]
Mongolian (adj)	monqol	[mo'ŋol]

Malaysia	Malayziya	[ma'lajzija]
Malaysian (masc.)	malay	[ma'laj]
Malaysian (fem.)	malay qadın	[ma'laj ga'dın]
Malaysian (adj)	Malayziya	[ma'lajzija]

Pakistan	Pakistan	[pakis'tan]
Pakistani (masc.)	pakistanlı	[pakistan'lı]
Pakistani (fem.)	pakistanlı qadın	[pakistan'lı ga'dın]
Pakistani (adj)	Pakistan	[pakis'tan]

Saudi Arabia	Səudiyyə Ərəbistanı	[sæudi'j:ə æræbista'nı]
Arab (masc.)	ərəb	[æ'ræb]
Arab (fem.)	ərəb qadını	[æ'ræb gadı'nı]
Arabian (adj)	ərəb	[æ'ræb]

Thailand	Tailand	[tai'land]
Thai (masc.)	tay	[taj]
Thai (fem.)	tay qadını	['taj gadı'nı]
Thai (adj)	tay	[taj]

Taiwan	Tayvan	[taj'van]
Taiwanese (masc.)	tayvanlı	[tajvan'lı]
Taiwanese (fem.)	tayvanlı qadın	[tajvan'lı ga'dın]
Taiwanese (adj)	Tayvan	[taj'van]

Turkey	Türkiyə	['tyrkijə]
Turk (masc.)	türk	[tyrk]
Turk (fem.)	türk qadını	['tyrk gadı'nı]
Turkish (adj)	türk	[tyrk]

Japan	Yaponiya	[ja'ponija]
Japanese (masc.)	yapon	[ja'pon]
Japanese (fem.)	yapon qadın	[ja'pon ga'dın]
Japanese (adj)	yapon	[ja'pon]

Afghanistan	Afqanistan	[afganis'tan]
Bangladesh	Banqladeş	[baŋla'deʃ]
Indonesia	İndoneziya	[indo'nezija]

Jordan	İordaniya	[ior'danija]
Iraq	İraq	[i'rak]
Iran	İran	[i'ran]
Cambodia	Kamboca	[kam'bodʒa]
Kuwait	Küveyt	[ky'vejt]

Laos	Laos	[la'os]
Myanmar	Myanma	['mjanma]
Nepal	Nepal	[ne'pal]
United Arab Emirates	Birləşmiş Ərəb Əmirlikləri	[birlæʃmiʃ æ'ræb æmirliklæ'ri]

Syria	Suriya	['surija]
Palestine	Fələstin muxtariyyatı	[fælæs'tin muhtarij:a'tı]
South Korea	Cənubi Koreya	[dʒænu'bi ko'reja]
North Korea	Şimali Koreya	[ʃima'li ko'reja]

238. North America

United States of America	Amerika Birləşmiş Ştatları	[a'merika birlæʃmiʃ ʃtatla'rı]
American (masc.)	amerikalı	[a'merikalı]
American (fem.)	amerikalı qadın	[a'merikalı ga'dın]
American (adj)	amerikan	[ameri'kan]

Canada	Kanada	[ka'nada]
Canadian (masc.)	kanadalı	[ka'nadalı]
Canadian (fem.)	kanadalı qadın	[ka'nadalı ga'dın]
Canadian (adj)	Kanada	[ka'nada]

Mexico	Meksika	['meksika]
Mexican (masc.)	meksikalı	['meksikalı]
Mexican (fem.)	meksikalı qadın	['meksikalı ga'dın]
Mexican (adj)	Meksika	['meksika]

239. Central and South America

Argentina	Argentina	[argen'tina]
Argentinian (masc.)	argentinalı	[argen'tinalı]
Argentinian (fem.)	argentinalı qadın	[argen'tinalı ga'dın]
Argentinian (adj)	Argentina	[argen'tina]

Brazil	Braziliya	[bra'zilija]
Brazilian (masc.)	braziliyalı	[bra'zilijalı]
Brazilian (fem.)	braziliyalı qadın	[bra'zilijalı ga'dın]
Brazilian (adj)	Braziliya	[bra'zilija]

Colombia	Kolumbiya	[ko'lumbija]
Colombian (masc.)	kolumbiyalı	[ko'lumbijalı]
Colombian (fem.)	kolumbiyalı qadın	[ko'lumbijalı ga'dın]
Colombian (adj)	Kolumbiya	[ko'lumbija]
Cuba	Kuba	['kuba]

Cuban (masc.)	kubalı	['kubalı]
Cuban (fem.)	kubalı qadın	['kubalı ga'dın]
Cuban (adj)	Kuba	['kuba]

Chile	Çili	['tʃili]
Chilean (masc.)	çilili	['tʃilili]
Chilean (fem.)	çilili qadın	['tʃilili ga'dın]
Chilean (adj)	Çili	['tʃili]

Bolivia	Boliviya	[bo'livija]
Venezuela	Venesuela	[venesu'æla]
Paraguay	Paraqvay	[parag'vaj]
Peru	Peru	[pe'ru]
Suriname	Surinam	[suri'nam]
Uruguay	Uruqvay	[urug'vaj]
Ecuador	Ekvador	[ækva'dor]

The Bahamas	Baqam adaları	[ba'gam adala'rı]
Haiti	Haiti	[ha'iti]
Dominican Republic	Dominikan Respublikası	[domini'kan res'publikası]
Panama	Panama	[pa'nama]
Jamaica	Yamayka	[ja'majka]

240. Africa

Egypt	Misir	[mi'sir]
Egyptian (masc.)	misirli	[misir'li]
Egyptian (fem.)	misirli qadın	[misir'li ga'dın]
Egyptian (adj)	Misir	[mi'sir]

Morocco	Mərakeş	[mæra'keʃ]
Moroccan (masc.)	mərakeşli	[mærakeʃ'li]
Moroccan (fem.)	mərakeşli qadın	[mærakeʃ'li ga'dın]
Moroccan (adj)	Mərakeş	[mæra'keʃ]

Tunisia	Tunis	[tu'nis]
Tunisian (masc.)	tunisli	[tunis'li]
Tunisian (fem.)	tunisli qadın	[tunis'li ga'dın]
Tunisian (adj)	Tunis	[tu'nis]

Ghana	Qana	['gana]
Zanzibar	Zənzibar	[zænzi'bar]
Kenya	Keniya	['kenija]
Libya	Liviya	['livija]
Madagascar	Madaqaskar	[madagas'kar]

Namibia	Namibiya	[na'mibija]
Senegal	Seneqal	[sene'gal]
Tanzania	Tanzaniya	[tan'zanija]
South Africa	Cənubi Afrika respublikası	[dʒænu'bi 'afrika res'publikası]

African (masc.)	afrikalı	['afrikalı]
African (fem.)	afrikalı qadın	['afrikalı ga'dın]
African (adj)	afrikalı	['afrikalı]

241. Australia. Oceania

Australia	Avstraliya	[avst'ralija]
Australian (masc.)	avstraliyalı	[avst'ralijalı]
Australian (fem.)	avstraliyalı qadın	[avst'ralijalı ga'dın]
Australian (adj)	Avstraliya	[avst'ralija]

New Zealand	Yeni Zelandiya	[e'ni ze'landija]
New Zealander (masc.)	yeni zelandiyalı	[e'ni ze'landijalı]
New Zealander (fem.)	yeni zelandiyalı qadın	[e'ni ze'landijalı ga'dın]
New Zealand (as adj)	Yeni Zelandiya	[e'ni ze'landija]

Tasmania	Tasmaniya	[tas'manija]
French Polynesia	Fransız Polineziyası	[fran'sız poli'nezijası]

242. Cities

Amsterdam	Amsterdam	[amster'dam]
Ankara	Ankara	[aŋka'ra]
Athens	Afina	[a'fina]
Baghdad	Bağdad	[bay'dad]
Bangkok	Banqkok	[baŋ'kok]
Barcelona	Barselona	[barse'lona]

Beijing	Pekin	[pe'kin]
Beirut	Beyrut	[bej'rut]
Berlin	Berlin	[ber'lin]
Bombay, Mumbai	Bombey	[bom'bej]
Bonn	Bonn	[boŋ]

Bordeaux	Bordo	[bor'do]
Bratislava	Bratislava	[bratisla'va]
Brussels	Brüssel	[brys'sel]
Bucharest	Buxarest	[buha'rest]
Budapest	Budapeşt	[buda'peʃt]

Cairo	Qahirə	[gahi'ræ]
Calcutta	Kalkutta	[kal'kutta]
Chicago	Çikaqo	[tʃi'kago]
Copenhagen	Kopenhaqen	[kopen'hagen]

Dar-es-Salaam	Dar Əs Salam	['dar 'æs sa'lam]
Delhi	Dehli	[deh'li]
Dubai	Dubay	[du'baj]
Dublin	Dublin	['dublin]
Düsseldorf	Düsseldorf	['dysseldorf]

Florence	Florensiya	[flo'rensija]
Frankfurt	Frankfurt	['fraŋkfurt]
Geneva	Cenevrə	[dʒe'nevræ]

The Hague	Haaga	[ha'aga]
Hamburg	Hamburq	['hamburg]

215

Hanoi	**Hanoy**	[ha'noj]
Havana	**Havana**	[ha'vana]
Helsinki	**Helsinki**	['helsiŋki]
Hiroshima	**Xirosima**	[hiro'sima]
Hong Kong	**Honkonq**	[ho'ŋkoŋ]
İstanbul	**İstanbul**	[istan'bul]
Jerusalem	**Yeruselim**	[erusæ'lim]
Kiev	**Kiyev**	['kiev]
Kuala Lumpur	**Kuala Lumpur**	[ku'ala lum'pur]
Lisbon	**Lissabon**	[lissa'bon]
London	**London**	['london]
Los Angeles	**Los Anjeles**	['los 'anʒeles]
Lyons	**Lion**	[li'on]
Madrid	**Madrid**	[mad'rid]
Marseille	**Marsel**	[mar'sel]
Mexico City	**Mexiko**	['mehiko]
Miami	**Mayami**	[ma'jami]
Montreal	**Monreal**	[monre'al]
Moscow	**Moskva**	[mosk'va]
Munich	**München**	['mynhen]
Nairobi	**Nayrobi**	[naj'robi]
Naples	**Neapol**	[ne'apol]
New York	**Nyu-York**	['ɲjy 'jork]
Nice	**Nitsa**	['nitsa]
Oslo	**Oslo**	['oslo]
Ottawa	**Ottava**	[ot'tava]
Paris	**Paris**	[pa'ris]
Prague	**Praqa**	['praga]
Rio de Janeiro	**Rio-de-Janeyro**	['rio 'de ʒa'nejro]
Rome	**Roma**	['roma]
Saint Petersburg	**Sankt-Peterburq**	['saŋkt peter'burg]
Seoul	**Seul**	[se'ul]
Shanghai	**Şanxay**	[ʃan'haj]
Singapore	**Sinqapur**	[siŋa'pur]
Stockholm	**Stokholm**	[stok'holm]
Sydney	**Sidney**	['sidnej]
Taipei	**Taypey**	[taj'pej]
Tokyo	**Tokio**	['tokio]
Toronto	**Toronto**	[to'ronto]
Venice	**Venesiya**	[ve'nesija]
Vienna	**Vena**	['vena]
Warsaw	**Varşava**	[var'ʃava]
Washington	**Vaşinqton**	[vaʃiŋ'ton]

243. Politics. Government. Part 1

politics	**siyasət**	[sija'sæt]
political (adj)	**siyasi**	[sija'si]

politician	siyasətçi	[sijasæ'tʃi]
state (country)	dövlət	[døv'læt]
citizen	vətəndaş	[vætæn'daʃ]
citizenship	vətəndaşlıq	[vætændaʃ'lıg]
national emblem	milli herb	[mil'li 'herb]
national anthem	dövlət himni	[døv'læt him'ni]
government	hökümət	[høky'mæt]
head of state	ölkə başçısı	[øl'kæ baʃtʃı'sı]
parliament	parlament	[par'lament]
party	partiya	['partija]
capitalism	kapitalizm	[kapita'lizm]
capitalist (adj)	kapitalist	[kapita'list]
socialism	sosializm	[sotsia'lizm]
socialist (adj)	sosialist	[sotsia'list]
communism	kommunizm	[kommu'nizm]
communist (adj)	kommunist	[kommu'nist]
communist (n)	kommunist	[kommu'nist]
democracy	demokratiya	[demok'ratija]
democrat	demokrat	[demok'rat]
democratic (adj)	demokratik	[demokra'tik]
Democratic party	demokratik partiyası	[demokra'tik 'partijası]
liberal (n)	liberal	[libe'ral]
Liberal (adj)	liberal	[libe'ral]
conservative (n)	mühafizəkar	[myhafizæ'kar]
conservative (adj)	mühafizəkar	[myhafizæ'kar]
republic (n)	respublika	[res'publika]
republican (n)	respublikaçı	[res'publikatʃı]
Republican party	respublikaçılar partiyası	[res'publikatʃılar 'partijası]
poll, elections	seçkilər	[setʃki'lær]
to elect (vt)	seçmək	[setʃ'mæk]
elector, voter	seçici	[setʃi'dʒi]
election campaign	seçki kampaniyası	[setʃ'ki kam'panijası]
voting (n)	səs vermə	['sæs ver'mæ]
to vote (vi)	səs vermək	['sæs ver'mæk]
suffrage, right to vote	səs vermə hüququ	['sæs ver'mæ hygu'gu]
candidate	namizəd	[nami'zæd]
to be a candidate	namizədliyini	[namizædliji'ni]
	irəli sürmək	iræ'li syr'mæk]
campaign	kampaniya	[kam'panija]
opposition (as adj)	müxalif	[myha'lif]
opposition (n)	müxalifət	[myhali'fæt]
visit	səfər	[sæ'fær]
official visit	rəsmi səfər	[ræs'mi sæ'fær]

international (adj)	beynəlxalq	[bejnæl'halg]
negotiations	danışıqlar	[danıʃıg'lar]
to negotiate (vi)	danışıqlar aparmaq	[danıʃıg'lar apar'mag]

244. Politics. Government. Part 2

society	cəmiyyət	[dʒæmi'j:ət]
constitution	konstitusiya	[konsti'tusija]
power (political control)	hakimiyyət	[hakimi'j:ət]
corruption	korrupsiya	[kor'rupsija]

| law (justice) | qanun | [ga'nun] |
| legal (legitimate) | qanuni | [ganu'ni] |

| justice (fairness) | ədalət | [æda'læt] |
| just (fair) | ədalətli | [ædalæt'li] |

committee	komitə	[komi'tæ]
bill (draft of law)	qanun layihəsi	[ga'nun laihæ'si]
budget	büdcə	[byd'dʒæ]
policy	siyasət	[sija'sæt]
reform	islahat	[isla'hat]
radical (adj)	radikal	[radi'kal]

power (strength, force)	qüdrət	[gyd'ræt]
powerful (adj)	qüdrətli	[gydræt'li]
supporter	tərəfdar	[tæræf'dar]
influence	təsir	[tæ'sir]

regime (e.g. military ~)	rejim	[re'ʒim]
conflict	münaqişə	[mynagi'ʃæ]
conspiracy (plot)	sui-qəsd	['sui 'gæsd]
provocation	provokasiya	[provo'kasija]

to overthrow (regime, etc.)	devirmək	[devir'mæk]
overthrow (of government)	devrilmə	[devril'mæ]
revolution	inqilab	[iŋi'lab]

| coup d'état | çevriliş | [ʧevri'liʃ] |
| military coup | hərbi çevriliş | [hær'bi ʧevri'liʃ] |

crisis	böhran	[bøh'ran]
economic recession	iqtisadi zəifləmə	[igtisa'di zæiflæ'mæ]
demonstrator (protester)	nümayişçi	[nymaiʃ'ʧi]
demonstration	nümayiş	[nyma'iʃ]
martial law	hərbi vəziyyət	[hær'bi væzi'j:ət]
military base	baza	['baza]

| stability | stabillik | [stabil'lik] |
| stable (adj) | stabil | [sta'bil] |

exploitation	istismar	[istis'mar]
to exploit (workers)	istismar etmək	[istis'mar æt'mæk]
racism	irqçilik	[irgʧi'lik]

racist	irqçi	[irg'tʃi]
fascism	faşizm	[fa'ʃizm]
fascist	faşist	[fa'ʃist]

245. Countries. Miscellaneous

foreigner	xarici	[hari'dʒi]
foreign (adj)	xarici	[hari'dʒi]
abroad (adv)	xaricdə	[haridʒ'dæ]
emigrant	mühacir	[myha'dʒir]
emigration	mühacirət	[myhadʒi'ræt]
to emigrate (vi)	mühacirət etmək	[myhadʒi'ræt æt'mæk]

the West	Qərb	[gærb]
the East	Şərq	[ʃærg]
the Far East	Uzaq Şərq	[u'zag 'ʃærg]

civilization	sivilizasiya	[sivili'zasija]
humanity (mankind)	bəşəriyyət	[bæʃæri'j:ət]
world (earth)	dünya	[dyn'ja]
peace	əmin-amanlıq	[æ'min aman'lıg]
worldwide (adj)	dünya	[dyn'ja]

homeland	vətən	[væ'tæn]
people (population)	xalq	[halg]
population	əhali	[æha'li]
people (a lot of ~)	adamlar	[adam'lar]
nation (people)	milliyət	[milli'jət]
generation	nəsil	[næ'sil]

territory (area)	ərazi	[æra'zi]
region	bölqə	[bøl'gæ]
state (part of a country)	ştat	[ʃtat]
tradition	ənənə	[ænæ'næ]
custom (tradition)	adət	[a'dæt]
ecology	ekoloqiya	[æko'logija]

Indian (Native American)	hindi	[hin'di]
Gipsy (masc.)	qaraçı	[gara'tʃı]
Gipsy (fem.)	qaraçı qadın	[gara'tʃı ga'dın]
Gipsy (adj)	qaraçı	[gara'tʃı]

empire	imperatorluq	[impe'ratorlug]
colony	müstəmləkə	[mystæmlæ'kæ]
slavery	köləlik	[kølæ'lik]
invasion	basqın	[bas'gın]
famine	aclıq	[adʒ'lıg]

246. Major religious groups. Confessions

| religion | din | [din] |
| religious (adj) | dini | [di'ni] |

belief (in God)	etiqad	[æti'gad]
to believe (in God)	etiqad etmək	[æti'gad æt'mæk]
believer	dindar	[din'dar]
atheism	ateizm	[ate'izm]
atheist	ateist	[ate'ist]
Christianity	xristianlıq	[hristian'lıg]
Christian (n)	xristian	[hristi'an]
Christian (adj)	xristian	[hristi'an]
Catholicism	Katolisizm	[katoli'sizm]
Catholic (n)	katolik	[ka'tolik]
Catholic (adj)	katolik	[kato'lik]
Protestantism	Protestantlıq	[protestant'lıg]
Protestant Church	Protestant kilsəsi	[protes'tant kilsæ'si]
Protestant	protestant	[protes'tant]
Orthodoxy	Pravoslavlıq	[pravoslav'lıg]
Orthodox Church	Pravoslav kilsəsi	[pravos'lav kilsæ'si]
Orthodox	pravoslav	[pravos'lav]
Presbyterianism	Presviterianlıq	[presviterian'lıg]
Presbyterian Church	Presviterian kilsəsi	[presviteri'an kilsæ'si]
Presbyterian (n)	presviterian	[presviteri'an]
Lutheranism	Lüteran kilsəsi	[lyte'ran kilsæ'si]
Lutheran	lüteran	[lyte'ran]
Baptist Church	Baptizm	[bap'tizm]
Baptist	baptist	[bap'tist]
Anglican Church	Anqlikan kilsəsi	[aŋli'kan kilsæ'si]
Anglican	anqlikan	[aŋli'kan]
Mormonism	Mormonluq	[mormon'lug]
Mormon	mormon	[mor'mon]
Judaism	Yahudilik	[jahudi'lik]
Jew	yahudi	[jahu'di]
Buddhism	Buddizm	[bud'dizm]
Buddhist	buddist	[bud'dist]
Hinduism	Hinduizm	[hindu'izm]
Hindu	hinduist	[hindu'ist]
Islam	İslam	[is'lam]
Muslim (n)	müsəlman	[mysæl'man]
Muslim (adj)	müsəlman	[mysæl'man]
Shiism	Şiəlik	[ʃiæ'lik]
Shiite (n)	şiə	[ʃi'æ]
Sunni (religion)	Sünnülük	[syŋy'lyk]
Sunnite (n)	sünnü	[sy'ŋy]

247. Religions. Priests

priest	keşiş	[keˈʃiʃ]
the Pope	Roma Papası	[ˈroma ˈpapası]
monk, friar	rahib	[raˈhib]
nun	rahibə	[rahiˈbæ]
pastor	pastor	[ˈpastor]
abbot	abbat	[abˈbat]
vicar	vikari	[viˈkari]
bishop	yepiskop	[eˈpiskop]
cardinal	kardinal	[kardiˈnal]
preacher	moizəçi	[moizæˈtʃi]
preaching	moizə	[moiˈzæ]
parishioners	kilsəyə gələn dindarlar	[kilsæˈjə gæˈlæn dindarˈlar]
believer	dindar	[dinˈdar]
atheist	ateist	[ateˈist]

248. Faith. Christianity. Islam

Adam	Adəm	[aˈdæm]
Eve	Həvva	[hævˈva]
God	Tanrı	[tanˈrı]
the Lord	Tanrı	[tanˈrı]
the Almighty	Qüdrətli	[gydrætˈli]
sin	günah	[gyˈnah]
to sin (vi)	günaha batmaq	[gynaˈha batˈmag]
sinner (masc.)	günahkar	[gynahˈkar]
sinner (fem.)	günahkar qadın	[gynahˈkar gaˈdın]
hell	cəhənnəm	[dʒæhæˈŋæm]
paradise	cənnət	[dʒæˈŋæt]
Jesus	İsa	[iˈsa]
Jesus Christ	İsa Məsih	[iˈsa mæˈsih]
the Holy Spirit	ruhülqüds	[ˈruhylgyds]
the Saviour	İsa	[iˈsa]
the Virgin Mary	İsanın anası	[isaˈnın anaˈsı]
the Devil	Şeytan	[ʃejˈtan]
devil's (adj)	şeytan	[ʃejˈtan]
Satan	İblis	[ibˈlis]
satanic (adj)	iblisanə	[iblisaˈnæ]
angel	mələk	[mæˈlæk]
guardian angel	mühafiz mələk	[myhaˈfiz mæˈlæk]
angelic (adj)	mələk	[mæˈlæk]

apostle	həvvari	[hævva'ri]
archangel	Cəbrayıl	[dʒæbra'il]
the Antichrist	dəccəl	[dæ'dʒæl]
Church	Kilsə	[kil'sæ]
Bible	bibliya	['biblija]
biblical (adj)	bibliya	['biblija]
Old Testament	Əhdi-ətiq	['æhdi æ'tig]
New Testament	Əhdi-cədid	['æhdi dʒæ'did]
Gospel	İncil	[in'dʒil]
Holy Scripture	əhdi-ətiq və əhdi-cədid	['æhdi æ'tig 'væ 'æhdi dʒæ'did]
heaven	Səma Səltənəti	[sæ'ma sæltænæ'ti]
Commandment	ehkam	[æh'kam]
prophet	peyğəmbər	[pejɣæm'bær]
prophecy	peyğəmbərlik	[pejɣæmbær'lik]
Allah	Allah	[al'lah]
Mohammed	Məhəmməd	[mæhæm'mæd]
the Koran	Quran	[gu'ran]
mosque	məsçid	[mæs'tʃid]
mullah	molla	[mol'la]
prayer	dua	[du'a]
to pray (vi, vt)	dua etmək	[du'a æt'mæk]
pilgrimage	zəvvarlıq	[zævvar'lıg]
pilgrim	zəvvar	[zæv'var]
Mecca	Məkkə	[mæk'kæ]
church	kilsə	[kil'sæ]
temple	məbəd	[mæ'bæd]
cathedral	baş kilsə	['baʃ kil'sæ]
Gothic (adj)	qotik	[go'tik]
synagogue	sinaqoq	[sina'gog]
mosque	məsçid	[mæs'tʃid]
chapel	kişik kilsə	[ki'tʃik kil'sæ]
abbey	abbatlıq	[abbat'lıg]
convent	qadın monastırı	[ga'dın monastı'rı]
monastery	kişi monastırı	[ki'ʃi monastı'rı]
bell (in church)	zənq	[zæŋ]
bell tower	zənq qülləsi	['zæŋ gyllæ'si]
to ring (ab. bells)	zənq etmək	['zæŋ æt'mæk]
cross	xaç	[hatʃ]
cupola (roof)	günbəz	[gyn'bæz]
icon	ikona	[i'kona]
soul	can	[dʒan]
fate (destiny)	qismət	[gis'mæt]
evil (n)	pislik	[pis'lik]
good (n)	yaxşılıq	[jahʃı'lıg]

vampire	**xortdan**	[hort'dan]
witch (sorceress)	**caduger qadın**	[ʤadu'gær ga'dın]
demon	**iblis**	[ib'lis]
devil	**şeytan**	[ʃej'tan]
spirit	**ruh**	[ruh]
redemption (giving us ~)	**günahdan təmizlənmə**	[gynah'dan tæmizlæn'mæ]
to redeem (vt)	**günahı təmizləmək**	[gyna'hı tæmizlæ'mæk]
church service, mass	**ibadət etmə**	[iba'dæt æt'mæ]
to say mass	**ibadət etmək**	[iba'dæt æt'mæk]
confession	**tövbə etmə**	[tøv'bæ æt'mæ]
to confess (vi)	**tövbə etmək**	[tøv'bæ æt'mæk]
saint (n)	**övliya**	[øvli'ja]
sacred (holy)	**müqəddəs**	[mygæd'dæs]
holy water	**müqəddəs su**	[mygæd'dæs 'su]
ritual (n)	**mərasim**	[mæra'sim]
ritual (adj)	**mərasimə aid**	[mærasi'mæ a'id]
sacrifice	**qurban kəsmə**	[gur'ban kæs'mæ]
superstition	**xurafat**	[hura'fat]
superstitious (adj)	**xurafatçı**	[hurafa'tʃı]
afterlife	**axirət dünyası**	[ahi'ræt dynja'sı]
eternal life	**əbədi həyat**	[æbæ'di hæ'jat]

MISCELLANEOUS

249. Various useful words

background (green ~)	fon	[fon]
balance (of situation)	balans	[ba'lans]
barrier (obstacle)	sədd	[sædd]
base (basis)	baza	['baza]
beginning	başlanqıc	[baʃla'ŋıʤ]
category	kateqoriya	[kate'gorija]
cause (reason)	səbəb	[sæ'bæb]
choice	seçim	[se'tʃim]
coincidence	üst-üstə düşmə	['yst ys'tæ dyʃ'mæ]
comfortable (~ chair)	əlverişli	[ælveriʃ'li]
comparison	müqayisə	[mygajı'sæ]
compensation	kompensasiya	[kompen'sasija]
degree (extent, amount)	dərəcə	[dæræ'ʤæ]
development	inkişaf	[iŋki'ʃaf]
difference	fərqlənmə	[færglæn'mæ]
effect (e.g. of drugs)	təsir	[tæ'sir]
effort (exertion)	səy	[sæj]
element	element	[æle'ment]
end (finish)	son	[son]
example (illustration)	misal	[mi'sal]
fact	fakt	[fakt]
frequent (adj)	tez-tez	['tez 'tez]
growth (development)	boy atma	['boj at'ma]
help	kömək	[kø'mæk]
ideal	ideal	[ide'al]
kind (sort, type)	növ	['nøv]
labyrinth	labirint	[labi'rint]
mistake, error	səhv	[sæhv]
moment	an	[an]
object (thing)	obyekt	[ob'jekt]
obstacle	maneə	[mane'æ]
original (original copy)	əsl	[æsl]
part (~ of sth)	hissə	[his'sæ]
particle, small part	zərrə	[zær'ræ]
pause (break)	pauza	['pauza]
position	pozisiya	[po'zisija]
principle	prinsip	['prinsip]
problem	problem	[prob'lem]

process	proses	[pro'ses]
progress	tərəqqi	[tæræg'gi]
property (quality)	xüsusiyyət	[hysusi'j:ət]

| reaction | reaksiya | [re'aksija] |
| risk | risk | [risk] |

secret	sirr	[sirr]
section (sector)	seksiya	['seksija]
series	seriya	['serija]
shape (outer form)	forma	['forma]
situation	situasiya	[situ'asija]

solution	həll	[hæll]
standard (adj)	standart	[stan'dart]
standard (level of quality)	standart	[stan'dart]
stop (pause)	fasilə	[fasi'læ]
style	üslub	[ys'lub]
system	sistem	[sis'tem]

table (chart)	cədvəl	[ʤæd'væl]
tempo, rate	temp	[temp]
term (word, expression)	termin	['termin]
thing (object, item)	əşya	[æ'ʃa]
truth	həqiqət	[hægi'gæt]
turn (please wait your ~)	növbə	[nøv'bæ]
type (sort, kind)	tip	[tip]

urgent (adj)	təcili	[tæʤi'li]
urgently	təcili	[tæʤi'li]
utility (usefulness)	xeyir	[he'jɪr]
variant (alternative)	variant	[vari'ant]
way (means, method)	üsul	['ysul]
zone	zona	['zona]

250. Modifiers. Adjectives. Part 1

additional (adj)	əlavə	[æla'væ]
ancient (~ civilization)	qədim	[gæ'dim]
artificial (adj)	süni	[sy'ni]

back, rear (adj)	arxa	[ar'ha]
bad (adj)	pis	[pis]
beautiful (~ palace)	gözəl	[gø'zæl]
beautiful (person)	gözəl	[gø'zæl]
big (in size)	böyük	[bø'yk]
bitter (taste)	acı	[a'ʤɪ]
blind (sightless)	kor	[kor]

calm, quiet (adj)	sakit	[sa'kit]
careless (negligent)	səliqəsiz	[sæligæ'siz]
caring (~ father)	qayğıkeş	[gajɣɪ'keʃ]
central (adj)	mərkəzi	[mærkæ'zi]
cheap (adj)	ucuz	[u'ʤuz]

cheerful (adj)	şən	[ʃæn]
children's (adj)	uşaq	[uˈʃag]
civil (~ law)	mülki	[myʎˈki]

clandestine (secret)	xəlvət	[hælˈvæt]
clean (free from dirt)	təmiz	[tæˈmiz]
clear (explanation, etc.)	aydın	[ajˈdın]
clever (intelligent)	ağıllı	[aɣılˈlı]
close (near in space)	yaxın	[jaˈhın]
closed (adj)	bağlı	[baɣˈlı]
cloudless (sky)	buludsuz	[buludˈsuz]

cold (drink, weather)	soyuq	[soˈyg]
compatible (adj)	bir birinə uyğun gələn	[ˈbir biriˈnæ ujɣˈun gæˈlæn]
contented (adj)	məmnun	[mæmˈnun]
continuous (adj)	sürəkli	[syrækˈli]
continuous (incessant)	aramsız	[aramˈsız]
cool (weather)	sərin	[sæˈrin]

dangerous (adj)	təhlükəli	[tæhlykæˈli]
dark (room)	qaranlıq	[garanˈlıg]
dead (not alive)	ölü	[øˈly]
dense (fog, smoke)	qalın	[gaˈlın]

different (adj)	fərqli	[færgˈli]
difficult (decision)	çətin	[ʧʲeˈtin]
difficult (problem, task)	mürəkkəb	[myrækˈkæb]
dim, faint (light)	zəif	[zæˈif]

dirty (not clean)	çirkli	[ʧʲirkˈli]
distant (faraway)	uzaqda olan	[uzagˈda oˈlan]
distant (in space)	uzaq	[uˈzag]
dry (climate, clothing)	quru	[guˈru]

easy (not difficult)	sadə	[saˈdæ]
empty (glass, room)	boş	[boʃ]
exact (amount)	dəqiq	[dæˈgig]
excellent (adj)	əla	[æˈla]
excessive (adj)	həddindən artıq	[hæddinˈdæn arˈtıg]
expensive (adj)	bahalı	[bahaˈlı]
exterior (adj)	xarici	[hariˈʤi]

fast (quick)	cəld	[ʤæld]
fatty (food)	yağlı	[jaɣˈlı]
fertile (land, soil)	münbit	[mynˈbit]
flat (~ panel display)	yastı	[jasˈtı]
flat (e.g. ~ surface)	hamar	[haˈmar]

foreign (adj)	xarici	[hariˈʤi]
fragile (china, glass)	incə	[inˈʤæ]
free (at no cost)	pulsuz	[pulˈsuz]
free (unrestricted)	azad	[aˈzad]

fresh (~ water)	şirin	[ʃiˈrin]
fresh (e.g. ~ bred)	təzə	[tæˈzæ]
frozen (food)	dondurulmuş	[dondurulˈmuʃ]

full (completely filled)	dolu	[do'lu]
good (book, etc.)	yaxşı	[jah'ʃı]
good (kindhearted)	xeyirxah	[hejır'hah]
grateful (adj)	minnətdar	[miɳæt'dar]

happy (adj)	xoşbəxt	[hoʃ'bæht]
hard (not soft)	bərk	[bærk]
heavy (in weight)	ağır	[aɣ'ır]

hostile (adj)	düşməncəsinə	[dyʃ'mændʒæsinæ]
hot (adj)	isti	[is'ti]
huge (adj)	nəhənk	[næ'hæɳk]
humid (adj)	rütubətli	[rytubæt'li]
hungry (adj)	ac	[adʒ]

| ill (sick, unwell) | xəstə | [hæs'tæ] |
| incomprehensible | anlaşılmaz | [anlaʃıl'maz] |

immobile (adj)	hərəkətsiz	[hærækæ'tsiz]
important (adj)	vacib	[va'dʒib]
impossible (adj)	mümkünsüz	[mymkyn'syz]

indispensable (adj)	zəruri	[zæru'ri]
inexperienced (adj)	təcrübəsiz	[tædʒrybæ'siz]
insignificant (adj)	əhəmiyyətsiz	[æhæmij:ə'tsiz]
interior (adj)	daxili	[dahi'li]
joint (~ decision)	birgə	[bir'gæ]

last (e.g. ~ week)	keçən	[ke'tʃən]
last (final)	sonuncu	[sonun'dʒu]
left (e.g. ~ side)	sol	[sol]
legal (legitimate)	qanuni	[ganu'ni]

light (in weight)	yüngül	[y'ɳyl]
light (pale color)	açıq rəngli	[a'tʃıg ræɳ'li]
limited (adj)	məhdud	[mæh'dud]
liquid (fluid)	duru	[du'ru]
long (e.g. ~ way)	uzun	[u'zun]
loud (voice, etc.)	gurultulu	[gyrultu'lu]
low (voice)	yavaş	[ja'vaʃ]

251. Modifiers. Adjectives. Part 2

main (principal)	baş	[baʃ]
matt (paint)	donuq	[do'nug]
meticulous (job)	səliqəli	[sæligæ'li]
mysterious (adj)	müəmmalı	[myæmma'lı]

narrow (street, etc.)	dar	[dar]
native (of country)	doğma	[doɣ'ma]
necessary (adj)	lazımi	[lazı'mi]
negative (adj)	mənfi	[mæn'fi]
neighbouring (adj)	qonşu	[gon'ʃu]
nervous (adj)	əsəbi	[æsæ'bi]

new (adj)	yeni	[e'ni]
next (e.g. ~ week)	növbəti	[nøvbæ'ti]
nearby	yaxın	[ja'hın]
nice (kind)	iltifatlı	[iltifat'lı]
nice (voice)	məlahətli	[mælahæt'li]

normal (adj)	normal	[nor'mal]
not big (adj)	balaca	[bala'dʒa]
not clear (adj)	qeyri-müəyyən	['gejri myæ'j:ən]
not difficult (adj)	çətin olmayan	[tʃə'tin 'olmajan]

obligatory (adj)	məcburi	[mædʒbu'ri]
old (house)	qoca	[go'dʒa]
open (adj)	açıq	[a'tʃɪg]
opposite (adj)	müqabil	[myga'bil]
ordinary (usual)	adi	[a'di]
original (unusual)	orijinal	[oriʒi'nal]

past (recent)	keçmiş	[ketʃ'miʃ]
permanent (adj)	daimi	[dai'mi]
personal (adj)	şəxsi	[ʃæh'si]
polite (adj)	nəzakətli	[næzakæt'li]
poor (not rich)	kasıb	[ka'sıb]
possible (adj)	mümkün ola bilən	[mym'kyn o'la bi'læn]
poverty-stricken (adj)	dilənçi	[dilæn'tʃi]

present (current)	hazırki	[hazır'ki]
previous (adj)	əvvəlki	[ævvæl'ki]
principal (main)	əsas	[æ'sas]
private (~ jet)	xüsusi	[hysu'si]
probable (adj)	mümkün ola bilən	[mym'kyn o'la bi'læn]

public (open to all)	ictimai	[idʒtima'i]
punctual (person)	dəqiq	[dæ'gig]
quiet (tranquil)	sakit	[sa'kit]

rare (adj)	nadir	[na'dir]
raw (uncooked)	çiy	[tʃij]
right (not left)	sağ	[saɣ]
right, correct (adj)	düzgün	[dyz'gyn]
ripe (fruit)	dəymiş	[dæj'miʃ]
risky (adj)	riskli	[risk'li]

sad (~ look)	qəmli	[gæm'li]
sad (depressing)	qəmgin	[gæm'gin]
safe (not dangerous)	təhlükəsiz	[tæhlykæ'siz]
salty (food)	duzlu	[duz'lu]
satisfied (customer)	məmnun	[mæm'nun]
second hand (adj)	istifadədə olmuş	[istifadæ'dæ ol'muʃ]

shallow (water)	dayaz	[da'jaz]
sharp (blade, etc.)	iti	[i'ti]
short (in length)	qısa	[gı'sa]
short, short-lived (adj)	qısamüddətli	[gısamyddæt'li]
short-sighted (adj)	uzağı görməyən	[uzaɣ'ı 'gørmæjən]
significant (notable)	əhəmiyyətli	[æhæmij:ət'li]

similar (adj)	oxşar	[oh'ʃar]
simple (easy)	adi	[a'di]
slim (person)	arıq	[a'rıg]

small (in size)	kiçik	[ki'tʃik]
smooth (surface)	hamar	[ha'mar]
soft (to touch)	yumşaq	[ym'ʃag]
solid (~ wall)	möhkəm	[møh'kæm]
somber, gloomy (adj)	tutqun	[tut'gun]
sour (flavour, taste)	turş	[turʃ]

spacious (house, etc.)	geniş	[ge'niʃ]
special (adj)	xüsusi	[hysu'si]
straight (line, road)	düz	[dyz]
strong (person)	güclü	[gydʒ'ly]
stupid (foolish)	axmaq	[ah'mag]

convenient (adj)	yararlı	[jarar'lı]
sunny (day)	günəşli	[gynæʃ'li]
superb, perfect (adj)	əla	[æ'la]
swarthy (adj)	qarabuğdayı	[garabuɣda'jı]
sweet (sugary)	şirin	[ʃi'rin]

tanned (adj)	gündən qaralmış	[gyn'dæn garal'mıʃ]
tasty (adj)	dadlı	[dad'lı]
tender (affectionate)	zərif	[zæ'rif]

the highest (adj)	ali	[a'li]
the most important	ən vacib	['æn va'dʒib]
the nearest	ən yaxın	['æn ja'hın]
the same, equal (adj)	eyni	['æjni]

thick (e.g. ~ fog)	sıx	[sıh]
thick (wall, slice)	qalın	[ga'lın]
tired (exhausted)	yorğun	[jorɣ'un]
tiring (adj)	yorucu	[joru'dʒu]
too thin (emaciated)	arıq	[a'rıg]
transparent (adj)	şəffaf	[ʃæf'faf]

unique (exceptional)	bənzərsiz	[bænzær'siz]
various (adj)	müxtəlif	[myhtæ'lif]

warm (moderately hot)	isti	[is'ti]
wet (e.g. ~ clothes)	islanmış	[islan'mıʃ]
whole (entire, complete)	tam	[tam]
wide (e.g. ~ road)	enli	[æn'li]
young (adj)	cavan	[dʒa'van]

MAIN 500 VERBS

252. Verbs A-C

to accompany (vt)	müşaidə etmək	[myʃai'dæ æt'mæk]
to accuse (vt)	ittiham etmək	[itti'ham æt'mæk]
to act (take action)	hərəkət etmək	[hæræ'kæt æt'mæk]
to add (supplement)	əlavə etmək	[æla'væ æt'mæk]
to address (speak to)	müraciət etmək	[myradʒi'æt æt'mæk]
to admire (vi)	heyran olmaq	[hej'ran ol'mag]
to advertise (vt)	reklam etmək	[rek'lam æt'mæk]
to advise (vt)	məsləhət vermək	[mæslæ'hæt ver'mæk]
to affirm (vt)	iddia etmək	[iddi'a æt'mæk]
to agree (say yes)	razı olmaq	[ra'zı ol'mag]
to allow (sb to do sth)	icazə vermək	[idʒa'zæ ver'mæk]
to allude (vi)	eyham vurmaq	[æj'ham vur'mag]
to amputate (vt)	amputasiya etmək	[ampu'tasija æt'mæk]
to make angry	əsəbiləşdirmək	[æsæbilæʃdir'mæk]
to answer (vi, vt)	cavab vermək	[dʒa'vab ver'mæk]
to apologize (vi)	üzr istəmək	['yzr istæ'mæk]
to appear (come into view)	görünmək	[gøryn'mæk]
to applaud (vi, vt)	alqışlamaq	[algıʃla'mag]
to appoint (assign)	təyin etmək	[tæ'jin æt'mæk]
to approach (come nearer)	yaxınlaşmaq	[jahınlaʃ'mag]
to arrive (ab. train)	gəlmək	[gæl'mæk]
to ask (~ sb to do sth)	xahiş etmək	[ha'iʃ æt'mæk]
to aspire to ...	can atmaq	['dʒan at'mag]
to assist (help)	kömək etmək	[kø'mæk æt'mæk]
to attack (mil.)	hücum etmək	[hy'dʒum æt'mæk]
to attain (objectives)	əldə etmək	[æl'dæ æt'mæk]
to avenge (vt)	intiqam almaq	[inti'gam al'mag]
to avoid (danger, task)	qaçmaq	[gatʃ'mag]
to award (give medal to)	təltif etmək	[tæl'tif æt'mæk]
to bath (~ one's baby)	çimdirmək	[tʃimdir'mæk]
to battle (vi)	vuruşmaq	[vuruʃ'mag]
to be (~ on the table)	olmaq	[ol'mag]
to be (vi)	olmaq	[ol'mag]
to be afraid	qorxmaq	[gorh'mag]
to be angry (with ...)	əsəbiləşmək	[æsæbilæʃ'mæk]
to be at war	müharibə etmək	[myhari'bæ æt'mæk]
to be based (on ...)	əsaslanmaq	[æsaslan'mag]

to be bored	darıxmaq	[darıh'mag]
to be convinced	inanmaq	[inan'mag]
to be enough	yetərli olmaq	[etær'li ol'mag]
to be envious	paxıllıq etmək	[pahıl'lıg æt'mæk]
to be indignant	hiddətlənmək	[hiddætlæn'mæk]
to be interested in ...	maraqlanmaq	[maraglan'mag]
to be lying down	uzanmaq	[uzan'mag]
to be needed	tələb olunmaq	[tæ'læb olun'mag]
to be perplexed	heyrətlənmək	[hæjrætlæn'mæk]
to be preserved	qalmaq	[gal'mag]
to be required	zəruri olmaq	[zæru'ri ol'mag]
to be surprised	təəccüblənmək	[tæ:dʒyblæn'mæk]
to be worried	narahat olmaq	[nara'hat ol'mag]
to beat (dog, person)	vurmaq	[vur'mag]
to become (e.g. ~ old)	olmaq	[ol'mag]
to become pensive	fikrə dalmaq	[fik'ræ dal'mag]
to behave (vi)	özünü aparmaq	[øzy'ny apar'mag]
to believe (think)	inanmaq	[inan'mag]
to belong to ...	mənsub olmaq	[mæn'sub ol'mag]
to berth (moor)	sahilə yaxınlaşmaq	[sahi'læ jahınlaʃ'mag]
to blind (of flash of light)	göz qamaşdırmaq	['gøz gamaʃdır'mag]
to blow (wind)	üfürmək	[yfyr'mæk]
to blush (vi)	qızarmaq	[gızar'mag]
to boast (vi)	lovğalanmaq	[lovɣalan'mag]
to borrow (money)	borc pul almaq	['bordʒ 'pul al'mag]
to break (branch, toy, etc.)	qırmaq	[gır'mag]
to snap (vi, ab. rope)	cırılmaq	[dʒırıl'mag]
to breathe (vi)	nəfəs almaq	[næ'fæs al'mag]
to bring (sth)	gətirmək	[gætir'mæk]
to burn (paper, logs)	yandırmaq	[jandır'mag]
to buy (purchase)	almaq	[al'mag]
to call (for help)	çağırmaq	[tʃaɣır'mag]
to calm down (vt)	sakitləşdirmək	[sakitlæʃdir'mæk]
can (v aux)	bacarmaq	[badʒar'mag]
to cancel (call off)	ləğv etmək	['læɣv æt'mæk]
to cast off	sahildən ayrılmaq	[sahil'dæn ajrıl'mag]
to catch (e.g. ~ a ball)	tutmaq	[tut'mag]
to catch sight (of ...)	görmək	[gør'mæk]
to cause ...	səbəb olmaq	[sæ'bæb ol'mag]
to change (~ one's opinion)	dəyişmək	[dæiʃ'mæk]
to change (exchange)	dəyişmək	[dæiʃ'mæk]
to charm (vt)	məftun etmək	[mæf'tun æt'mæk]
to choose (select)	seçmək	[setʃ'mæk]
to chop off (with an axe)	kəsmək	[kæs'mæk]
to clean (from dirt)	təmizləmək	[tæmizlæ'mæk]
to clean (shoes, etc.)	təmizləmək	[tæmizlæ'mæk]
to clean (tidy)	yığışdırmaq	[jıɣıʃdır'mag]
to close (vt)	bağlamaq	[baɣla'mag]

to comb one's hair	başını daramaq	[baʃɪ'nɪ dara'mag]
to come down (the stairs)	aşağı düşmək	[aʃaɣ'ɪ dyʃ'mæk]
to come in (enter)	içəri daxil olmaq	[itʃə'ri da'hil ol'mag]
to come out (book)	çıxmaq	[tʃɪh'mag]

to compare (vt)	müqayisə etmək	[mygajɪ'sæ æt'mæk]
to compensate (vt)	kompensasiya etmək	[kompen'sasija æt'mæk]
to compete (vi)	rəqabət aparmaq	[ræga'bæt apar'mag]

to compile (~ a list)	tərtib etmək	[tær'tib æt'mæk]
to complain (vi, vt)	şikayət etmək	[ʃika'jət æt'mæk]
to complicate (vt)	mürəkkəbləşdirmək	[myrækkæblæʃdir'mæk]
to compose (music, etc.)	bəstələmək	[bæstælæ'mæk]
to compromise (vt)	nüfuzdan salmaq	[nyfuz'dan sal'mag]

to concentrate (vi)	fikrini cəmləşdirmək	[fikri'ni dʒæmlæʃdir'mæk]
to confess (criminal)	boynuna almaq	[bojnu'na al'mag]
to confuse (mix up)	dolaşıq salmaq	[dola'ʃɪg sal'mag]
to congratulate (vt)	təbrik etmək	[tæb'rik æt'mæk]

to consult (doctor, expert)	...məsləhət almaq	[mæslæ'hæt al'mag]
to continue (~ to do sth)	davam etdirmək	[da'vam ætdir'mæk]
to control (vt)	nəzarət etmək	[næza'ræt æt'mæk]
to convince (vt)	inandırmaq	[inandɪr'mag]

to cooperate (vi)	əməkdaşlıq etmək	[æmækdaʃ'lɪg æt'mæk]
to coordinate (vt)	uzlaşdırmaq	[uzlaʃdɪr'mag]
to correct (an error)	düzəltmək	[dyzælt'mæk]
to cost (vt)	qiyməti olmaq	[gijmæ'ti ol'mag]

to count (money, etc.)	hesab aparmaq	[hæ'sab apar'mag]
to count on ...	bel bağlamaq	['bel baɣla'mag]
to crack (ceiling, wall)	çatlamaq	[tʃatla'mag]
to create (vt)	yaratmaq	[jarat'mag]
to cry (weep)	ağlamaq	[aɣla'mag]
to cut off (with a knife)	kəsmək	[kæs'mæk]

253. Verbs D-G

to dare (~ to do sth)	cürət etmək	[dʒy'ræt æt'mæk]
to date from ...	tarixi qoyulmaq	[tari'hi goyl'mag]
to deceive (vi, vt)	aldatmaq	[aldat'mag]
to decide (~ to do sth)	qərar vermək	[gæ'rar ver'mæk]

to decorate (tree, street)	bəzəmək	[bæzæ'mæk]
to dedicate (book, etc.)	həsr etmək	['hæsr æt'mæk]
to defend (a country, etc.)	müdafiə etmək	[mydafi'jə æt'mæk]
to defend oneself	müdafiə olunmaq	[mydafi'jə olun'mag]

to demand (request firmly)	tələb etmək	[tæ'læb æt'mæk]
to denounce (vt)	xəbərçilik etmək	[hæbærtʃi'lik æt'mæk]
to deny (vt)	inkar etmək	[i'ŋkar æt'mæk]
to depend on ...	asılı olmaq	[asɪ'lɪ ol'mag]
to deprive (vt)	məhrum etmək	[mæh'rum æt'mæk]

to deserve (vt)	layiq olmaq	[la'jıg ol'mag]
to design (machine, etc.)	layihələşdirmək	[lajıhælæʃdir'mæk]
to desire (want, wish)	istəmək	[istæ'mæk]
to despise (vt)	xor baxmaq	['hor bah'mag]
to destroy (documents, etc.)	məhv etmək	['mæhv æt'mæk]

to differ (from sth)	fərqlənmək	[færglæn'mæk]
to dig (tunnel, etc.)	qazmaq	[gaz'mag]
to direct (point the way)	istiqamətləndirmək	[istigamætlændir'mæk]

to disappear (vi)	yox olmaq	['joh ol'mag]
to discover (new land, etc.)	kəşf etmək	['kæʃf æt'mæk]
to discuss (vt)	müzakirə etmək	[myzaki'ræ æt'mæk]
to distribute (leaflets, etc.)	yaymaq	[jaj'mag]
to disturb (vt)	mane olmaq	[ma'ne ol'mag]

to dive (vi)	dalmaq	[dal'mag]
to divide (math)	bölmək	[bøl'mæk]

to do (vt)	etmək	[æt'mæk]
to do the laundry	yumaq	[y'mag]
to double (increase)	ikiqat artırmaq	[iki'gat artır'mag]
to doubt (have doubts)	şübhələnmək	[ʃybhælæn'mæk]

to draw a conclusion	nətice çıxarmaq	[næti'dʒæ tʃıhar'mag]
to dream (daydream)	xəyal etmək	[hæ'jal æt'mæk]
to dream (in sleep)	yuxu görmək	[y'hu gør'mæk]

to drink (vi, vt)	içmək	[itʃ'mæk]
to drive a car	maşın sürmək	[ma'ʃın syr'mæk]
to drive away	qovmaq	[gov'mag]

to drop (let fall)	yerə salmaq	[e'ræ sal'mag]
to drown (ab. person)	suda boğulmaq	[su'da boɣul'mag]
to dry (clothes, hair)	qurutmaq	[gurut'mag]

to eat (vi, vt)	yemək	[e'mæk]
to eavesdrop (vi)	xəlvətçə qulaq asmaq	[hæl'væʧæ gu'lag as'mag]
to enter (on the list)	yazmaq	[jaz'mag]
to entertain (amuse)	əyləndirmək	[æjlændir'mæk]
to equip (fit out)	təchiz etmək	[tædʒ'hiz æt'mæk]

to examine (proposal)	baxmaq	[bah'mag]
to exchange (sth)	mübadilə etmək	[mybadi'læ æt'mæk]
to exclude, to expel	xaric etmək	[ha'ridʒ æt'mæk]
to excuse (forgive)	bağışlamaq	[baɣıʃla'mag]
to exist (vi)	mövcud olmaq	[møv'dʒud ol'mag]

to expect (anticipate)	gözləmək	[gøzlæ'mæk]
to expect (foresee)	qabaqcadan görmək	[ga'bagdʒadan gør'mæk]
to explain (vt)	izah etmək	[i'zah æt'mæk]
to express (vt)	ifadə etmək	[ifa'dæ æt'mæk]
to extinguish (a fire)	söndürmək	[søndyr'mæk]

to fall in love (with …)	aşiq olmaq	[a'ʃig ol'mag]
to fancy (vt)	xoşuna gəlmək	[hoʃu'na gæl'mæk]

to feed (provide food)	yedirmək	[edir'mæk]
to fight (against the enemy)	vuruşmaq	[vuruʃ'mag]
to fight (vi)	dalaşmaq	[dalaʃ'mag]

to fill (glass, bottle)	doldurmaq	[doldur'mag]
to find (~ lost items)	tapmaq	[tap'mag]
to finish (vt)	qurtarmaq	[gurtar'mag]
to fish (vi)	balıq tutmaq	[ba'lıg tut'mag]
to fit (ab. dress, etc.)	münasib olmaq	[myna'sib ol'mag]

to flatter (vt)	yaltaqlıq etmək	[jaltag'lıg æt'mæk]
to fly (bird, plane)	uçmaq	[utʃ'mag]

to follow ... (come after)	ardınca getmək	[ar'dındʒa get'mæk]
to forbid (vt)	qadağan etmək	[gaday'an æt'mæk]
to force (compel)	məcbur etmək	[mædʒ'bur æt'mæk]
to forget (vi, vt)	unutmaq	[unut'mag]
to forgive (pardon)	bağışlamaq	[bayıʃla'mag]
to form (constitute)	əmələ gətirmək	[æmæ'læ gætir'mæk]

to get dirty (vi)	çirklənmək	[tʃirklæn'mæk]
to get infected (with ...)	yoluxmaq	[joluh'mag]
to get irritated	acıqlanmaq	[adʒıglan'mag]
to get married	evlənmək	[ævlæn'mæk]
to get rid of ...	yaxa qurtarmaq	[ja'ha gurtar'mag]
to get tired	yorulmaq	[jorul'mag]
to get up (arise from bed)	qalxmaq	[galh'mag]

to give a hug, to hug (vt)	qucaqlamaq	[gudʒagla'mag]
to give in (yield to)	güzəştə getmək	[gyzæʃ'tæ gæt'mæk]

to go (by car, etc.)	getmək	[get'mæk]
to go (on foot)	getmək	[get'mæk]
to go for a swim	çimmək	[tʃim'mæk]
to go out (for dinner, etc.)	çıxmaq	[tʃıh'mag]
to go to bed	yatağa girmək	[jatay'a gir'mæk]

to greet (vt)	salamlamaq	[salamla'mag]
to grow (plants)	yetişdirmək	[etiʃdir'mæk]
to guarantee (vt)	təminat vermək	[tæmi'nat ver'mæk]
to guess right	tapmaq	[tap'mag]

254. Verbs H-M

to hand out (distribute)	paylamaq	[pajla'mag]
to hang (curtains, etc.)	asmaq	[as'mag]

to have (vt)	malik olmaq	['malik ol'mag]
to have a bath	yuyunmaq	[y:n'mag]
to have a try	cəhd etmək	['dʒæhd æt'mæk]
to have breakfast	səhər yeməyi yemək	[sæ'hær emæ'ji e'mæk]
to have dinner	axşam yeməyi yemək	[ah'ʃam emæ'jı e'mæk]
to have fun	şənlənmək	[ʃænlæn'mæk]
to have lunch	nahar etmək	[na'har æt'mæk]

to head (group, etc.)	başçılıq etmək	[baʃtʃı'lıg æt'mæk]
to hear (vt)	eşitmək	[æʃit'mæk]
to heat (vt)	qızdırmaq	[gızdır'mag]
to help (vt)	kömək etmək	[kø'mæk æt'mæk]

to hide (vt)	gizlətmək	[gizlæt'mæk]
to hire (e.g. ~ a boat)	kirayə etmək	[kira'jə æt'mæk]
to hire (staff)	işə götürmək	[i'ʃæ gøtyr'mæk]
to hope (vi, vt)	ümid etmək	[y'mid æt'mæk]

to hunt (for food, sport)	ova çıxmaq	[o'va tʃıh'mag]
to hurry (vi)	tələsmək	[tælæs'mæk]
to hurry (sb)	tələsdirmək	[tælæsdir'mæk]

to imagine (to picture)	təsəvvür etmək	[tæsæv'vyr æt'mæk]
to imitate (vt)	təqlid etmək	[tæg'lid æt'mæk]
to implore (vt)	yalvarmaq	[jalvar'mag]
to import (vt)	idxal etmək	[id'hal æt'mæk]

to increase (vi)	artmaq	[art'mag]
to increase (vt)	artırmaq	[artır'mag]
to infect (vt)	yoluxdurmaq	[joluhdur'mag]
to influence (vt)	təsir göstərmək	[tæ'sir gøstær'mæk]

to inform (~ sb about ...)	xəbər vermək	[hæ'bær ver'mæk]
to inform (vt)	məlumat vermək	[mælu'mat ver'mæk]
to inherit (vt)	varis olmaq	['varis ol'mag]
to inquire (about ...)	bilmək	[bil'mæk]

to insist (vi, vt)	təkid etmək	[tæ'kid æt'mæk]
to inspire (vt)	ruhlandırmaq	[ruhlandır'mag]
to instruct (teach)	təlimat vermək	[tæli'mat ver'mæk]
to insult (offend)	təhkir etmək	[tæh'kir æt'mæk]

to interest (vt)	maraqlandırmaq	[maraglandır'mag]
to intervene (vi)	müdaxilə etmək	[mydahi'læ æt'mæk]
to introduce (present)	tanış etmək	[ta'nıʃ æt'mæk]
to invent (machine, etc.)	ixtira etmək	[ihti'ra æt'mæk]
to invite (vt)	dəvət etmək	[dæ'væt æt'mæk]

to iron (laundry)	ütüləmək	[ytylæ'mæk]
to irritate (annoy)	acıqlandırmaq	[adʒıglandır'mag]
to isolate (vt)	təcrid etmək	[tædʒ'rid æt'mæk]

| to join (political party, etc.) | qoşulmaq | [goʃul'mag] |
| to joke (be kidding) | zarafat etmək | [zara'fat æt'mæk] |

to keep (old letters, etc.)	saxlamaq	[sahla'mag]
to keep silent	susmaq	[sus'mag]
to kill (vt)	öldürmək	[øldyr'mæk]
to knock (at the door)	taqqıldatmaq	[taggıldat'mag]
to know (sb)	tanımaq	[tanı'mag]
to know (sth)	bilmək	[bil'mæk]

| to laugh (vi) | gülmək | [gyʎ'mæk] |
| to launch (start up) | işə salmaq | [i'ʃæ sal'mag] |

to leave (~ for Mexico)	getmək	[get'mæk]
to leave (forget)	yaddan çıxartmaq	[jad'dan tʃıhart'mag]
to leave (spouse)	tərk etmək	['tærk æt'mæk]

to liberate (city, etc.)	azad etmək	[a'zad æt'mæk]
to lie (tell untruth)	aldatmaq	[aldat'mag]
to light (campfire, etc.)	yandırmaq	[jandır'mag]
to light up (illuminate)	işıqlandırmaq	[iʃıglandır'mag]

to limit (vt)	məhdudlaşdırmaq	[mæhdudlaʃdır'mag]
to listen (vi)	qulaq asmaq	[gu'lag as'mag]
to live (~ in France)	yaşamaq	[jaʃa'mag]
to live (exist)	yaşamaq	[jaʃa'mag]

to load (gun)	doldurmaq	[doldur'mag]
to load (vehicle, etc.)	yükləmək	[yklæ'mæk]
to look (I'm just ~ing)	baxmaq	[bah'mag]
to look for ... (search)	axtarmaq	[ahtar'mag]
to look like (resemble)	oxşamaq	[ohʃa'mag]

to lose (umbrella, etc.)	itirmək	[itir'mæk]
to love (sb)	sevmək	[sev'mæk]
to love (sth)	sevmək	[sev'mæk]
to lower (blind, head)	aşağı salmaq	[aʃaɣ'ı sal'mag]

to make (~ dinner)	hazırlamaq	[hazırla'mag]
to make a mistake	səhv etmək	['sæhv æt'mæk]
to make copies	çoxaltmaq	[tʃohalt'mag]
to make easier	yüngülləşdirmək	[yŋyllæʃdir'mæk]
to make the acquaintance	tanış olmaq	[ta'nıʃ ol'mag]
to make use (of ...)	istifadə etmək	[istifa'dæ æt'mæk]

to manage, to run	idarə etmək	[ida'ræ æt'mæk]
to mark (make a mark)	işarələmək	[iʃarælæ'mæk]
to mean (signify)	əhəmiyyət kəsb etmək	[æhæmi'j:ət 'kæsb æt'mæk]
to memorize (vt)	yadda saxlamaq	[jad'da sahla'mag]
to mention (talk about)	adını çəkmək	[adı'nı tʃək'mæk]

to miss (school, etc.)	buraxmaq	[burah'mag]
to mix (combine, blend)	qarışdırmaq	[garıʃdır'mag]
to mock (deride)	rişxənd etmək	[riʃ'hænd æt'mæk]
to move (wardrobe, etc.)	keçirmək	[ketʃir'mæk]
to multiply (math)	vurmaq	[vur'mag]
must (v aux)	borclu olmaq	[bordʒ'lu ol'mag]

255. Verbs N-S

to name, to call (vt)	adlandırmaq	[adlandır'mag]
to negotiate (vi)	danışıqlar aparmaq	[danıʃig'lar apar'mag]
to note (write down)	qeyd etmək	['gejd æt'mæk]
to notice (see)	görmək	[gør'mæk]

to obey (vi, vt)	tabe olmaq	[ta'be ol'mag]
to object (vi, vt)	etiraz etmək	[æti'raz æt'mæk]

to observe (see)	müşaidə etmək	[myʃai'dæ æt'mæk]
to offend (vt)	incitmək	[indʒit'mæk]
to omit (word, phrase)	buraxmaq	[burah'mag]

to open (vt)	açmaq	[atʃ'mag]
to order (in restaurant)	sifariş etmək	[sifa'riʃ æt'mæk]
to order (mil.)	əmr etmək	['æmr æt'mæk]
to organize (concert, party)	təşkil etmək	[tæʃ'kil æt'mæk]
to overestimate (vt)	yenidən qiymətləndirmək	[eni'dæn gijmætlændir'mæk]
to own (possess)	sahib olmaq	[sa'hib ol'mag]

to participate (vi)	iştirak etmək	[iʃti'rak æt'mæk]
to pass (go beyond)	keçmək	[kætʃ'mæk]
to pay (vi, vt)	pulunu ödəmək	[pulu'nu ødæ'mæk]
to peep, to spy on	xəlvətçə baxmaq	[hæl'vætʃæ bah'mag]
to penetrate (vt)	içəri daxil olmaq	[itʃə'ri da'hil ol'mag]
to permit (vt)	icazə vermək	[idʒa'zæ ver'mæk]

to pick (flowers)	dərmək	[dær'mæk]
to place (put, set)	yerləşdirmək	[erlæʃdir'mæk]
to plan (~ to do sth)	planlaşdırmaq	[planlaʃdır'mag]
to play (actor)	oynamaq	[ojna'mag]
to play (children)	oynamaq	[ojna'mag]

to point (~ the way)	göstərmək	[gøstær'mæk]
to pour (liquid)	tökmək	[tøk'mæk]
to pray (vi, vt)	dua etmək	[du'a æt'mæk]

to predominate (vi)	çoxluq təşkil etmək	[tʃoh'lug tæʃ'kil æt'mæk]
to prefer (vt)	üstünlük vermək	[ystyn'lyk ver'mæk]
to prepare (~ a plan)	hazırlamaq	[hazırla'mag]
to present (sb to sb)	təmsil etmək	[tæm'sil æt'mæk]
to preserve (peace, life)	saxlamaq	[sahla'mag]

to progress (move forward)	irəli getmək	[iræ'li get'mæk]
to promise (vt)	vəd etmək	['væd æt'mæk]
to pronounce (vt)	tələffüz etmək	[tælæf'fyz æt'mæk]
to propose (vt)	təklif etmək	[tæk'lif æt'mæk]

to protect (e.g. ~ nature)	mühafizə etmək	[myhafi'zæ æt'mæk]
to protest (vi)	etiraz etmək	[æti'raz æt'mæk]
to prove (vt)	sübut etmək	[sy'but æt'mæk]
to provoke (vt)	təhrik etmək	[tæh'rik æt'mæk]

to pull (~ the rope)	çəkmək	[tʃək'mæk]
to punish (vt)	cəzalandırmaq	[dʒæzalandır'mag]
to push (~ the door)	itələmək	[itælæ'mæk]

to put away (vt)	gizlətmək	[gizlæt'mæk]
to put in (insert)	salmaq	[sal'mag]
to put in order	qaydaya salmaq	[gajda'ja sal'mag]
to put, to place	qoymaq	[goj'mag]
to quote (cite)	sitat gətirmək	[si'tat gætir'mæk]

| to reach (arrive at) | çatmaq | [tʃat'mag] |
| to read (vi, vt) | oxumaq | [ohu'mag] |

to realise (achieve)	həyata keçirmək	[hæja'ta ketʃir'mæk]
to recall (~ one's name)	xatırlamaq	[hatırla'mag]

to recognize (admit)	etiraf etmək	[æti'raf æt'mæk]
to recognize (identify sb)	tanımaq	[tanı'mag]
to recommend (vt)	məslahət görmək	[mæslæ'hæt gør'mæk]
to recover (~ from flu)	sağalmaq	[sayal'mag]

to redo (do again)	yenidən düzəltmək	[eni'dæn dyzælt'mæk]
to reduce (speed, etc.)	azaltmaq	[azalt'mag]
to refuse (~ sb)	rədd cavabı vermək	['rædd ʤava'bı ver'mæk]
to regret (be sorry)	heyfsilənmək	[hejfsilæn'mæk]

to remember (vt)	yadda saxlamaq	[jad'da sahla'mag]
to remind of ...	xatırlatmaq	[hatırlat'mag]
to remove (~ a stain)	aparmaq	[apar'mag]
to remove (~ an obstacle)	aradan qaldırmaq	[ara'dan galdır'mag]
to rent (sth from sb)	kiraya etmək	[kira'jə æt'mæk]

to repair (mend)	təmir etmək	[tæ'mir æt'mæk]
to repeat (say again)	təkrar etmək	[tæk'rar æt'mæk]
to report (make a report)	məlumat vermək	[mælu'mat ver'mæk]
to reproach (vt)	üz vurmaq	['yz vur'mag]

to reserve, to book	təxsis etmək	[tæh'sis æt'mæk]
to restrain (hold back)	saxlamaq	[sahla'mag]
to return (come back)	qayıtmaq	[gajıt'mag]
to risk, to take a risk	risk etmək	['risk æt'mæk]
to rub off (erase)	silmək	[sil'mæk]
to run (move fast)	qaçmaq	[gatʃ'mag]

to satisfy (please)	təmin etmək	[tæ'min æt'mæk]
to save (rescue)	xilas etmək	[hi'las æt'mæk]
to say (~ thank you)	demək	[de'mæk]
to scold (vt)	danlamaq	[danla'mag]
to scratch (with claws)	cızmaq	[ʤız'mag]

to select (to pick)	seçmək	[setʃ'mæk]
to sell (goods)	satmaq	[sat'mag]
to send (a letter)	göndərmək	[gøndær'mæk]
to send back (vt)	geri göndərmək	[ge'ri gøndær'mæk]

to sense (danger)	hiss keçirmək	['hiss ketʃir'mæk]
to sentence (vt)	məhkum etmək	[mæh'kum æt'mæk]
to serve (in restaurant)	xidmət göstərmək	[hid'mæt gøstær'mæk]
to settle (a conflict)	düzəltmək	[dyzælt'mæk]

to shake (vt)	silkələmək	[silkælæ'mæk]
to shave (vi)	üzünü qırxmaq	[yzy'ny gırh'mag]
to shine (vi)	parıldamaq	[parılda'mag]
to shiver (with cold)	titrəmək	[titræ'mæk]

to shoot (vi)	atəş açmaq	[a'tæʃ atʃ'mag]
to shout (vi)	çığırmaq	[tʃıɣır'mag]
to show (to display)	göstərmək	[gøstær'mæk]
to shudder (vi)	diksinmək	[diksin'mæk]

to sigh (vi)	nəfəs almaq	[næ'fæs al'mag]
to sign (document)	imzalamaq	[imzala'mag]
to signify (mean)	ifadə etmək	[ifa'dæ æt'mæk]
to simplify (vt)	sadələşdirmək	[sadælæʃdir'mæk]
to sin (vi)	günaha batmaq	[gyna'ha bat'mag]
to sit (be sitting)	oturmaq	[otur'mag]
to sit down (vi)	oturmaq	[otur'mag]
to smash (~ a bug)	əzmək	[æz'mæk]
to smell (have odour)	ətir saçmaq	[æ'tir satʃ'mag]
to smell (sniff at)	iyləmək	[ijlæ'mæk]
to smile (vi)	gülümsəmək	[gylymsæ'mæk]
to solve (problem)	həll etmək	['hæll æt'mæk]
to sow (seed, crop)	əkmək	[æk'mæk]
to spill (liquid)	tökmək	[tøk'mæk]
to spit (vi)	tüpürmək	[typyr'mæk]
to emit (smell)	saçmaq	[satʃ'mag]
to stand (toothache, cold)	dözmək	[døz'mæk]
to start (begin)	başlamaq	[baʃla'mag]
to steal (money, etc.)	oğurlamaq	[oɣurla'mag]
to stop (cease)	kəsmək	[kæs'mæk]
to stop (for pause, etc.)	dayanmaq	[dajan'mag]
to stop talking	susmaq	[sus'mag]
to strengthen	möhkəmləndirmək	[møhkæmlændir'mæk]
to stroke (caress)	sığallamaq	[sɪɣalla'mag]
to study (vt)	öyrənmək	[øjræn'mæk]
to suffer (feel pain)	əzab çəkmək	[æ'zab tʃək'mæk]
to support (cause, idea)	dəstəkləmək	[dæstæklæ'mæk]
to suppose (assume)	fərz etmək	['færz æt'mæk]
to surface (ab. submarine)	üzə çıxmaq	[y'zæ tʃɪh'mag]
to surprise (amaze)	təəccübləndirmək	[tæːʤyblændir'mæk]
to suspect (vt)	şübhələnmək	[ʃybhælæn'mæk]
to swim (vi)	üzmək	[yz'mæk]
to switch on (vt)	qoşmaq	[goʃ'mag]

256. Verbs T-W

to take (get hold of)	almaq	[al'mag]
to take a rest	dincəlmək	[dinʤæl'mæk]
to take aim (at ...)	nişan almaq	[ni'ʃan al'mag]
to take away	aparmaq	[apar'mag]
to take off (aeroplane)	havaya qalxmaq	[hava'ja galh'mag]
to take off (remove)	yığmaq	[jɪɣ'mag]
to take pictures	fotoşəkil çəkmək	[fotoʃæ'kil tʃək'mæk]
to talk to ...	...danışmaq	[danɪʃ'mag]
to teach (give lessons)	öyrətmək	[øjræt'mæk]
to tear off (vt)	qopartmaq	[gopart'mag]

to tell (story, joke)	söyləmək	[søjlæ'mæk]
to thank (vt)	təşəkkür etmək	[tæʃæk'kyr æt'mæk]
to think (believe)	hesablamaq	[hesabla'mag]
to think (vi, vt)	düşünmək	[dyʃyn'mæk]

to threaten (vt)	hədələmək	[hædælæ'mæk]
to throw (stone)	atmaq	[at'mag]
to tie to ...	bağlamaq	[baɣla'mag]
to tie up (prisoner)	bağlamaq	[baɣla'mag]
to tire (make tired)	yormaq	[jor'mag]

to touch (one's arm, etc.)	toxunmaq	[tohun'mag]
to tower (over ...)	yüksəlmək	[yksæl'mæk]

to train (animals)	heyvanı təlim etmək	[hejva'nı tæ'lim æt'mæk]
to train (vi)	məşq etmək	['mæʃg æt'mæk]
to train (sb)	məşq keçmək	['mæʃg ketʃ'mæk]

to transform (vt)	transformasiya etmək	[transfor'masija æt'mæk]
to translate (vt)	tərcümə etmək	[tærdʒy'mæ æt'mæk]
to treat (patient, illness)	müalicə etmək	[myali'dʒæ æt'mæk]
to trust (vt)	etibar etmək	[æti'bar æt'mæk]
to try (attempt)	cəhd göstərmək	['dʒæhd gøstær'mæk]

to turn (~ to the left)	döndərmək	[døndær'mæk]
to turn away (vi)	üz döndərmək	['yz døndær'mæk]
to turn off (the light)	söndürmək	[søndyr'mæk]
to turn over (stone, etc.)	çevirmək	[tʃevir'mæk]

to underestimate (vt)	lazımi qədər qiymətləndirməmək	[lazı'mi gæ'dær gijmætlæn'dirmæmæk]
to underline (vt)	altından xətt çəkmək	[altın'dan 'hætt tʃək'mæk]
to understand (vt)	başa düşmək	[ba'ʃa dyʃ'mæk]
to undertake (vt)	başlamaq	[baʃla'mag]

to unite (vt)	birləşdirmək	[birlæʃdir'mæk]
to untie (vt)	açmaq	[atʃ'mag]
to use (phrase, word)	istifadə etmək	[istifa'dæ æt'mæk]

to vaccinate (vt)	peyvənd etmək	[pej'vænd æt'mæk]
to vote (vi)	səs vermək	['sæs ver'mæk]

to wait (vt)	gözləmək	[gøzlæ'mæk]
to wake (sb)	oyatmaq	[ojat'mag]
to want (wish, desire)	istəmək	[istæ'mæk]
to warn (of the danger)	xəbərdarlıq etmək	[hæbærdar'lıg æt'mæk]

to wash (clean)	yumaq	[y'mag]
to water (plants)	sulamaq	[sula'mag]
to wave (the hand)	yelləmək	[ellæ'mæk]
to weigh (have weight)	çəkisi olmaq	[tʃeki'si ol'mag]

to work (vi)	işləmək	[iʃlæ'mæk]
to worry (make anxious)	narahat etmək	[nara'hat æt'mæk]
to worry (vi)	həyacan keçirmək	[hæja'dʒan ketʃir'mæk]
to wrap (parcel, etc.)	bükmək	[byk'mæk]

to wrestle (sport)	**mübarizə etmək**	[mybari'zæ æt'mæk]
to write (vt)	**yazmaq**	[jaz'mag]
to write down	**yazmaq**	[jaz'mag]

CPSIA information can be obtained at www.ICGtesting.com
Printed in the USA
LVOW12s0120290414

383563LV00029B/1401/P